全国高等学校外语教师丛书

U0587304

Case Study Research in Applied Linguistics

应用语言学中的
个案研究方法

Patricia A. Duff（加拿大） 著

外语教学与研究出版社
FOREIGN LANGUAGE TEACHING AND RESEARCH PRESS
北京 BEIJING

京权图字：01-2011-6107

图书在版编目 (CIP) 数据

应用语言学中的个案研究方法 = Case Study Research in Applied Linguistics：英文 /（加）达夫 (Duff, P. A.) 著. -- 北京：外语教学与研究出版社，2011.11（2022.4 重印）
（全国高等学校外语教师丛书. 科研方法系列）
ISBN 978-7-5135-1453-8

I. ①应… II. ①达… III. ①应用语言学 - 个案研究 - 研究方法 - 英文 IV. ①H08-3

中国版本图书馆 CIP 数据核字 (2011) 第 224915 号

出 版 人　王　芳
项目负责　段长城
责任编辑　毕　争　金　玲
封面设计　覃一彪
版式设计　吴德胜
出版发行　外语教学与研究出版社
社　　址　北京市西三环北路 19 号（100089）
网　　址　http://www.fltrp.com
印　　刷　北京九州迅驰传媒文化有限公司
开　　本　650×980　1/16
印　　张　17
版　　次　2011 年 12 月第 1 版　2022 年 4 月第 11 次印刷
书　　号　ISBN 978-7-5135-1453-8
定　　价　62.90 元

购书咨询：(010) 88819926　电子邮箱：club@fltrp.com
外研书店：https://waiyants.tmall.com
凡印刷、装订质量问题，请联系我社印制部
联系电话：(010) 61207896　电子邮箱：zhijian@fltrp.com
凡侵权、盗版书籍线索，请联系我社法律事务部
举报电话：(010) 88817519　电子邮箱：banquan@fltrp.com
物料号：214530101

记载人类文明
沟通世界文化
www.fltrp.com

Contents

总　序

　　"全国高等学校外语教师丛书"是外语教学与研究出版社高等英语教育出版分社近期精心策划、隆重推出的系列丛书，包含理论指导、科研方法和教学研究三个子系列。本套丛书既包括学界专家精心挑选的国外引进著作，又有特邀国内学者执笔完成的"命题作文"。作为开放系列，该丛书还将根据外语教学与科研的发展不断增加新的专题，以便教师研修与提高。

　　笔者有幸参与了这套系列丛书的策划工作。在策划过程中，我们分析了高校英语教师面临的困难与挑战，考察了一线教师的需求，最终确立这套丛书选题的指导思想为：想外语教师所想，急外语教师所急，顺应广大教师的发展需求；确立这套丛书的写作特色为：突出科学性、可读性和操作性，做到举重若轻、条理清晰、例证丰富、深入浅出。

　　第一个子系列是"理论指导"。该系列力图为教师提供某学科或某领域的研究概貌，期盼读者能用较短的时间了解某领域的核心知识点与前沿研究课题。以《二语习得重点问题研究》一书为例。该书不求面面俱到，只求抓住二语习得研究领域中的热点、要点和富有争议的问题，动态展开叙述。每一章的写作以不同意见的争辩为出发点，对取向相左的理论、实证研究结果的差异进行分析、梳理和评述，最后介绍或者展望国内外的最新发展趋势。全书阐述清晰，深入浅出，易读易懂。再比如《认知语言学与二语教学》一书，全书分为理论篇、教学篇与研究篇三个部分。理论篇阐述认知语言学视角下的语言观、教学观与学习观，以及与二语教学相关的认知语言学中的主要概念与理论；教学篇选用认知语言学领域比较成熟的理论，探讨其应用到中国英语教学实践的可能性；研究篇包括国内外将认知语言学理论应用到教学实践中的研究综述、研究方法介绍以及对未来研究的展望。

第二个子系列是"科研方法"。该系列介绍了多种研究方法，通常是一书介绍一种方法，例如问卷调查、个案研究、行动研究、有声思维、语料库研究、微变化研究和启动研究等。也有一书涉及多种方法，综合描述量化研究或者质化研究，例如：《应用语言学中的质性研究与分析》、《应用语言学中的量化研究与分析》和《第二语言研究中的数据收集方法》等。凡入选本系列丛书的著作人，无论是国外著者还是国内著者，均有高度的读者意识，乐于为一线教师开展教学科研服务，力求做到帮助读者"排忧解难"。例如，澳大利亚安妮•伯恩斯教授撰写《英语教学中的行动研究方法》一书，从一线教师的视角，讨论行动研究的各个环节，每章均有"反思时刻"、"行动时刻"等新颖的形式设计。同时，全书运用了丰富的例证来解释理论概念，便于读者理解、思考和消化所读内容。凡是应邀撰写研究方法系列的中国著作人均有博士学位，并对自己阐述的研究方法有着丰富的实践经验。他们有的运用了书中的研究方法完成了硕士、博士论文，有的是采用书中的研究方法从事过重大科研项目。以秦晓晴教授撰写的《外语教学问卷调查法》一书为例，该书著者将系统性与实用性有机结合，根据实施问卷调查法的流程，系统地介绍了问卷调查研究中问题的提出、问卷项目设计、问卷试测、问卷实施、问卷整理及数据准备、问卷评价以及问卷数据汇总及统计分析方法选择等环节。书中的各个环节的描述都配有易于理解的研究实例。

第三个子系列是"教学研究"。该系列与前两个系列相比，有两点显著不同：第一，本系列侧重同步培养教师的教学能力与教学研究能力；第二，本系列所有著作的撰稿人主要为中国学者。有些著者虽然目前在海外工作和生活，但他们出国前曾在国内高校任教，期间也经常回国参与国内的教学与研究工作。本系列包括《听力教学与研究》、《写作教学与研究》、《阅读教学与研究》、《口语教学与研究》、《翻译教学与研究》等。以《听力教学与研究》一书为例，著者王艳博士拥有十多年的听力教学经验，同时听力教学研究又是她完成博士论文的选题领域。《听力教学与研究》一书，浓缩了她多年听力教学与听力教学研究的宝贵经验。全书分为两部分：教学篇与研究篇。教学篇涉及了听力教学的各个重要环节以及学生在听力学习中可能碰到的困难与应对的办法，所选用的案例均来自著者课堂教学的真实活动。研究篇中既有著者的听力教学研究案例，也有著者从国内外文献中筛选出的符合中国国情的听力教学研究案例，综合在一起加以分析阐述。

教育大计，教师为本。"全国高等学校外语教师丛书"内容全面，出版及时，必将成为高校教师提升自我教学能力、研究能力与合作能力的良师益友。笔者相信本套丛书的出版对高校外语教师个人专业能力的提高，对教师队伍整体素质的提高，必将起到积极的推动作用。

文秋芳
北京外国语大学中国外语教育研究中心
2011年7月3日

导　读

　　导读分三个部分：一、本书的主要内容、目标和特点；二、个案研究法概述；三、各章节主要内容和导读。

一、本书的主要内容、目标和特点

　　本书是一部关于研究方法的专著，即如何在应用语言学研究中开展个案研究的专著。作者帕特里夏•达夫是加拿大不列颠哥伦比亚大学（University of British Columbia）语言与文化教育系教授[1]。她研究兴趣广泛，著述丰厚，其主要学术研究领域包括应用语言学和社会语言学、二语习得、语言社会化、研究方法（如课堂研究、个案研究、人种志研究、语篇分析、基于任务的研究）、语言教学等。本书正是作者近年（2008年）出版的一部将自己的研究兴趣（应用语言学与个案研究）有机结合的专著。

　　按照作者的描述，本书的目标有三个：（1）帮助读者了解个案研究作为一种质的研究范式的方法论基础；（2）检视二语习得领域中一些重要的个案研究实例；（3）在实用的层面上，就如何在应用语言学中开展和评估个案研究以及如何撰写个案研究报告，给读者提供一些指导（详见 p. 1）。本书的目标读者是本科生、研究生以及其他希望学习并使用个案研究的学者，特别是运用个案研究法研究不同环境下的语言学习和使用的学者。

　　本书有三个特点：（1）是第一部介绍用个案研究法研究应用语言学问题的研究方法专著。虽然关于外 / 二语学习者的个案研究是整个应用语言学领域的重要基础，也有越来越多的应用语言学研究者开始使用个案研究法，但一直以来并没有一部全面、深入介绍如何在应用语言学中开展个案研究的专著，应该说，本书填补了这样一个空白。（2）本书的

1　引自 http://educ.ubc.ca/faculty/pduff

"全面"和"深入"表现在作者不仅从个案研究的哲学基础和历史渊源两方面较好地阐述了个案研究的理据，还用大量的个案研究的实例有效地说明了这些理据的现实意义，理据与个案讨论相得益彰，有很强的说服力。(3)"应用语言学中的个案研究"的书名，名副其实。每一章都有相关的案例细节，所引案例丰富、翔实、生动、示范性强，便于读者理解并得到启发，进而在自己的研究实践中得以模仿。

二、个案研究法概述

1. 什么是个案研究?

　　"个案研究"（case study）（也称"案例研究"）[1] 是社会科学研究中常用的研究方法之一，被广泛地应用于社会学、政治学、心理学、经济学、管理学、教育学、应用语言学、二语习得及语言教学等研究领域。那么，什么是个案研究? 它的核心要素或基本特征是什么? 什么时候使用个案研究最为合适? 三个问题互相关联，是学习使用个案研究法的基本问题。就文献来看，不同的学者似有不同的说法，其中最大的不同源自他们不同的研究背景，例如，有着自然主义研究背景的学者和尊崇实验研究传统的学者对这些问题的看法自然不同（Nunan & Bailey, 2009）。在研究实践中，试图将变量从自然环境中抽离出来并加以控制是非常困难的，也是无益的，所以，大多数学者倾向于把个案研究归为质性研究。Yin (1984) 这样定义个案研究："个案研究是一种实证性探究，它研究真实生活场景中的当前现象，特别适用于现象与其背景的界限并不明显的状况"（p. 13）。Merriam（1988）则把个案研究明确定义为："对单位事件、现象或社会单位所进行的密集的、整体的描述和分析"（p. 21）。两人的角度和侧重点似有不同。为了更好地厘清定义并理解这些基本问题、找到共识，一个好方法是把常见的几种定义或看法进行比较 (参见表 1)。

1　其他常见的说法是 case studies, case study method/methodology 或 case study research 和 qualitative case study 等（ 参见 Miles & Huberman, 1994; Stake, 1995; Denzin & Lincoln, 2000; Dörnyei, 2007; Cohen *et al.*, 2007 等）。在本导读中，案例研究和个案研究同义。

表 1　个案研究定义比照

Yin (1984, p. 13)	…an empirical inquiry that investigates a contemporary pheno-menon within its real-life context when the boundaries between the phenomenon and the context are not clearly evident, and in which multiple sources of evidence are used.
Merriam (1988, p. 16)	…an intensive, holistic description and analysis of a single entity, phenomenon, or social unit. Case studies are particularistic, descriptive, and heuristic and rely heavily on inductive reasoning in handling multiple data sources.
Johnson (1992, p. 84).	…to understand the complexity and dynamic nature of the particular entity, and to discover systematic connections among experiences, behaviors, and relevant features of the context.
Miles & Huberman (1994, p. 24)	…a phenomenon of some sort occurring in a bounded context.
Stake (1995, p. xi)	…the study of particularity and complexity of a single case.
Gall *et al.* (2003, p. 436)	…the in-depth study of instances of a phenomenon in its natural context and from the perspective of the participants involved in the phenomenon.
Dörnyei (2007, p. 152)	…not a specific technique but rather a method of collecting and organizing data so as to maximize our understanding of the unitary character of the social being or object studied.
Nunan & Bailey (2009, p. 162)	…typically observing "the characteristics of an individual entity—a child, a clique, a class, an educational program, or a community—in that entity's natural really occurring situation".

　　通过比较可以看出，虽然各种说法表达各异，但四点共识依然鲜明：(1) 个案研究的本质是实证的，其核心要素是对真实的生活环境的精细观察，即对研究对象在其现实环境中所展开的全面、翔实、深入的描述和分析；(2) 研究对象可以是一个或若干个人，也可以是一个或若干个小组、机构、项目、事件或现象；(3) 因真实的生活，即研究场景的特性，研究的基础是多元视角和数据，注重从整体的角度了解事件或现象的活动脉络而非某一特定变量；(4) 研究的关注点是个案的特殊性 (particularity)、复杂性 (complexity) 和启发性 (heuristic nature)，而非超越个案的共性，如可推而广之的模型或概念。本书作者在回顾并评析了几个较有代表性的定义后也总结出几条共识原则，它们分别是："有界性

或单一性（boundedness or singularity）、深度研究 (in-depth study)、多元视角或三角互证 (multiple perspectives or triangulation)、特殊性 (particularity)、情境性和解释 (contextualization and interpretation)"（详见 p. 21）。

可明显看出，在这些重要共识的背后实际上是个案研究的认识论基础：描写、理解和诠释个体的意义。换言之，研究并认识事物的特殊性和复杂性之重要性不亚于对事物共性的发现和求证，在个体中寻找共性并非不能。而这一点通常被看做质性研究和定性研究的主要区别（Cohen, Manion & Morrison, 2007）。也正因为这个特点，个案研究通常被自然地划归为质性研究范式（qualitative research paradigm）[1]。从常见的几本研究方法专著中可看出这是一种普遍做法，如 Yin (1984) 的《个案研究：设计与方法》(*Case Study Research: Designand Methods*)、Miles & Huberman (1994) 的《质性数据分析》(*Qualitative Data Analysis: An Expanded Sourcebook*)、Stake (1995) 的《个案研究的艺术》(*The Art of Case Study Research*)、Merriam (1988) 的《教育个案研究：一种质性方法》(*Case Study Research in Education: A Qualitative Approach*) 和 Merriam (1998) 的《质性研究与教育个案研究的应用》(*Qualitative Research and Case Study Applications in Education*)、Denzin & Lincoln (2000) 的《质性研究手册》(*Handbook of Qualitative Research*) 以及 Cohen, Manion & Morrison (2007) 的《教育研究方法》(*Research Methods in Education*)。在这些书中，个案研究均被置于质性研究的大框架下进行专案讨论。另外，也因为个案研究对研究对象所处的现实的全面、精细的"特写式"观察和检视（Cohen *et al.*, 2007, p. 254），个案研究已成为应用语言学、二语习得和语言教学等相关领域特别受欢迎的研究方法。多位学者就个案研究在上述领域的使用和意义著书立说，其中近期较有代表性的有 Dörnyei (2007) 的《应用语言学研究方法》(*Research Methods in Applied Linguistics*)、Nunan & Bailey (2009) 的《第二语言课堂研究》(*Exploring Second Language Classroom Research*) 和本书。事实上，正如 van Lier (2005) 和本书作者指出的那样，整个应用语言学领域的基础正是 20 世纪 70 至 80 年代第一拨关于语言学习者的个案研究，其中重要的研究者包括 Hatch (1978), Schmidt (1983)（关于日本艺术家在夏威夷时的语言发展的个案研究), Schumann (1978) 及 Wong-Fillmore (1979) 等

---

1 但是，也有学者可能对此持有不同看法。Yin (2003) 曾特别区分逻辑实证个案研究和更具解释性、现象学意义的个案研究，但同时他也指出前者的目的是"把个案研究置于科学研究（scientific methods）的框架之下，在科学数据分析的基础上生成假设、采集实证数据并得出结论 (p. 47)。

人，他们的研究成果对应用语言学中许多重要问题的理解和看法形成了重要的影响，至今仍被广泛引用。

2. 个案研究的类别

从不同的角度可以将个案研究分为几类。Yin (1984) 依照研究的功能把个案研究分为探索性 (exploratory) 个案研究、描述性 (descriptive) 个案研究和解释性 (explanatory) 个案研究。所谓探索性个案研究通常适用于两种情况：一是研究者试图用新的视角、假设、观点和方法来解析某一社会现象或问题，为新理论的形成 (theory-seeking) 作铺垫；二是研究者为了明确后续研究的问题和假设或者为了确定研究计划和程序是否恰当而开展的研究任务（虽然后续研究不一定是个案研究），所以数据采集通常先于理论和研究问题的形成。在社会研究中，这样的探索性个案研究通常被看做研究的前奏。描述性个案研究是研究者在已有理论框架的指导下对事件、现象和问题的全面描述，以叙述、描摹为主，理论先于数据。解释性个案研究适用的情形则是研究者运用现有理论理解并解释事件或现象的相关性及因果关系。在研究实践中，为达到探索和描述现象的目的，个案研究可以有多种设计构想，如：验证理论、形成理论或解释、生成假设、检验假设或者用个案表现理论观点 (Merriam, 1988, 1998)。

另一个常见的分类来自 Stake (1995, 2005)。他依照研究的目的把个案研究分为内发性个案研究 (intrinsic case study)、工具性个案研究 (instrumental case study) 和集体性个案研究 (collective case study) 三类。所谓"内发性"是指某一特定个案，如一个人、班级、事件或现象，引发了研究者的兴趣。研究者希望了解个案的特质，如：大部分孩子八岁时都已学会了识字，但某一八岁的男孩还没有学会，是什么原因？这便是典型的内发性个案研究。研究者的目的是了解和认识这一个案本身的特殊性，而不是通过研究该个案去了解别的个案或谋求对某一普遍性问题的认识 (Merriam, 1998)。工具性个案研究则发生在另一种情形下。研究者观察到了某一问题或现象，需要并希望找到具有普遍意义的解释或理解，如某种新的"作业评阅标准"（参见 Stake, 1995, pp. 2-4）。与之相关的问题可能是：新标准可用吗？怎么用？对教学有什么影响？推广者可能希望在某一个体教师的教学中开始试行新标准，这便构成了研究个案。与内发性个案研究不同的是，工具性个案研究的焦点不是个案中的教师或他/她的教学，而是了解新标准是否可行，也就是说，研究的目的不是为了了解和认识所涉个案本身，而是个案以外的东西，有着"项庄舞剑，意在沛公"的意味。多数情况下，研究者可能希望不只研究单一个案，而是选择多个个案以了解个案间的关联度或共性，Stake (1995) 把这种情形下的个案研究称为集体性个案研究，即把工具性个案研究延伸至数个案例，以更好地理解现象和问题或作出推论。

在研究实践中，这些类别并不是彼此完全独立或相互排斥的。虽作出如此分类，Stake (2005) 也承认所谓内发性个案研究和工具性个案研究只是它们各自某一方面的特征更突出，但在很多情况下又同时具有两种类别的某些特质。他特别指出："甚至内发性个案研究也可以被看做迈向宏大普遍性的一小步，特别是在个案反证了某一普遍原则的情况下" (p. 448)。

也有学者在实际研究中会根据运用个案数量的不同把个案研究分为单一案例 (single case) 研究和多案例 (multiple cases) 研究 (Miles & Huberman, 1994)。前者多用于分析一个极端的、独特的和罕见的现象、事件或情形（如上述内发性个案），也可以用于证实或证伪已有理论假设的某一个方面的问题。单一案例研究的学者认为，单一案例研究更能够深入、细致地揭示个案的本质和全貌，从而能够保证个案研究的信度。多案例研究者通常会开展两个层面的分析：个案内分析 (within-case analysis) 和个案间分析 (cross-case analysis) (Miles & Huberman, 1994)。所谓个案内分析是研究者将每一个个案作为独立的整体进行全面、深入的分析；个案间分析则是在彼此独立的个案内分析的基础上，研究者对所有个案再进行横向比较、归纳、总结并得出研究结论。与单一案例研究相比，这样的做法能够更好、更全面地反映研究问题的个案背景，尤其是在多个个案同时指向同一结论的时候，提高了研究结论的可再现性 (replicability)。换句话说，从某种角度来看，多案例研究可显著提高个案研究的效度。正如 Miles & Huberman (1994) 所言，虽然案例研究的初衷不是为了寻求普遍真理，但人类之本能诉求之一是了解事物的规律、掌握普遍性的知识，而多案例研究中的个案间分析能够从某种程度上满足这种诉求。

Yin (1984) 和 Stake (1995) 的分类是两种最为常见的个案研究分类，在相关文献中引用甚广。细观之下，可见这些分类间相通或交叉重叠之处，如 Stake (1995) 的内发性个案研究与 Yin (1984) 的描述性和解释性个案研究有共通之处，工具性个案研究和探索性个案研究则本质相同。Yin (1984) 也曾特别提示研究者们不要试图将这些类别割裂开来或者把它们看做某种等级。他说："一个常见的错误观念是，把不同的研究策略都按等级排列。于是，我们所接受的教导是，个案研究只适用于研究的探索阶段，调查和历史追溯适用于描写阶段，而实验则是探索和因果关系研究的唯一方法"（p. 15）。上述观念错误的原因是，研究实践表明，个案研究不仅仅是一种探索研究方法。

从表面看，对个案研究的分类，特别是相似的分类，似乎没有实质意义，但本导读认为，这样的分类和分类分析在帮助个案研究者明确研究目的、厘清研究构想以及更准确地设计并开展个案研究有着十分重要的意义。

3. 个案研究适用的范围和数据来源

个案研究最初主要用于医学，应用于研究病人的个案，之后陆续用于心理学、社会学及工商管理学等领域。在法律、医学和工商管理学中，个案研究早已成为最基本的教学工具之一。它在教学及学习研究方面的应用也十分广泛，特别是关于超常儿童、学习落后或低度缺陷儿童等类型的学习者的心理研究。Johnson (1992, p. 84) 认为，个案研究的目的是理解某一特定存在或实体（entity）的复杂性和动态本质，找到经验、行为和相关环境特征之间的系统性联系（详见 Duff, 2008, p. 32）。因强调其对事物的复杂性和动态本质的有效捕捉和分析，个案研究在某些研究情形下显得特别有吸引力。Yin（1994）曾提到四种情形下适用个案研究：

(1) 解释 (to explain) 现实生活干预 (intervention) 中存在的复杂因果关系

(2) 描述 (to describe) 干预已然发生的现实生活场景

(3) 描述 (to describe) 干预本身

(4) 探索 (to explore) 干预没有生效的情景

首先，四种情形下的个案研究有两个共同点：一是研究一定发生在真实的生活环境下，亦即所谓自然的探询（naturalistic inquiry）；二是研究的侧重点可有不同。其次，对上述四种情形的细读和解析有助于理解前面所提到的两个现象：(1) 20 世纪 70 至 80 年代的关于语言学习者的个案研究何以成为整个应用语言学领域的基础；(2) 个案研究何以成为应用语言学、二语习得和语言教学等相关领域特别受欢迎的研究方法。就二语习得的情景而言，进入二语环境对于学习者来说是一种真实的生活干预（或一种变化），至于干预是否生效、如何生效或者干预的质或量等都是二语习得的研究问题。课堂语言教学的情况与此类似。所以，应该说，对二语习得和语言教学过程的理解包含了对全部四种情形的研究和考量。正如本书作者指出的那样，对人们学习语言或尝试融入新的（语言或文化）群体的研究已经生成了非常详细的描述，这些描述包括

（学习或融入的）过程、结果和影响语言学习、使用或磨蚀的因素，这样的研究是应用语言学研究，特别是二语习得研究中一个非常重要的部分（详见本书 p. 35）。

Stake（2000）认为个案研究不是关于方法的选择，而是关于研究什么的选择（p. 435）。这可能正是案例研究作为一种研究方法的名称的由来。方法可以多种多样，但关注的核心始终是个案本身。在应用语言学研究中，这些研究的研究对象（或研究的案例）来源广泛，可能是单一母语环境中的幼儿和儿童、双语或多语环境下的儿童、少年移民或者成年外派劳务工人、成年外语学习者、留学生，或者因年龄、伤害、残疾等原因造成的成年失语症患者等。相关的研究议题和领域也十分广泛，可以是关于词汇、句法或语篇层面的特征、语用、叙事结构、读和写的过程的研究，也可以是关于社会或语言身份、态度和动机、学习策略和焦虑等方面的研究。

案例研究的一个重要特质是其研究视角和数据的多元化和多样性，其常见的主要数据来源包括以下六种（Yin, 2003）。

（1）文件（Documentation）：信函、备忘录、会议议程和记录报告、简报或评价以及大众媒体上出现的文章等都可以为个案研究提供有价值的信息。文件最重要的用途是为其他数据来源提供佐证。

（2）档案记录（Archival Records）：个人日记、工作日志、研究参与者个人信息、研究现场的相关资料等均可成为个案研究的相关数据链接以及可供广泛检索和分析的对象。

（3）访谈（Inteviews）：访谈是个案研究最重要的基本数据来源之一。访谈通常可采取三种形式：1）开放式访谈，即以谈话的方式要求被访者陈述有关事实或提出自己对事件的看法和意见；2）焦点式访谈，即就研究计划事先拟定的一组特定问题展开半开放式访谈；3）结构式访谈，即以问卷调查的方式展开面对面的交谈。

（4）直接观察（Direct Observation）：研究者进入研究的现场就创造了直接观察的机会。这种观察包括正式和非正式的数据收集活动，如观察会议、课堂或其他类似的场所或场景中一段时间内某种行为发生的频率等。这是个案研究另一重要的数据来源。需要特别注意的是这种观察可能需要得到书面许可。

（5）参与式观察（Participant Observation）：当研究者融入研究对象的环境，成为现象或事件中的一部分时所开展的观察。这种观察为个案研究提供了特殊的收集数据的机会，其特殊性在于对现象或事件的理解有可能来自个案内部人（insider）的视角，而不是外人（outsider）的观点。但也有人认为这种特殊的机会毫无价值，因为这样的参与可能意味着对案例的操纵，对准确地描述案例并无益处。

（6）实物（Physical Artifacts）：实物是个案研究的另一种数据源，包括工具、仪器、艺术作品及其他实体的证据。

Sturman (1997，转引自 Cohen *et al.*, 2007, p. 262) 则把个案研究中的数据收集、类型和分析概括总结为一个连续体（见表2），更为清晰地描述了个案研究的数据收集之本质，也从另一个侧面反映了个案研究可能适用的范围。

表 2　个案研究数据收集、类型和分析

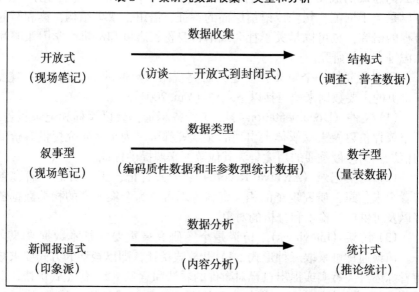

虽然不是所有的个案研究都需要同时引入这些数据，但多元视角和多样化数据使研究者能够增加证据的分量。

4. 个案研究的方法与步骤

在研究实践中，不同的个案研究者可能会有不同的安排，但一般认为实施个案研究有三大阶段（Yin, 1984）：第一阶段是定义与研究设计，包括发展理论、界定分析单元、确定单一案例或多案例和选择案例与研究设计四个步骤。其中，研究设计需考虑五个问题：（1）研究什么？（2）回答什么问题？（3）如何展开分析？（4）数据与研究问题之间的逻辑关系是什么？（5）如何解释研究发现？第二阶段是准备、数据收集和分析，包括资料准备、决定数据收集的方法和分析策略与方式两个步骤。第三阶段则是分析与提出结论的阶段，包括数据分析、数据解释与综合报告三个步骤。Nisbet & Watt (1984) 提出，个案研究应遵循由宽泛到逐渐聚焦的过程。这个过程也包括三个阶段，因为个案研究的目的是捕捉逐渐展开的情形之动态特征，所以它的第一个阶段应该是开放的，即开始于一个非常宽泛的视域，之后则是逐渐聚焦的过程，以确保识别后续研究的关键点和数据的采集，即第二阶段。第三阶段是草拟数据的诠释以备多方验证。

本书作者则以流程图的方式介绍了个案研究实施的过程以及各环节和要素之间的关联和交互，如数据收集和分析环节使解读环节成为可能，而解读环节又反过来确保了进一步的数据收集（详见本书 p. 92）。

研究问题和设计	数据收集	数据分析	解读	写作并修改案例报告
*研究目的 *概念或理论框架 *研究问题 *确定环境、案例、分析单位、抽样策略、时间表等	*观察 *访谈 *多方检视 *实物 *记研究日志	*转写 *整理数据库 *建立概念图 *备忘录 *编码 *比较案例 *缩小数据分析的范围 *多方检视 *模式配比 *引出主题 *找到反证等	*识别、理解关键主题或模式 *考虑对立的解释或数据 *得出结论	*确定读者和体裁 *选择有代表性的证据 *数据陈列 *写出连贯、完整的叙事或说明报告 *提交最终研究报告

综合几位学者的观点，个案研究实施的流程可归纳为三个阶段：(1) 确定个案研究对象或研究问题；(2) 以各种方式调查并收集相关数据和资料；(3) 分析数据并写出分析报告。三个阶段又可细分为以下六个具体步骤(Simons, 1980; Nisbet & Watt, 1984; Yin, 1984, 2003; Merriam, 1988; Stake, 1995, 2000; Duff, 2008)：

◆ 确立 / 定义研究问题
◆ 选择个案并确定收集和分析数据的方法
◆ 准备收集数据
◆ 进入现场并开始收集数据
◆ 评估与分析数据
◆ 撰写个案研究报告

5. 关于个案研究的长短之争

　　如前所述，个案研究法通常被归入质性研究范式，那些针对质性研究范式的传统的批评与诟病也都自然演变成对个案研究的批评和指责。换言之，关于个案研究的长短之争通常与两大研究"范式之争"(paradigm wars)（Gage, 1989）的诸多方面有着紧密的联系。纵观文献，在诸多的研究方法中，可能没有一种方法如个案研究法一般因其长短、优劣有过如此广泛、深入且频繁的探讨。探讨的场景和方式基本一致，即和量化研究方法，特别是大规模的实验或调查作比照，其结果往往是提出一个问题：仅凭个别个案研究如何求得真知？ Campbell & Stanley (1966) 曾把单一个案研究看做研究方法中的垃圾："这样的研究完全没有控制，导致其结果几乎没有科学价值……"(pp. 6-7)[1]。Smith (1991) 也曾评论道，个案研究是逻辑性最弱的知的方式（the logically weakest method of knowing）(p. 375, 引自 Cohen, Manion & Morrison, 2007, p. 257)。Cohen, Manion & Morrison (2007) 认为这样的观点不能称之为批评，而是一种"偏见或意识形态"，但其指认的问题值得重视，即个案研究必须回应信度和效度的问题，以确保其研究的"权威性和合法性"(p. 257)。类似的争议和讨论此起彼伏，迁延数十载，似乎仍无尘埃落定之时。

　　许多个案研究者或个案研究的推崇者以各自的方式对这些争议作出了回应或反驳（Simons, 1980; Yin, 1984, 2003; Miles & Huberman, 1994; Stake, 1995, 2000）。Flyvbjerg (2004) 也是其中一位。他将这些争议和讨论精简地归纳为人们对个案研究的五大误解，并一一给予批驳或校正 (pp. 421-434，见表 3)。

---

1 虽然几年后，Campbell (1975) 完全改变了自己关于个案研究的判断，用他自己的话说是彻底放弃了早期对个案研究的武断的藐视（an extreme oscillation away from my earlier dogmatic disparagement of case studies）(p. 179)。他的解释是，……量化的知的方式不会取代质性的、常识性知的方式……这并不是说常识性的自然主义观察就是客观的、可靠的或者无偏见的。但这就是我们所拥有的一切。虽然喧闹、易出错且存有偏见，它仍然是通向知识的唯一之路 (pp. 179, 191)。

表 3　关于个案研究的五大误解

	误解	批驳或校正
1	一般化的理论知识（独立于语境之外的）比具体的实践性知识（依赖于语境的）更有价值。	个案知识是人类认知的核心，社会科学尚无法提供概括性的、独立于语境的预测性理论（predictive theory），所以依赖语境的知识和经验是专家能力的核心，而这样的知识也正是个案研究法和个案教学法的核心，或者说，认知的核心。因此，具体的、依赖于语境的知识比徒劳地寻找预测性理论和普遍性更有价值 (p. 422-423)。
2	在个案的基础上无法概括出一般性，所以个案研究不能对科学发展作出贡献。	我们经常从个别个案概括出一般性（如：伽利略从一个个案观察就彻底推翻了亚里士多德延续近两千年的落体运动法则），作为其他研究方法的补充或备选，个案研究可以生成一般性，对科学的发展有关键作用；只是我们高估了一般性（知识）在科学发展中的作用的同时却低估了例子的力量 (p. 425)。
3	个案研究只是研究过程的第一步，即提出假设的时候最有用，而在验证假设和建构理论时其他方法则更合适。	个案研究对假设的生成和验证都是很有用的方法，而且并不限于这些研究活动 (p. 425)。
4	个案研究偏重证实（verification），其常见倾向是确认研究者先入为主的观念。	个案研究不比其他的研究方法更偏重证实研究者先入为主的观点，相反，经验表明，个案研究更偏重对先入为主之观念的证伪（falsification），而不是证实（verification）(p. 429)。
5	在具体的个案研究基础上很难总结、概括出一般性命题和理论。	总结个案研究常常比较困难，特别是牵涉到个案过程。这样的看法是正确的，但不太正确的是认为个案结果也难以总结。总结个案研究之困难主要在于研究现实的特性而非方法的原因。总结并概括个案研究并不可取，好的研究理应被当做完整的叙事来解读 (pp. 431-432)。

　　本书作者在本书中也对这些争议作了比较清楚、透彻的讨论（详见本书 pp. 39-55）。她认为："与其他任何研究方法一样，个案研究有其本身固有的长处和短处。然而，只要研究者意识到它的潜力和局限，就能作出扎实、周密、内容充实且有意义的研究" (p. 40)。在她看来，因其

自身特点，个案研究有着明显的优势，如果设计、实施恰当，个案研究的"完整性、深度分析和可读性"不容置疑，其主要长处有以下四点：

(1) 丰富且厚重的描写和多方验证
(2) 在理论建构中所展现出的探索和创新的潜能与作用
(3) 特异或非典型性案例的选用有助于开拓某一领域的新知识和认识
(4) 便于进行历时性设计，从而使考察变化成为可能

同时，作者也总结并回应了一些所谓个案研究法的"短处"或"弱点"，它们主要包括以下几点：(1) 缺乏概括性；(2) 如何用"非正常"案例构建"正常"行为的模型？ (3) 海量的描写和多远视角对数据分析和呈现构成巨大挑战；(4) 不够客观；(5) 缺乏理论指引，无法提出理论洞见；(6) 历时性案例设计或导致参与者流失或终止参与；(7) 小样本数据量化分析的限制；(8) 研究伦理的关切，如难以保护研究参与者的隐私等。细读之下，可以看出这些所谓的"短处"或"弱点"大多是在特定的情境下显得特别突出。正如作者指出的那样，个案研究法"常常是被置于大规模的实验法的对立面进行负面的比照……一种方法的长处通常是另一种方法的短处"（详见本书 p. 39）。反之亦然。真正值得思考或尝试的应该是如何在"研究多案例中的个别变量和研究个别案例中的多个变量之间"找到平衡 (Lewin, 1979)。

三、各章节主要内容和导读

第一章以介绍作者本人曾经完成的一个二语习得个案研究为基础，生动、有效地引入了关于个案研究的理论和方法问题。吉姆是移民到加拿大的柬埔寨难民，作者跟踪观察他长达两年半，详细记录并研究了吉姆在这段时间习得、使用英语的过程以及努力融入新环境所遇到的困难和挫折。书中有大量叙事和原始语料摘录片段，生动地再现了个案研究的要点和特点，使读者对个案研究的本质有了初步但清晰的了解。作者对该个案的分析则不仅再次突出了个案研究作为一种研究方法的种种特质和优势，也较好地展现了个案研究在揭示二语习得研究中一些重大理论和方法问题方面的作用。这个主题一直贯穿于之后的五章。

在第二章中，作者首先在之前个案研究的定义中提取了关键的几个原则，即有界性或单一性、深度研究、多元视角或三角互证、特殊性、情境性和解释。然后，作者概括地论述了个案研究在社会科学研究中的

历史本源、质性研究的一般特点以及质性研究方法在应用语言学中的应用。在此背景下，作者又进一步阐释了个案研究的目的和哲学基础及其在应用语言学研究中的作用。作者还用了较多篇幅介绍了个案研究的类别（如：探索式、描述式和解释式）、长短优劣之争以及她自己对这些问题的回应和观点。

第三章主要介绍过去三十多年间应用语言学个案研究的实例，数量达五十多个。这些个案类别各有不同，例证翔实、细腻，既展现了个案间的共性，也点出了它们之间的差异。个案所涉议题均为第二语言习得过程中的基本问题，详列如下：

（1）儿童语言习得、双语和语言丢失的早期研究（Ronjat, 1913; Kenyeres, 1938; Leopold,1939, 1947, 1949a, 1949b, 1954/1978; Hatch, 1978a, 1978b）[1]

（2）20世纪60至80年代的自然习得顺序研究和绩效分析（performance analysis）（Brown, 1973; Wong-Fillmore, 1979; Huebner, 1983; Schmidt, 1983; Long & Sato, 1984）

（3）个体差异：特例、有天赋的和没有天赋的学习者（Wong-Fillmore, 1979; Abraham & Vann, 1987; Ioup, 1989; Obler, 1989; Ioup, Boustagui, El Tigi & Moselle, 1994等）

（4）语言经历的日记、回忆录和自传（Schmidt & Frota, 1986; Hoff-man, 1989; Kaplan, 1993; Schumann, 1997; Mori, 1997; Pavlenko & Lantolf, 2000）

（5）语言学习中的身份、投入和性别问题（Norton, 2000; Day, 2002; McKay & Wong, 1996; Miller, 2003; Toohey, 2001）

（6）语言学习、固化和石化现象（Lardiere, 1998a, 1998b, 2006; Han, 1998; Long, 2003）

（7）语言遗失（或磨蚀）现象（Kouritzen, 1999）

（8）语用和社会语言能力发展（Ellis, 1992; Belz & Kinginger, 2002; Li, 1998, 2000; Siegal, 1996）

（9）家庭个案：双语社会化和维系的研究（de la Pietra & Romo, 2003; Schecter & Bayley, 1997, 2002）

（10）主流二语学习者：身份、表征与定位（Harklau, 1994a, 1994b; Willett，1995; McKay & Wong, 1996; Hunter, 1997; Toohey, 2000）

（11）二语写作和学术话语的社会化（Leki, 1995; Spack, 1997;

---

1 参见本书的参考文献。下同。

Casanave, 2002）

（12）在线语言发展和使用：融入虚拟空间（Lam, 2000, 2004; Yim, 2005）

（13）双语和双文化：移民、旅居者和海归者的身份意识（Kanno, 2003; Shi, 2003; Marx, 2002）

（14）教师作为语言和文化社会化的促进者（Borg, 1998; Duff, 1995, 2002a, 2002b; Duff & Li, 2004; Duff & Uchida, 1997 等）

这些实例反映了个案研究的多面性和立体性，也证实了个案研究对应用语言学研究趋势的影响。一个重要的结论是个案研究必须把语言学习者看做多维度的个体，有着自己的历史、希望和期待。

第四、五和六章分别介绍个案研究的三个主要阶段：第四章描述实施个案研究的起始阶段，即研究设计、数据收集和相关研究伦理问题；第五章重点描述个案数据分析、诠释和评估；第六章则论述如何撰写个案研究报告。

作者在第四章中首先介绍了这三个主要阶段以及具体步骤间的互动关系。她特别强调，在个案研究中，因为研究问题的本质会影响后续数据收集、分析、诠释和报告撰写的方法或步骤，所以研究者在设计时必须充分、透彻地理解自己的研究焦点和目的。设计的关键是个案选择和抽样策略，如：是选用单一还是多个个案、封闭式还是开放式个案等。这些选择和决定背后的理据是一定的理论前提和假设，它们既是现场研究活动的基础，也是确立研究问题时的原则。关于如何提取高质量的个案数据，作者又用较大篇幅特别介绍了数据收集过程的一些重要方面：数据来源（选取哪一种、各有什么特点等）、访谈类型和方法（结构式、主题式、焦点式访谈或口述历史）、观察技巧（直接观察或参与式观察）、多方验证以及相关研究伦理的考量（如何确保个案参与者的权益不会受到任何损害）。在介绍中，作者使用了大量的表格，总结对比各种技巧、方法和问题类型，给读者提供了很大方便，使读者一目了然。

第五章是第四章后续部分，主要描述个案研究的第二阶段，即数据分析、诠释和评估阶段。作者首先介绍了个案数据转写、分析、诠释和评估的一些实用性指导原则，包括转写符号的样例、转写片断示例、编码和个案分析（如个案内和个案间分析）以及一些必要的评估标准。读者则可以学习如何确立哪些是不必要的转写内容（如停顿长度、非语言交流等）以减轻转写任务的强度，更好地服务于研究目的。无论是手工还是机助方式，数据编码都是数据分析的第一步，编码系统则可能来自数据本身（如字、词、句或表述）隐含的主题或者来自特定的概念框架

（如动机或归因等）。通过阅读本章提供的实例，读者可以了解编码相关技巧和问题。最后，作者讨论了个案研究的评估标准以回应个案研究之效度和准确度的问题。作者认为对个案研究的评估应包括三个方面的内容：（1）体恤到读者的需要；（2）合理扎实的研究方法；（3）彻底、完整的数据收集和分析。作者一个重要的提醒是：个案研究实施的过程中，研究者不仅要在微观上明确自己的研究问题和设计，也要在宏观上确立自己的认识论立场和相应的研究范式。

　　第六章主要介绍如何撰写个案研究书面报告。作者首先介绍了撰写个案研究书面报告的重要性，然后概括介绍了可能影响研究报告呈现形式的几大因素，如目标读者、目的和焦点、内容、结构、体裁、语态、立场和自反性以及相关研究伦理。作者详细介绍了个案报告的主要类型、结构和特征，并佐以大量实例和样例片段进行说明。这对读者和个案研究学习者有很大帮助。之后，作者介绍了如何在报告中用流程图、概念图、柱状图、表格等呈现视觉信息，如何在报告中谨守研究伦理规范，确保个案参与者的权益不受损害。本章结尾处，作者介绍了附录的必要性和评价个案研究书面报告的标准。

参考文献：

Campbell, D. T. (1975). Degrees of freedom and the case study. *Comparative Political Studies*, 8: 178–191.

Campbell, D. T. & Stanley, J. C. (1966). *Experimental and quasi-experimental designs for research*. Chicago: Rand McNally.

Cohen, L., Manion, L. & Morrison, K. (2007). *Research methods in education* (6th ed.). London: Routledge.

Denzin, N. K. & Lincoln, Y. S. (2000). *The handbook of qualitative research* (2nd ed.). Thousand Oaks, CA: Sage.

Dörnyei, Z. (2007). *Research methods in applied linguistics*. Oxford: Oxford University Press.

Duff, P. (2008). *Case study research in applied linguistics*. New York: Taylor & Francis Group, LLC.

Flyvbjerg, B. (2004). Five misunderstandings about case study research. In Seale *et al.*, (Eds.). *Qualitative research practice*. London & Thousand Oaks, CA: Sage.

Gage, N. L. (1989). The paradigm wars and their aftermath: A "historical" sketch of research on teaching since 1989. *Educational Researcher*, 18: 4-10.

Gall, M. D., Gall, J. P. & Borg, W. T. (2003). *Educational research* (7th ed.). White Plains, NY: Pearson Education.

Hatch, E. (Ed.). (1978). *Second language acquisition: A book of readings*. Rowley, MA:

Newbury House.

Johnson, D. M. (1992). *Approaches to research in second language learning*. New York: Longman.

Lewin, M. (1979). *Understanding psychological research*. New York: John Wiley & Sons.

Merriam, S. B. (1988). *Case study research in education: A qualitative approach*. San Francisco: Jossey-Bass Publishers.

Merriam, S. B. (1998). *Qualitative research and case study applications in education*. San Francisco: Jossey-Bass Publishers.

Miles, M. B. & Huberman, A. M. (1994). *Qualitative data analysis: An expanded sourcebook* (2nd ed.). Thousand Oaks, CA: Sage.

Nisbet, J. & Watt, J. (1984). Case study. In J. Bell, T. Bush, A. Fox, J. Goodey & S. Goulding (Eds.). *Conducting small-scale investigation in educational management* (pp. 79-92). London: Harper & Row.

Nunan, D. & Bailey, K. M. (2009). *Exploring second language classroom research*. Boston: Heinle & Heinle.

Schmidt, R. (1983). Interaction, acculturation and the acquisition of communicative competence: A case study of an adult. In N. Wolfson & E. Judd (Eds.). *Sociolinguistics and second language acquisition* (pp.137-174). Rowley, MA: Newbury House.

Schmidt, R. W., & Frota, S. N. (1986). Developing basic conversational ability in a second language: A case study of an adult learner of Portuguese. In R. R. Day (Ed.). *Talking to learn: Conversations in second language acquisition* (pp. 237-322). Rowley, MA: Newbury House.

Schumann, J. (1978). *The pidginization process: A model for second language acquisition*. Rowley, MA: Newbury House.

Simons, H. (1980). *Towards a science of the singular: Essays about case study in educational research and evaluation*. Norwich, UK: University of East Anglia, Centre for Applied Research in Education.

Smith, H. W. (1991). *Strategies of social research: The methodological imagination*. London: Prentice Hall.

Stake, R. E. (1995). *The art of case study research*. Thousand Oaks, CA: Sage.

Stake, R. E. (2000). Case studies. In N. K. Denzin & Y. S. Lincoln (Eds.). *The handbook of qualitative research*. Thousand Oaks, CA: Sage.

Stake, R. R. (2005). Qualitative case studies. In N. K. Denzin & Y. S. Lincoln (Eds.). *The handbook of qualitative research* (3rd ed., pp. 443–466). Thousand Oaks, CA: Sage.

van Lier, L. (2005). Case study. In E. Hinkel (Ed.). *Handbook of research in second language teaching and learning* (pp. 195–208). Mahwah, NJ: Erlbaum.

Wong-Fillmore, L. (1979). Individual differences in second language acquisition. In C. Fillmore, D. Kempler & W. Wang (Eds.). *Individual differences in language ability and language behaviour* (pp. 203–228). New York: Academic Press.

Yin, R. K. (1984). *Case study research: Design and methods*. California: Sage Publications.

Yin, R. K. (1994). *Case study research: Design and methods* (2nd ed.). California: Sage
　　Publications.
Yin, R. K. (2003). *Applications of case study research* (2nd ed.). Thousand Oaks, CA: Sage.

张莲

北京外国语大学

2011年7月20日

Preface

As a graduate student at the University of Hawaii, I learned a great deal about important advances made in the field of second-language acquisition (SLA) on the basis of a relatively small number of well-documented cases of learners of English as a second language (ESL) by scholars there and at the University of California at Los Angeles (UCLA), where I later studied. The researchers included Evelyn Hatch, Roger Andersen, Thom Huebner, John Schumann, Richard Schmidt, Charlene Sato, and their colleagues and students. Their case studies were accessible, intriguing accounts of individual language learners that had a huge impact on the young subfield of SLA within applied linguistics. Vivid, complex, and theoretically interesting, the case studies were a valuable means of illustrating developmental issues connected with learning another language.

Although my master's degree research was a large cross-sectional study of the syntactic development of English language learners from Mandarin and Japanese backgrounds that did not involve the in-depth analysis of any particular case, I began a study of a Cambodian learner of English in 1986 (see Chapter 1). The impetus for this book came from that research and my earlier graduate studies. My first publication on case study research methods in SLA (Duff, 1990) convinced me that some of the complexities of applied linguistic research can be studied and presented meaningfully within the fullness of cases, and that an introductory text on case study research was needed in our field. Despite the many intervening years and delays in completing this manuscript, no other applied linguistics textbooks on this method have been written.

Yet, increasing numbers of case studies have been conducted by graduate students and established scholars without coursework or dedicated applied linguistics research methods texts to guide the process. This book does not argue that case studies or other qualitative approaches to applied linguistics research are the best or most valid approaches. The research methods one employs may be a matter of personal preference, but choice of method is also determined in large part by the questions one seeks answers to, the body of knowledge that already exists on that topic, the domain of inquiry and context, and the methods the questions lend themselves to. I learned from Brian Lynch at UCLA that all research has an underlying epistemology and ontology as well as methodology. Researchers using case study may approach it from different philosophical positions and may also favor different approaches to data analysis, accordingly.

This book is intended for undergraduate and graduate students and other scholars wishing to understand more about case study methods and also about their application in research on language learners and language users in a variety of contexts. Since the number of case studies conducted each year is growing steadily, this book provides an overview, but is not a comprehensive survey of all significant existing case studies. In addition, although I have tried to include case studies of people's encounters with languages other than English, most of the research reported involves teachers and learners of English in Canada and the United States, since I am most familiar with that work. Finally, applied linguistics is more than language teaching and learning, but most of my examples are related to these topics. The book should contribute to our understanding of the complexities, difficulties, and discoveries of how people learn or are taught another language. However, it is my hope that applied linguists working in other subfields will find the book useful as they undertake their own studies and evaluate those by others.

This book could not have been published without the supreme patience and goodwill of the series editor, Susan Gass, and the publishing team at Lawrence Erlbaum, especially Cathleen Petree. Sue and Cathleen have prodded me along for many years, since I first started—and stopped—then restarted this project (many times over). I also acknowledge the inspiration of my former professors and their own case study research, referred to earlier. However, my interest in case studies was piqued even before that, by the celebrated urban researcher and anthropologist Oscar Lewis. His 1961 book *The Children of Sanchez*, an "autobiographical" account of five members of a poor family in a Mexico City slum, had an enormous impact on me as a young teenager and convinced me of the power of case study.

To my many graduate students over the years (and particularly my Amigos group), and to colleagues near and far, friends and family, I give big thanks not only for putting up with me while I talked endlessly about this project, but also for giving me excellent examples of case studies to draw upon. I thank Kathi Bailey, Wayne Wright, and especially Lourdes Ortega for their helpful comments on an earlier version of the manuscript. My wonderful research assistant, Sandra Zappa-Hollman, helped me with library and editorial tasks, and provided some graphic support as well, for which I am very grateful. To my former case study participants and research collaborators, I also extend my deep gratitude. Additional special thanks go to Nancy Duff, Jane Duff, Nelly and Bonnie Duff, Linda Corrigan, Maria Andersson, and Duanduan Li for helping me to keep a balanced perspective and for allowing me to drone on, far too often, about my fears that I would never finish. As an indication of just how long its incubation has been, I started the manuscript using WordStar, later migrated to WordPerfect, and in more recent years switched to Microsoft Word. In the meantime, I have acquired multiple revised editions of the same case study and qualitative research methods textbooks, which have been updated every few years. My own research epistemologies have also shifted in the interim, from (post)positivist to interpretive.

Funding for my research and for the writing of this book has been provided by the Social Sciences and Humanities Research Council of Canada and the (U.S.) National Academy of Education/Spencer Foundation. I am very grateful to both organizations.

Finally, I dedicate this book to my loving parents, Lawrence and Elizabeth Duff, who have looked forward to its completion perhaps most of all. I also acknowledge, with deep thanks, their unwavering encouragement and support over the years, and my father's assistance with my case study of the Cambodian learner of English presented in Chapter 1.

Patsy Duff

Vancouver, Canada

Case Study Research in Applied Linguistics

1.1 Introduction

The goal of this book is threefold: (1) to help readers understand the methodological foundations of case study research as one type of qualita- tive research, (2) to examine seminal case studies in the area of second- language (L2) teaching, learning, and use, in order to illustrate the approach across thematic areas, and (3) to provide some guidance, on a more practical level, about how to conduct, evaluate, and write up case studies in applied linguistics. The book expands on the overviews provided in other methods textbooks and also draws on the burgeoning literature on qualitative research, and case study in particular, from the fields of psychology, sociology, and education primarily (e.g., Bromley, 1986; Denzin & Lincoln, 2000; Merriam, 1998; Stake, 1995; Yin, 2003a, 2003b).

I begin, as many case studies do, with a concrete example, a narrative description of a language learner named "Jim", with short interspersed excerpts of his oral English language production at different stages in time. Details are provided about my original analysis of Jim's L2 development and the rationale for that focus. Then, for the more general purposes of this book, a fuller description of Jim's life and circumstances is provided, including his experiences learning English and his challenges in Canada as a government-assisted refugee, a new immigrant, and an English as a second language (ESL) student with a wife and young children to support. Later in this chapter and elsewhere in the book, I reflect on other kinds of analysis that could be conducted with an individual such as Jim, especially given current directions in our field related to language and literacy socialization, family multiliteracies, identity and language learning, and sociopolitical and economic aspects of immigration. I also consider the strengths and limitations of case studies such as this one.

Although the case presented here is that of a language learner, many of the same principles of case study research apply when conducting other kinds of case studies within the realm of applied linguistics, including descriptions and analyses of an individual language teacher or learner, a school, or a country's language policies, communication in a multilingual workplace setting, language shift in a postcolonial small-scale society, and so on.

1.2 Case Study of a Language Learner: "Jim"

In February 1986, Jim[1] was a 28-year-old Cambodian man who had just been granted refugee status in Canada, where he and his family had lived for two months.[2] The experiences leading up to that significant milestone in his life included harrowing years of being on the run in Cambodia and later living and working at refugee camps in Thailand, while seeking opportunities to immigrate to North America. Two years earlier, in 1984, as the following excerpt reveals, he had married a Cambodian woman who had already obtained a United Nations refugee number that would allow her and her (first) husband and their two infants to leave Thailand. However, before their immigration could be finalized, her husband was killed by Thai soldiers, a tragedy that had a positive outcome for Jim. By marrying this young widow, Jim gained refugee status in the place of her late husband, and thus the chance of a new life in Canada. His wife's chances of immigration were increased because Jim knew some English, which was rewarded by the Canadian Embassy interviewers at the time, according to Jim. In Excerpt 1, Jim describes some of this background:

---

1 In previous publications I referred to Jim as "JDB," my abbreviation for the Cambodian king, Jayavarman the Seventh (pronounced Jayavarman Dibrombul in Khmer), who built Angkor Wat (e.g., Duff, 1993a, 1993b).

2 Approximately 18,600 Cambodians entered Canada in this way between 1980 and 1992, according to one Canadian source (http://www.multiculturalcanada.ca/ecp/content/cambodians_khmer. html).

Excerpt 1 [1]

Four person [in my family]. My wife, her husband die. I was arri(ve) in
Thailand on [1984] so I haven't raison [food rations] and UN number ...
and impossible interviews other embassy, so I must to live with my wife.
Because my wife, her husband die by Thai soldier, and my wife has
the UN number and raison [rations] ... So now I no + children but my
wi(fe) has two children ... four year and two year ... After that I was to
+ examination at IRC + International Committee Red Cross + after that
and + was pass a + examination and + teacher Cambodian-Cambodian
teacher at school + in Thailand ... In Cambodian, when I stop study,
because my fatherland has big fighting, so I must stop ...

[There are four people in my family. My wife's husband died. I
arrived in Thailand in 1984 and I didn't have food rations or a
United Nations number, and it was impossible to get interviews at
other embassies, so I had to live with [marry] my wife. Because my
wife's husband, who was killed by a Thai soldier, had a UN number
and rations. So I have no children but my wife has two children, a
four-year-old and two-year-old. After that I had an examination at
the International Red Cross and passed and became a Cambodian
teacher at school in Thailand. In Cambodia, I had to stop studying
because of the war ...]

Jim's story was a fascinating but sad one that over the next 20 years
would take various twists and turns, not unlike those of others who immigrate under similar circumstances. During his first winter in Canada, Jim
began to take intensive English courses five hours a day at a government-
sponsored adult education center and had just begun to deliver newspapers
in my neighborhood, a new job for him and his first in Canada. I myself had
just moved back to Canada from Asia and had a new job as well, teaching
university courses on L2 education and acquisition. Jim's wife and young
children spoke no English. I met Jim a few times that January and February,
and asked whether he would agree to participate in this research about his
English language learning. I would pay him to discuss various topics and he
would have a chance to practice his English. He was very willing to comply. I

---

1   Transcription conventions: + is a short untimed pause; ... denotes talk I have ellipted;
    commas mark sharp rising intonation; timed pauses appear as numbers, in seconds, for
    example (1.0); (x) denotes unclear word; (xx) denotes two unclear words. Words in square
    brackets are provided by the researcher to aid interpretation of the utterance or excerpt; a
    half-attached dash represents a false-start or self-correction; a colon represents lengthening of
    a sound or syllable. For other conventions, see Chapter 5, Table 5.2.

had other interactions with him outside of this study as well, taking his family grocery shopping sometimes, helping them in emergencies, offering Jim additional paid employment (e.g., gardening), and attending Cambodian cultural events with his family. He was part of a small, rather fragile community of Cambodian refugees who had recently arrived in Canada. Like many of them, he was anxious about not having had any contact with, or news from, relatives in Cambodia for nearly 15 years, despite many attempts to locate them.[1]

At that stage in Jim's life, it was unclear how his oral English would develop over time, with his daily exposure to English in classes and his encounters with a range of English speakers in the community, such as government agencies, charities, neighbors, church members, and the general English-speaking public. Would he exhibit developmental patterns similar to those reported in Huebner's (1979, 1983) influential case study of a Hmong-speaking Laotian immigrant (refugee) in Hawaii named Ge? Whereas Ge had received no formal English instruction in either Laos or Hawaii, Jim had studied some English. Would he therefore make more rapid progress in his acquisition of English based on his intensive language courses and contact in the community?

Huebner's longitudinal study focused mainly on Ge's evolving nominal reference system, which involved learning to use appropriate articles with nouns and supplying required sentence subjects in English (e.g., with specific/definite nouns or with information known to the hearer). For example, he tended to produce utterances of the following type (with the sentence topics, minus the definite article *the*, shown in italics):

> *chainis* tertii—tertii fai. bat *jaepanii* isa twentii eit. (1-224)
> [*The Chinese man* is thirty-five. But *the Japanese* is twenty-eight.]
> en *beibii,* isa in da moder, en da owder broder. (1-115)
> [And *the babies* were placed between the adults.]

> (Huebner, 1979, p. 27)

Huebner detected several traits in Ge's interlanguage (his developing second-language system) that reflected the topic prominence of his first

---

1 He received his first news from Cambodia a few months later, in 1986, when he received a letter and a small, wrinkled black-and-white photo that his parents had sent of his family. Although they had survived the war, several of them were in need of medical treatment and Jim began sending them medical supplies. Jim subsequently (in the 1990s) made two trips back to Cambodia.

language (L1), Hmong, especially in his earliest stages of development (see Chapter 3 for more details). The traits were similar to those I observed in Jim and among Chinese and Japanese learners of English in other studies I was conducting (Duff, 1985, 1988): the use of *have* constructions that functioned as existentials and introducers of new information/noun phrases (e.g., *Have four man in my family* [There are four people in my family] and *On hill have much man* [There are many people on the hill]); the omission of subjects that could be guessed from context; and the frequent use of a topicalizing device (e.g., *As for me,* I am a student).[1] In Ge's case, the topic marker was the invented (but copula-like) form "isa", as in *gow howm, isa plei da gerl* [When we went home, we would visit with the girls] (Huebner, 1979, p. 27).

Thus, Ge and Jim had rather similar personal and linguistic backgrounds, with topic-prominent L1s that influenced their English. My research was not meant to be a replication of Huebner's study examining the exact same sets of structures. I had two goals: (1) to examine Jim's English as it became less topic prominent and more subject prominent over time (Duff, 1993a), and (2) to consider task-related variation in his performance (Coughlan & Duff, 1994; Duff, 1993b). Here I mainly discuss observations related to the first goal. The study, which took place over a 2.5-year period, yielded about 36 hours of interviews and hundreds of narratives about Jim's personal experiences, and other kinds of elicited language production, including picture descriptions, picture-sequence narratives, and Cambodian folktale narratives (Duff, 1993a, 1993b).

A brief sketch of Jim's background as an English language learner helps to contextualize his observed language development. The son of a school principal, Jim had started studying English at a public school in Cambodia at the age of 15. Six months later, the Khmer Rouge, under Pol Pot's leadership, closed all schools and began a campaign of genocide that resulted in the killing of more than a million Cambodians and the devastation of the country. Some years later, Jim had studied English for about six months in refugee camps and had also attended a teacher-training course offered partly in English in order to learn how to teach Cambodian[2] to Cambodian children in the camps. He was also briefly involved in developing materials for English teaching, just prior to his emigration. Along the way he had learned some Thai and Vietnamese as well.

---

1   Duff (1985) and Sasaki (1990) reported similar findings with Japanese learners of English.
2   I use the terms Cambodian and Khmer interchangeably here to refer to the language.

At the time we met, Jim was able to communicate in English at a fairly basic level, as Excerpt 1 illustrates, able to convey information about his family, the politics and history of Cambodia and Thailand, and aspects of his education and prior training. His English was heavily accented phonologically, influenced by his L1, Khmer (Cambodian). His English grammar also bore the traces of his L1 and other developmental factors, and certain recurring patterns were evident. Many aspects of his English interlanguage, as in *My wife, her husband die* and *I no children*, reflected topic-comment constructions found in many topic-prominent languages, including Khmer (Duff, 1985, 1993a; Givón, 1979; Huebner, 1983; Li & Thompson, 1976; Rutherford, 1983; see Mitchell & Miles, 2004, for a recent review of some of this work).[1] As described above with respect to Hmong, Chinese, and Japanese, these languages often feature the use of a sentence-initial noun phrase (e.g., *My wife*) or locative representing "old information" (e.g., *In Cambodia*) that is followed by a topic marker or a pause and rising intonation, and then an expression (comment) containing "new information" related to the first semantically or pragmatically, but not necessarily linked to the topic syntactically (e.g., *her husband die*). Word order is somewhat flexible and pragmatic, determined by the focus of the sentence, and unambiguous grammatical subjects are often omitted. Grammatical morphology is minimal. English and other subject-prominent languages, on the other hand, generally have syntactic devices for connecting subjects to predicates (e.g., subject-verb agreement) and have subordinate clauses, complex verb phrases, passives, and other constructions that either do not exist or are not as widely used in topic-prominent languages (Li & Thompson, 1976). As a result, those elements are often challenging for speakers of other types of languages, such as Khmer, when learning English.

Although there were definite signs of progress in Jim's English over time (Duff, 1993a, 1993b), certain structures had not fully developed (yet), such as his use of the existential expression *there is/are ...*, as in *There are a lot of people on the beach*. Early on, he frequently used the verb *has* (or *has-a*) instead, in the following ways: *Has many people on the beach, On beach has*

---

1   As reported in Duff (1993a), Khmer (Cambodian) belongs to the Mon-Khmer family. It is a non-tonal, isolating language with flexible, pragmatic word order reflecting topic-comment sentence organization (Ehrman, 1972). A typical topic-comment sentence is *kasaet nih kee lú? craen cbap (newspaper this, they sell many copy* = "they sell many copies of this newspaper"). The uninflected word *mian* marks both existence and possession in the affirmative: *niw nih mian menuh craen peek* (at here have people too many) [*menuh* = people, *craen* = many, *peek* = too (excessive), *craen peek* = too many].

many people, and *Hasa many people on beach*. Over time, he began to use a new form, *they has*, productively, as in *In the countryside they has no fruit* or *In the refugee camp they has a university*; this usage revealed a greater grammatical sensitivity to providing a subject before *has*, and not just locative phrases like *In the countryside* or *In the refugee camp*. Finally, by the end of the study he began to use *has* less in this ambiguous existential/possessive manner and more with animate subjects as a possessive verb (e.g., *the man has glasses*). In the last interview, a new sort of existential construction, somewhat more like a colloquial English form, also appeared: *'S many people on the beach*, with the initial *'S* functioning like the remnant of an elliptted *There's* (or *They has?*), but Jim never really articulated the "dummy" subject *there*. His former usage of *has* (*In Phnom Penh now hasa international ban(k)*) had not disappeared, however. Subject-verb agreement and other verb morphology (tense-aspect) and syntax were still inconsistent or nontarget-like, although developments were evident within some systems, such as negation, auxiliary verbs, and the copula (*is*) (Duff, 1993a, 1993b; Coughlan & Duff, 1994).

Excerpts below illustrate Jim's general English development from 1986 to 1988. Excerpt 2, within three months of his arrival in Canada, reveals his pervasive use of topic-comment constructions (main sentence topics are shown in boldface) and an interlanguage possessive/existential *has* in this description of a beach scene with a man sitting in a chair with some children playing nearby and other activities depicted (see Duff, 1993a). The expression *has-a* NP[1] (shown in italics below) was often used to introduce new noun phrases into the discussion, as in "*Has a lot of bird* flying on the sky" (Duff, 1993a).

Excerpt 2 (February 1986)

The old man is- the old man who + has the glasses and + with- and with hat + they sitting on the chair. **They** reading a newspaper, and **behinds him** *has the three children*, one girl and two s- two boy. Maybe **they** dancing because the radios turn ons- turn ons about music. And **they** happy. **They** dancing. And **over his head** *has a + ball?* Maybe ball yes. And **behinds far away** + **him** *has a + a lot of people*. Some peo- uh **some people** + they sitting + on the chair, and **some people** they standing ... And + **right-his-hand beside** + **at the sea**, *has the: + six bot.* Yeah six bot, + and (3.0) **a big boat** *has people sitting a lot of* and **some people** they - jum- uh they jum + into- the water and swimming. Maybe

---

1   NP = noun phrase.

they very happy. + And **over the sea** *has* + *a lot of bird* + flying on the sky. + And he is uh + **cameraman**, + they take un: potograss to (a/the) strongman + run into the sea …

[The old man with the glasses and hat is sitting on the chair. He's reading a newspaper. And behind him there are three children, one girl and two boys. Maybe they were dancing because the radio was playing music. And they were happy and were dancing. And there was a ball over his head. And far behind him there were many people, some sitting on chairs and some standing. And to his right, there were six boats at sea. And a lot of people were sitting in the big boat. And some people were jumping into the sea and swimming. Maybe they were very happy. And there were a lot of birds flying in the sky over the sea. And a cameraman takes photographs of a muscular man running into the sea ...]

When describing the same picture two and a half years later (in 1988), after more than two years of nearly full-time English instruction and residence in Canada, Jim produced the text in Excerpt 3:

Excerpt 3 (June 1988)

The picture on (x) on the beach (9.0). ((laugh)). I don't know what's happen. Maybe **the people** they go to - on vacation. (4.0) … (8.0) (x) **cameraman**? … Yeah. He's take- he:: he took a picture. I think maybe **the lady** (4.0) she's going drown on- in the water, and he (1.0) need(s) some help. (4.8) … (11.0) Ah **this man** I thin(k) he- he's not happy I think because **all the children** play (0.6) to make a noisy. (3.0) Ah I dunno …

[The picture is on a beach. I don't know what's happening. Maybe the people are on vacation. There's a cameraman taking a picture. I think maybe the lady is going to drown in the water and she needs some help. I think this man is not happy because all the children are playing noisily. I don't know ...]

In this excerpt, there are no uses of the existential *has* but still many topic-comment expressions (e.g., *this man I think he's not happy*). A few other verb forms are included, though they are not grammatically correct: *the lady, she's going [to] drown and [s]he need some help*. The excerpt is marked by many very long pauses, limited information about the content of the picture, and relatively simple grammar.

One of the aspects of the study I was interested in, beyond basic grammatical development, was how well the tasks themselves served as tools for eliciting language and demonstrating developmental patterns. Coughlan and Duff (1994) attributed Jim's apparent reticence on this particular task, as judged by his hesitations and lack of description of the picture, to its artificiality. It was the duplication of a description of exactly the same picture two years earlier (what we called "same task, different activity"). However, the picture description task was now recontextualized in an extended interview during which much more significant matters were discussed, such as Jim's latest employment, family matters, current politics in Cambodia and traditional Cambodian values and tales. In that discursive context, this simple, repeated picture description task seemed to catch him off guard, to trivialize the discussion.

Consider, for example, Jim's much more fluent and ample narration of a traditional Cambodian story about "the good wife" later in the same interview, as shown in Excerpt 4. He had just skimmed the short story (in Khmer) in a Cambodian library book I showed him, which contained traditional folk tales, and then told me the following story; it was therefore quite a different task from the repeated picture description just before.

Excerpt 4 (June 1988)

Many years ago has two families a rich family and one family has one daughter. An another one has one son and when their chil- child grow up, they marrieds. And then's uh the- that's parent is uh die- dead. Yeah but + the wife is a + very good she is very good wife. But the husband is not good. He spends lot money he is still- because their parent has + many thing the rich family has many land and too much- lot money, and he + he didn't find other job or or make other money. No just stay home or for a walk. And then's a they are going to uh they are poor because uh something that their parent gave, is noth- is he- he spend + + at all. But his wife is a good wife and + she she still have some + some uh gold that she hides. She never let her husband. If- if she give to her husband or she told her husband maybe her husband + took them to sell to make money and spend. And them . . . she hides some gold and some money and after her husband said "Oh we haves no more money and then we have to go to a countryside and make a farm". And his wife + she- she didn't tell her husband yet until the husband work in the farms very hard and maybe he sick and then his wife sold some gold and get the money

9

but some medicine some food- good food for her husband. And her husband said "How can you make money from"? And first time she she- she didn't tell her husband yet. Just- just tell him "You don't want to know about that". And her husband still ask her and she said "That money if I sold the gold". And she [=he] said "How can we still have the gold"? And she said she hides some gold that her husband + they- he- he didn't know. And then her husband think oh he's fault because uh . . . he- before he's a rich family. After his parent and now he's poor. But . . . his wife's good wife. She still keep some money on her. And then next time he- he- he won't go he won't do like that before anymore and she work hard- and he work hard yeah and then + he become a rich man again.

Here, then, in contrast to his fragmented description of the beach scene in Excerpt 3, Jim is able to introduce a number of characters and present a sequence of events in this story: parents in two rich families, whose children got married; the lazy husband squandering his inheritance after his parents died; the man was therefore forced to move his family to the countryside to farm the land; but he then demonstrated that he could actually work hard for a living—so much so that he got sick. Jim also uses reported speech between the husband and wife about the wife's secret stash of money (gold) she had kept hidden from him but produced after he proved he could work hard, and when the money was genuinely needed to feed the family. The story then concludes with a "happy ending": that the husband has now changed his ways and works hard, thanks to his wife's careful planning, and in this way he becomes rich again—not from his parents' riches but his own labor.

The next two paired excerpts, again more than two years apart, illustrate features of Jim's morphology (e.g., tense-aspect marking) and phonology as well as his topic-comment structures. Excerpt 5 took place in March, four months after Jim's arrival in Canada. He was describing Cambodia's recent history of war and colonization.

Excerpt 5 (March 1986)

I think in Cambodian when the Japan into Cambodian all the people gets + they don't likes. And then the Vietnam they don't like too. But French, *no problem* because French big country, they don't up pick up + everything for people- from people. *No problem*. And thens the soldier backs and has embassy in Cambodian *no problem*. Until- until United State into Cambodian + *no problem* for people Cam- the Cambodian people. Because the United State has a big country. They don't worry about + Cambodian people. *No problem.* And United State + give a lot of + special thing. Car airplane and a lot of gun in Cambodian. (From Duff, 1993a)

[I think when Japan came to (invaded) Cambodia, Cambodians didn't like them. And they didn't like the Vietnamese either. But with the earlier French (colonizers), there was no problem because France is a big country and they didn't take everything from the Cambodian people. And then the soldiers returned [to France] and had an embassy in Cambodia and there was no problem. Then the United States came into Cambodia but that was no problem. Because the United States is a big country. They didn't worry about Cambodian people. And the United States gave Cambodia a lot of special things: cars, airplanes, and a lot of guns.]

In Excerpt 5, Jim did not use past tense inflections and he used very few verbs. In their place were prepositions like *into* and *back* for actions, such as invading, entering, or returning to a country. The chunk phrase *no problem* (shown in italics) was used very frequently as well—five times in this short excerpt. (When I later learned there was a restaurant in Phnom Penh called Café No Problem, I realized that Jim was not the only Cambodian to use this expression so freely.) Topic noun phrases and comment phrases were loosely collocated to show their association, for example, *French big country* [France is a big country or The French have a big country]; *French, no problem* [The French weren't a problem].

In Excerpt 6, more than two years later, Jim explained how he now sent money back to his family in Cambodia. This explanation is also linked to the narrative in Excerpt 4 about how wives in the countryside customarily kept family assets (money, gold) at home, rather than at a bank.

Excerpt 6 (June 1988)

Yeah becau(se) uh in + Cambodian in the countrysi(de) 'z no ban(k). No, money or go(ld) jus(t) keep on their wice [wife]. No ban(k). If we has money + jus(t) keep in the hou(se) + an + an the wi(fe) stay home ... but I don('t) have mo- money in the ban(k) ... if I has my 's lot of money I keep in the international ban(k) ... because in Phnom Penh hasa- now hasa international ban(k). Yeah, one- one two two national ban(k) in Phnom Penh an(d) + then my brother tol(d) me + if I has money in international ban(k), I jus(t) go to + national ban(k) an tell them I wanto give money to my parent ... (Adapted from Duff, 1993a)

[Because in the Cambodian countryside there are no banks. Wives keep money or gold. If we have money we just keep it in the house and the wife stays home ... but I don't have money in the bank ... If I have a lot of money I keep it in the international bank ... because Phnom Penh now has one. There are two national banks in Phnom Penh, and then my brother told me that if I have money in an international bank, I just go to the national bank and tell them I want to give money to my parents ...]

Two and a half years after his immigration, as shown in Excerpt 6 (and earlier in Excerpt 4), Jim still did not demonstrate the development of the existential construction *there is/are*. Instead, he produced *in the countrysi(de) 'z no ban(k)* [There are no banks in the countryside], and *in Phnom Penh hasa-now hasa international ban(k)* [There is an international bank in Phnom Penh]. He generated several verbs (*go, keep, have*, and the irregular past *tol(d)* and negative verb phrases), but his pronunciation—especially the deletion of word-final stops or the plural *-s*—made it difficult to determine the extent of his word-final morphology. Later in the same interview, he produced utterances like: *Last year I live on [x]th avenue and then I move to front of [x]th avenue* and *That guy live near the [hospital] he work at a factory. Another guy live in southwest he go to school he has twin children*. Thus, past tense and other inflectional morphology (e.g., third-person *-s*) were mostly missing.

The simple transcription system I use in Excerpt 6 shows Jim's omission of final consonants (especially the stops *d, t*, and *k*, shown in parentheses), something Sato (1984, 1990) also found in her study of the English development of two Vietnamese brothers in Philadelphia. Because English morphemes tend to fall in consonant clusters word-finally, for many learners whose L1 reflects the universal tendency for open-syllable structure (a consonant followed by a vowel), the nonproduction of morphemes does not necessarily indicate the nonacquisition of those morphemes, but that there is a *production* problem (see also Lardiere, 2006). It shows how phonology interacts with, or may mask, morphology.[1] Sato reported similar kinds of crossover or "level-leaking" in the encoding of past tense morphology. She also found that, because learners could unambiguously establish time reference through preposed adverbials like *Yesterday I go*, they omitted many tense-aspect markers. Thus, topicalizing, scene-setting adverbial phrases interact

---

1   Writing samples from the same speaker or written error detection tasks would help clarify the situation.

with or reduce the need for tense-aspect morphology. These observations underscore the importance of incorporating multiple levels of linguistic analysis—phonological, morphological, syntactic, and discursive—in second-language acquisition (SLA) research of this nature.

1.3 Some Reflections on this Case Study

At the end of my analysis of Jim's L2 development in the early 1990s, it became clear to me just how lengthy and challenging it can be for an adult refugee whose education has been interrupted in his teenage years to become fully proficient in English and gainfully employed—even without significant health problems or trauma. A comparison of Excerpts 2 and 3, or 5 and 6 did not immediately reveal a substantial change in Jim's proficiency. Had his English become fossilized?

My original analysis and interpretations were that many linguistic factors, not to mention social and historical ones, conspired against Jim's rapid acquisition of English syntax:

- Language universals related to the syntactic and semantic conflation of forms for possession and existentials in many languages, encoding both in just one *be*-like or *have*-like form
- Transfer from his L1, with one *has*-like form serving both functions, and topic prominence
- The functionality of certain chunks he had adopted, such as *no problem*, and his topic-comment constructions, however simple, which made clear what he was talking about
- The redundancy in English that tolerates the deletion of grammatically necessary morphology without obscuring meaning too much, when temporal adverbs are used, for example
- The existence of semantically empty forms like dummy subject *it* or *there* in English (*It's raining* and *There's a child on the beach*), which are not salient in speech and therefore tended to be dropped and perhaps unnoticed by him (Duff, 1993a)

However, I could not conclude that there was across-the-board fossilization in his English development, as his English did seem to be slowly improving in various ways (see Han, 2004; Long, 2003).

On the basis of this single longitudinal case study of Jim, I could not predict whether other Cambodian learners in a similar situation would exhibit the exact same developmental patterns or difficulties as Jim because I do not know how linguistically typical Jim was as a Cambodian learner of

English (see Chapter 2).[1] Yet there is reason to believe that other Cambodian learners of English might also manifest similar syntactic patterns related to the conflation of the possessive *has/have* and the existential use of *has/have* for the syntactic, semantic, and pragmatic reasons given above, and in Duff (1993a), and certainly would share some of the same phonological and grammatical influences from Khmer. To understand the uniqueness or typicality of Jim's development, a larger study would be necessary, such as a cross-sectional study of many Cambodian learners of English or additional in-depth longitudinal case studies of several learners. With supplementary studies (not necessarily longitudinal or as in-depth) with learners from the same background, it might be possible to assert that specific interlanguage structures (e.g., the use of *have* vs. *has* as the default generic existential verb) were typically shared by Cambodian ESL learners in their earliest stages of development. If similar developmental trends were reported across even three Cambodian learners of English in a multiple-case study—a refugee with interrupted education, an instructed university student, and a child learner—or even three people in circumstances similar to Jim's, it would add to the robustness of the original observations. Conversely, if their development exhibited different patterns, that would beg the question: Why *those* patterns and not the ones Jim produced?

Most qualitative SLA research conducted in the 1970s to the 1990s, and especially SLA case studies such as mine, reflected a rather narrowly linguistic, positivist, or postpositivist orientation to research.[2] Although qualitative, the analyses were fairly unidimensional and less holistic than case studies in the social sciences and education generally are now, but they did look at clusters of related structures in learners' language (e.g., related to topic prominence), and not single features in isolation or outside of their discourse contexts. Microcontextual features such as task environment or discourse

---

1 I acknowledge, with thanks, Wayne Wright's (personal communication, September 28, 2006) recent examination of Jim's utterances to help me answer this question. Based on his extensive knowledge of Khmer and the Cambodian community in the United States, Wayne observed that Jim's utterances were "absolutely" typical of Cambodian ESL and "translated to perfectly acceptable Khmer".

2 According to Gall, Gall, and Borg (2003), positivism is "the epistemological doctrine that physical and social reality is independent of those who observe it, and that observations of this reality, if unbiased, constitute scientific knowledge" (p. 632). In contrast, postpositivism is "the epistemological doctrine that social reality is a construction, and that it is constructed differently by different individuals" (p. 632). Palys (1997) notes that the latter is "less rigidly realist" (p. 422) than positivism, and it acknowledges that verbal reports can contain valid and reliable data.

context were in some studies examined carefully, but larger macrocontextual social, political, and cultural factors were often minimized. My study of Jim fits this characterization, as a functional analysis of his oral production (and inferred development or acquisition) of particular constructions or forms over time, and the relationship between the elicitation tasks used in the longitudinal study and the types of language that were generated. Multiple perspectives of his language development or of his settlement in Canada (e.g., mine, his teachers' or children's, his own, or his government case worker's), different types of data (e.g., not only his oral language data but written production or grammaticality judgment tasks too), and his language use across a variety of natural contexts (e.g., when interacting with newspaper customers, social service workers, church members, neighbors) were not included. Furthermore, while my original publications provided some information about his history and current situation as a new Canadian, they did not present his life history in full or his ambivalence about learning English; his shifting identities and roles in society as a father, spouse, worker, Cambodian-Canadian, refugee, son, war veteran, and student (among others); his issues of gaining access to Anglo-Canadian social networks and employment; his role within the Cambodian-Canadian community; or the consequences of his language learning and immigration for his family members, both in Canada and Cambodia. That is, the social, cultural, political, and even economic dimensions of his life and his language learning were not fully explored because linguistic issues were of central concern to me and the SLA field (at that time).

Regrettably, I was unable to document his longer-term trajectory as a learner and user of English or as a member of Canadian society because the study, though longer than most, was not long enough to do so. I nevertheless did learn about Jim's post-1988 experiences as a language learner, a family member, and a Cambodian-Canadian. In 1997, he informed me that he had moved to another Canadian city and that he wanted to meet me again, which we arranged a short time later. He proudly declared that he now had an English name, which is why I now refer to him by the pseudonym Jim. His English remained somewhat limited, though. As a result of a stroke he had suffered in 1988, attributed to an old war injury, he continued to have difficulty expressing himself clearly in English and, sadly, had been unable to work for many years. My last interview in 1988 had taken place just days before his stroke—the same week as the birth of his fourth child—which is one of the reasons the interviews had ended when they did.[1] I had visited with him and his anxious wife and new baby as Jim convalesced from his brain surgery, none of us able to imagine what the future held in store for them.

By 1997, his four children were highly proficient in English and the two eldest were at the top of their respective high school classes. His eldest daughter aspired to study medicine so she could better understand her father's condition. His son had become a computer expert, and most of the family savings went to purchase computers for him. Jim's wife had just been hired to work at a fish packing shop, her first job. Until then, she had been taking care of the children and her husband. Her English remained quite limited. Both parents were worried about one of their two youngest daughters, who did not like to study and was spending time with the wrong types of children.

In 2006, 20 years after Jim's immigration, his eldest daughter (24 years of age) and his son had completed college and found full-time employment, the third child was still in college, and the youngest was finishing high school. His wife is working and has learned some English. They all live together in a large modern house in the suburbs. Jim is justifiably proud of his family, but he still suffers from ill-health. He has learned to take one day at a time.

1.4 Other Possible Applied Linguistic Analyses

As suggested above, case studies are driven by the researcher's and the discipline's current interests in theoretical and analytic phenomena in a range of possible domains—linguistic, psycholinguistic, cognitive, neurobiological/neuropsychological, sociolinguistic, sociocultural, political, discursive, textual, or educational. The research questions asked, the data collected, the duration and context of a study, and the analysis, interpretation, and reporting of results all depend on the central questions, the framing of the study, the traditions in the subfield, and the unit of analysis. My characterization of Jim mainly as a speaker from a topic-prominent language whose oral English developed or failed to develop in certain ways obscured or backgrounded other important dimensions of his life, although I was also very interested in these sociocultural and historical aspects and learned a lot about Cambodia in the process.

Other researchers might choose instead to study Jim's phonological or lexical development, or the way he presented new versus old information

---

1 I have no way of knowing, in retrospect, what kind of influence, if any, his brain injury a decade earlier had on his reported oral production or language acquisition.

in narratives, or produced other clusters of syntactic structures than those I examined. Discourse or text analysts, on the other hand, might study his narrative structure (e.g., different components of his stories) or how cohesive devices were used. Conversation analysts might examine turn-taking behaviors in the interviews or repair sequences when there were misunderstandings between interlocutors. Still other researchers might undertake a more (macro)sociological analysis, taking into account the settlement and integration patterns of similar types of families, or Cambodians in particular, who arrived in the United States, Canada, Australia, and the United Kingdom as refugees in the 1980s. They might also consider how long it takes such newcomers to integrate fully into society and into the labor market based on demographic and economic indicators.

Many current L2 researchers influenced by postmodernism, poststructuralism, and critical theory[1] (e.g., Norton, 2000) would argue for the importance of looking beyond just the linguistic details of a learner's or speaker's competence or production, and beyond the traditional categories and dichotomies that researchers use. They might focus on the interview *content* as opposed to linguistic dimensions, such as the changing social identity of the research subject, his social networks and sense of power and agency within them, or his investment in English language learning pre- and postimmigration. They would include more contextual and personal aspects of the research participant's experience, such as the social and political conditions under which speakers learn and produce language, or how the interaction between interviewer and interviewee constructs particular kinds of discourse and meanings or positions the language learner/user. Education researchers and phenomenologists might study how Jim portrayed the gains and losses in his life associated with immigration and learning English, and also how he reconstructed his sense of "self" and his experiences over time and across

---

1   Postmodernism and poststructuralism have common roots in "a broad social and philosophical movement that questions assumptions about the rationality of human action, the use of positivist epistemology, and any human endeavor (e.g., science) that claims a privileged position with respect to the search for truth" (Gall, Gall and Borg, 2003, p. 553). Critical theory is "the formulation of principles designed to clarify the power relationships and forms of oppression existing in society or culture, and thus to serve as a guide to efforts to emancipate its members from those forms of oppression" (Gall, Gall and Borg, 2003, p. 622).

narratives (e.g., Kouritzen, 1999; Pavlenko & Lantolf, 2000).[1]

Literacy researchers might examine the role of Khmer and English language and literacy practices in the lives of Jim's family members in Canada and analyze whether, how, and to what extent the children had learned or lost their L1, Khmer, and what the consequences had been in communication patterns within the family, especially between the youngest children, who spoke little Khmer in the home, and their mother, who spoke little English. Sociolinguists might consider code-switching behaviors in the home or in Jim's interactions with other Cambodians.

Thus, entirely different case studies could potentially be conducted with the same subject. Whatever the focus, the research would need to be informed by, and speak to, theory or broader principles, contextualized within other relevant research or literature, and supported by systematically collected, analyzed, and interpreted data with representative evidence for claims.

1.5 Summary

This chapter has stressed the importance of understanding different theoretical and methodological traditions and issues within a field such as applied linguistics or SLA, and thus different possibilities for new research. In this way, researchers can conduct case studies that not only are interesting for their own sake, but also speak to broader issues connected with learning, teaching, immigration, first-language transfer, and so on. In the short description of my case study of a Cambodian learner, I reflected on the decisions leading to my case selection, data collection, focus, analysis, and interpretations of L2 development. I also considered a range of other research problems that researchers might wish to address currently, especially if interested in a more complex portrayal of the research participant as a multifaceted social being and not just the "site" of L2 development.

The remainder of this book examines in more detail what a case study is, what we have learned from several generations of published case studies in applied linguistics, and, in more practical terms, how to conduct case studies, write about them, and evaluate them.

---

1   To my surprise, the content of Jim's life history narratives changed quite dramatically and substantively in my study over the first year of his interviews, especially about his years in Cambodia, as his trust in me increased.

CHAPTER 2

Defining, Describing, and Defending Case Study Research

2.1 Introduction

This chapter first provides a definition of case study, followed by a brief discussion of its historical roots. This is followed by an overview of the theoretical and methodological characteristics of qualitative research generally and case study specifically. The role of qualitative case studies in applied linguistics is then considered. Next, I present the advantages and (claimed) disadvantages of case study, devoting special attention to issues of generalizability. Finally, I discuss the significant role that case study research has played in the development of applied linguistics, especially within the subfield of SLA.

2.2 Defining Case Study

Case study is a type of research design and analysis, which Gall, Gall, and Borg (2003) characterize as the "most widely used approach to qualitative research in education" (p. 433). It is also referred to as a method, a "strategy" (Punch, 1998; Yin, 2003a), and an outcome of research: "The qualitative case study can be defined in terms of the process of actually carrying out the investigation, the unit of analysis (the bounded system, the case), or the end product" (Merriam, 1998, p. 34).

Most definitions of case study highlight the "bounded", singular nature of the case, the importance of context, the availability of multiple sources of information or perspectives on observations, and the in-depth nature of analysis. Education researchers Gall *et al.* (2003) describe case study research as "the in-depth study of instances of a phenomenon in its natural context and from the perspective of the participants involved in the phenomenon" (p. 436). Creswell (1998) and Merriam (1998), respectively, phrase it somewhat differently:

> A case study is an exploration of a "bounded system" or a case (or multiple cases) over time through detailed, in-depth data collection involving multiple sources of information rich in context. (Creswell, 1998, p. 61)

> The qualitative case study can be defined as an intensive, holistic description and analysis of a single entity, phenomenon, or social unit. Case studies are particularistic, descriptive, and heuristic and rely heavily on inductive reasoning in handling multiple data sources. (Merriam, 1988, p. 16)

Yin (2003a), a case study methodologist in education and management, provides a definition that addresses issues of scope, data collection, and analysis strategies:

1. A case study is an empirical inquiry that
   - investigates a contemporary phenomenon within its real-life context, especially when
   - the boundaries between phenomenon and context are not clearly evident.
2. The case study inquiry
   - copes with the technically distinctive situation in which there will be many more variables of interest than data points, and as one result
   - relies on multiple sources of evidence, with data needing to converge in a triangulating fashion, and as another result
   - benefits from the prior development of theoretical propositions to guide data collection and analysis. (pp. 13–14)

Bromley (1986), from the field of psychology, defines case study as

the description and analysis of a particular entity (object, person, group, event, state, condition, process, or whatever). Such singular entities are usually natural occurrences with definable boundaries, although they exist and function within a context of surrounding circumstances. Such entities also exist over a short period of time relative to that context. (p. 8)

In sociology, case study has been defined as follows:

a method of studying social phenomena through the thorough analysis of an individual case. The case may be a person, a group, an episode, a process, a community, a society, or any other unit of social life. All data relevant to the case are gathered, and all available data are organized in terms of the case. The case study method gives a unitary character to the data being studied by interrelating a variety of facts to a single case. It also provides an opportunity for the intensive analysis of many specific details that are often overlooked with other methods. (Theodorson & Theodorson, 1969; cited in Punch, 1998, p. 153)

Finally, in political science, where case study became known as "small-n" studies in the 1960s and 1970s, George and Bennett (2005) define the "case" in case study as

an instance of a class of events, ... a phenomenon of scientific interest, such as revolutions, types of governmental regimes, kinds of economic systems, or personality types that the investigator chooses to study with the aim of developing theory (or "generic knowledge") regarding the causes of similarities or differences among instances (cases) of that class of events.... The Cuban Missile Crisis, for example, is a historical instance of many classes of events: deterrence, coercive diplomacy, crisis management, and so on. (pp. 17–18)

A number of other definitions or attributes of case study research are found in Nunan (1992) and Merriam (1998). The key recurring principles are: boundedness or singularity, in-depth study, multiple perspectives or triangulation, particularity, contextualization, and interpretation. Case study is different from *case method, case work,* and *case history* (Merriam, 1998). Despite some shared elements with case study, these latter terms are more closely associated with business, social work, and medicine, respectively, in which cases often have a more specific clinical or pedagogical role than a research role.

21

2.3 Historical Roots of Case Study in the Social Sciences

This section provides a brief historical overview of case study in various disciplines. Researchers have systematically analyzed the observable behaviors of those around them, whether their children, students, clients, or patients, for generations, and applied linguists are no exception in this regard. They have also undertaken in-depth studies of their own or others' communities and social institutions.

Much influential research in the sciences and social sciences has started with or involved case studies at some point. Detailed, very important case studies of children are plentiful in the literature in developmental psychology, and even in the natural sciences, such as biology. As early as 1781 to 1783, Dietrich Tiedemann published one of the first case studies of its type: an in-depth "scientific observation" of the physical and psychological changes his infant son displayed over the first months of his life. Darwin, too, apparently published a study of his son in 1877 (both cited in Lamberth, McCullers, & Mellgren, 1976).

Also writing about the historical role of case study in psychology, Merriam (1988) provides other examples:

> Ebbinghaus in the late nineteenth century, for example, self-administered thousands of tasks in the study of memory (Dukes, 1965). His findings provided the basis for memory research for the next half century. Piaget in studying his own children developed states of cognitive structure that have had an enormous impact on curriculum and instruction. Indeed, his theory is still being tested and refined in educational research investigations.[1] Finally, many studies in child and adult development have employed a qualitative case study as the mode of inquiry. Vaillant's (1977) findings about mental health are derived from longitudinal case studies of ninety-five Harvard men; Levinson studied forty men and built a theory of male adult development (Levinson, 1978). (Merriam, 1988, p. 25)

In clinical psychology, Freud's most famous case study was that of a friend's patient, Anna O, which provided the foundations of Freud's theoretical framework of psychoanalysis. In that branch of psychology, case

---

1   However, the theoretical generalizations made by Piaget on the basis of those observations of his sons have, as a result, been challenged by some on the grounds that they lack objectivity (Dobson *et al.*, 1981).

studies are the primary method for the analysis and treatment of patients. To show how committed he was to his method, and to resolve his own psychological problems, Freud reportedly also became his own analyst on a daily basis until his death (Dobson, Hardy, Heyes, Humphreys, & Humphreys, 1981).

Although Merriam (1988) points out that case study in sociology was relatively uncommon until the 1960s, with large-scale quantitative methods being more the norm, Hamel, Dufour, and Fortin's (1993) review of case study in anthropology and sociology suggests otherwise.[1] They profile Malinowski's (1922/1953) acclaimed work in Melanesia in the early 20th century, which featured key participants (previously called informants or subjects), participant observation, contextualized data collection, prolonged on-site presence (three years), and researcher logs, all of which contributed to Malinowski's ethnographic case study of particular cultural communities. Hamel *et al.* (1993) note that, whereas in anthropological research the village often constituted *the case*, in French sociological fieldwork about working-class populations of European workers, such as miners, affected by postrevolutionary social changes, *the family* became the case or unit of analysis. That is because the family was seen to be the site of societal production and reproduction.[2]

Hamel *et al.* (1993) also provide an overview of the main trends in American sociology, notably the emphasis placed on case study by the Chicago School (associated with the University of Chicago) in the first half of the 20th century that coincided with dramatic demographic changes occurring in that city's urban ecology. Early studies examined such problems as unemployment, poverty, and violence among urban immigrant populations in Chicago and elsewhere. The influence of the overlapping disciplines of social psychology (e.g., George H. Mead), social work, journalism, anthropology, and sociology on studies was reflected in the fieldwork, methods, and written accounts of people studying delinquency and acculturation in another country. A methodological and institutional rift and competition ensued between the qualitative research of the Chicago School and the quantitative, statistical research favored at Columbia University in New York, which the latter institution appeared to win, at least until the 1960s. Criticisms related to the lack of representativeness, and thus generalizability, rigor, theoretical

---

1   Merriam (1998) does not repeat this claim.

2   Hamel *et al.* (1993) describe the family-based case study approach as the Le Play school, named after a French sociologist, which developed in the early 19th century.

validation, and micro- to macroscopic (or local to global) sociological analysis and explanation were leveled against case study's inductive approach (Hamel *et al.*, 1993). Another criticism was that the case studies "romanticized the subject" in cases of "deviant" behavior and produced "the illusion that a solution to a social problem had been found" (Hatch, 2002, p. 4).

However, seminal studies from the Chicago School have generated continued interest in case study despite such objections. Classic community and family case studies include Willis's (1977) *Learning to Labor*, Whyte's (1943/1993) *Street Corner Society*, and Lewis's (1961) *The Children of Sanchez*. All deal with life in urban slums and ghettos in the United States and Mexico and the "culture of poverty" (see Hamel *et al.*, 1993, for a list of other important case studies).

In political science, case study went through similar ups and downs in the 20th century. George and Bennett (2005) note that, although case study had been quite prominent in that field before the 1960s, there was a sharp decline in case study publications between the 1960s and 1970s as "more novel statistical and formal methods of research grew" (p. 3). Recently, though, there has been an "increasingly sophisticated and collaborative discourse on research methods in the social sciences" (p. 4):

> Over the past few decades, proponents of case study methods, statistics, and formal modeling have each scaled back their most ambitious goals regarding the kinds of knowledge and theories that they aspire to produce. Practitioners of each approach have improved and codified their techniques, reducing some of the problems identified by their critics but also gaining renewed appreciation for the remaining limits of their methods. (p. 2)

In addition to psychology, sociology, anthropology, and political science, case study research is used in the fields of education, medicine, law, management, social work, economics and business, history, journalism, public administration, policy, and urban planning (Merriam, 1998; Yin, 2003a).

2.4 General Features of Qualitative Research

In this section I describe briefly some features of qualitative research, which, in addition to case study, includes ethnography, ethnomethodology, phenomenology, biography or life history, semiotics, conversation/discourse analysis, and other types of research. There are a growing number of comprehensive textbooks on qualitative research, especially in education and sociology (e.g., Berg, 2007; Bogdan & Biklen, 2003; Creswell, 1998; Denzin & Lincoln, 2003, 2005b; Eisner & Peshkin, 1990; Hesse-Biber & Leavy, 2006; Holliday, 2002; LeCompte, Millroy, & Preissle, 1992; Merriam, 1998; Miles & Huberman, 1994; Patton, 1990; Richardson, 1996; Ritchie & Lewis, 2003; Stake, 1995; Silverman, 2000; Wolcott, 1994; Yin, 2003a). Although they were not written for applied linguists (in the next section I provide examples of textbooks and other resources designed precisely for our field), many of them provide a helpful philosophical, historically contextualized discussion of research paradigms and their attributes, and very specific examples of how to collect, analyze, and interpret linguistic data.

In the introduction to the third edition of their encyclopedic handbook, Denzin and Lincoln (2005a) write:

> Qualitative research involves the studied use and collection of a variety of empirical materials—case study; personal experience; introspection; life story; interviews; artifacts; cultural texts and productions; observational, historical, and visual texts—that describe routine and problematic moments and meanings in individuals' lives. Accordingly, qualitative researchers deploy a wide range of interconnected interpretive practices, hoping always to get a better understanding of the subject matter at hand. It is understood, however, that each practice makes the world visible in a different way. Hence there is frequently a commitment to using more than one interpretive practice in any study. (p. 4)

Qualitative research methods and practitioners are by no means monolithic or homogeneous, as the above quotation suggests. Research is conducted in different fields in various ways and reflects a continuum of "sensibilities" (Denzin & Lincoln, 2005a, p. 11) ranging from positivist to postpositivist and from modern to postmodern, and critical, using various combinations of methods.[1] In fact, Denzin and Lincoln (2005a) describe as many as eight "moments" or historical epistemological phases or sensibilities in qualitative research, from the "traditional" (1900–1950) to the "postmodern" (1990–1995) and "methodologically contested present" (2000–2004), and now the "fractured future" (2005–)[2]; but all of these orientations still operate today (p. 3). Denzin and Lincoln (2005a) also describe the tensions—and sometimes "crises"—that accompany qualitative research, citing and expanding on Nelson, Treichler, and Grossberg's (1992) account:

> On the one hand, [qualitative research] is drawn to a broad, interpretive, postexperimental, postmodern, feminist, and critical sensibility. On the other hand, it is drawn to more narrowly defined positivist, postpositivist, humanistic, and naturalistic conceptions of human experience and its analysis. Further, these tensions can be combined in the same project, bringing both postmodern and naturalistic, or both critical and humanistic, perspectives to bear. (Cited in Denzin & Lincoln, 2005a, p. 7)

This "tension" reflects one of the difficulties in discussing qualitative research as a singular approach or paradigm. Like all methods, it encompasses a number of components: *ontology*, *epistemology*, and *methodology*, and, as we have seen, covers a wide range of research beliefs or practices under the same rubric (Duff, 2002a; Duff & Early, 1996; Lincoln & Guba, 2000). Although it may not be made explicit, all research at some level represents an ideology concerning the nature of reality, a philosophical basis regarding the nature of knowing, and various practical methods for studying phenomena (Denzin & Lincoln, 2005a, 2005b). The *ontologies* (views of whether reality is constructed or exists independently of observers), *epistemologies* (or theories of knowledge, especially about the nature of truth and the objectivity or subjectivity of researchers), and *methodologies* (approaches to conducting

---

1   Yin (2003b), for example, contrasts logical positivist case study and more interpretive, ethnographic approaches to research, but notes that the aim and practice of the former approach (i.e., his own approach) "has been to base case study research within the framework of the scientific method—to develop hypotheses, collect empirical data, and develop conclusions based on the analysis of such data" (p. 47). Unlike most contemporary case study methodologists, he does not favor a more interpretive, less positivist, approach to case study.

2   The "future" (i.e., present) deals with the "methodological backlash associated with the evidence-based social movement" (p. 3), particularly in light of the current politics of research funding in the United States connected with George W. Bush's administration, which has rejected the validity of much (most) qualitative research.

research, such as experimental/manipulative or dialogical/dialectical) may vary quite widely, even among those who conduct qualitative case studies. Having said that, there are some tendencies across many qualitative studies, including case studies, in our field, and these will be explored in this and subsequent chapters.

Many—but certainly not all (e.g., Yin, 2003b)—qualitative researchers in the social sciences and humanities, especially in the 21st century, believe that the same phenomenon or event may be viewed from different perspectives or interpreted and explained differently by the research participant, researcher, or another observer (relative, teacher, tester, employer).[1] That is, they do not subscribe to a strong form of realism (as their ontology), nor do they believe they can carry out truly objective, value-free research (as their epistemology); they fall somewhere on the continuum between postpositivism and interpretivism. Because of differences in the way individuals perceive, interpret, and remember an event or behavior, accounts from different participants naturally vary. A researcher may observe that a person consistently uses language in a particular way, but the person may be quite oblivious to that behavior. A teacher may think she is doing a wonderful job of responding to students' questions, but the students may feel differently. A researcher might observe high levels of accuracy in an L2 speaker's language only to learn that the speaker had been consciously avoiding more difficult forms for fear of making errors (Schachter, 1974). It is this recognition of diverging observations and multiple realities that underlies *interpretivism*, which is arguably the most common approach to qualitative case studies in the social sciences (including applied linguistics) at present, although SLA studies examining linguistic development of a more discrete nature still tend to favor a less interpretive and more (post)positivist stance in the pursuit of evidence to support deductive theory testing or theory building.[2]

Therefore, in interpretive research focusing on English L2 students' social, cultural, and psychological orientation to language learning and use, researchers may interview not only the learners themselves, but also the people they work, live, or study with to understand aspects of their lives, their

---

1   Perhaps this is why Gall, Borg, and Gall (1996) and various others equate *qualitative* and *interpretive* research.

2   Intepretivism, according to Ritchie and Lewis (2003), acknowledges that "the researcher and the social world impact on each other"; that "findings are inevitably influenced by the researcher's perspective and values" and "the methods of the natural sciences are not appropriate because the social world is not governed by law-like regularities but is mediated through meaning and human agency" (p. 17).

adjustment to their English-speaking environment, and the occasions on which they use English. This knowledge can then be compared with the researcher's observations about the individual's ability to function in an L2 environment, at home, in the community, or even at work, and about the learner's own disclosures about the same. Similarly, postpositivist SLA research might interview or observe the learner as well as others, but perhaps with a greater emphasis on finding out the "truth" about the learner's orientation to language learning and use.

Drawing upon various kinds and sources of information for analysis is usually referred to as *triangulation*, which is thought to be a very useful research strategy. According to Bromley (1986), the term originates with the fields of surveying and navigation: "The navigational metaphor suggests that if several independent sources of evidence point to a common conclusion, then one's confidence in that conclusion is strengthened" (p. 10). Data, methods, perspectives, theories, and even researchers can be triangulated in order to produce either converging or diverging observations and interpretations. Although the notion of triangulation may have originally had positivist undertones (multiple sources of information leading to one "truth" to be discovered by the researcher), it can also be used to ascertain multiple forms of interpretation (or multiple realities) at work in order to "clarify meaning by identifying different ways the case is being seen" (Flick, 1998; Silverman, 1993) (Stake, 2005, p. 454).

Qualitative research also generally emphasizes the importance of examining and interpreting observable phenomena *in context*. These contexts tend to be naturally occurring ones, which in applied linguistics might include language testing sessions, classrooms, courtrooms, or job interviews. Although these settings may not seem very natural, the principle is that they were not arranged for research purposes alone; they are part of people's regular activities. In positivist research, various kinds of elicitation tasks may also be used, such as the narrative and descriptive tasks I asked Jim to do (Chapter 1) for research purposes alone. Finally, qualitative research typically involves an inductive, as opposed to deductive, approach to research (particularly in interpretive research): looking for, describing, and accounting for observed patterns, as opposed to testing explicitly stated hypotheses and making strong causal claims. More will be said about qualitative data analysis in Chapters 4 and 5.

2.5 Qualitative Research in Applied Linguistics

Just as there has been a growing acceptance of, and increase in, qualitative research conducted in the social sciences and education in recent years, the same has been true of research in applied linguistics: in classroom research, language testing research, or community- or workplace-based studies. There has also been a corresponding—and healthy—increase in the number of publications discussing qualitative methodological issues in our field (e.g., Chapelle & Duff, 2003; Davis, 1995; Duff, 2002a, 2002b; Holliday, 1994; Lazaraton, 1995, 2000, 2003; Lynch, 1996; McKay, 2006; Mackey & Gass, 2005; Richards, 2003). Nevertheless, as Duff and Early (1996) noted a decade ago, qualitative research is still sometimes characterized as a less robust or less mature form of scholarly inquiry than quantitative research. Such beliefs or misconceptions may result from there being too much so-called qualitative research published that does not reflect a theoretically grounded, systematic, methodical, in-depth, or original analysis, or appears to simply contain a few anecdotes or vignettes. In addition, old biases from the biological, physical, and social sciences still prevail in some circles about what constitutes legitimate scientific methodology. The situation is changing, however, and even "scientific" theory now acknowledges to a greater extent the nonlinear, emergent, dynamic, and complex interactions within systems, whether in the natural or physical world or in the social world (N. Ellis & Larsen-Freeman, 2006).

2.6 Purposes and Philosophical Underpinnings of Case Study

Against the backdrop of this general introduction to qualitative research, the remainder of this chapter deals with case study specifically. The purposes of a case study vary, depending on how much is already known about a topic, the amount of previous empirical research conducted on it, the nature of the case itself, and the philosophy of the researcher. Yin (2003b) suggests that there are three types of case study, categorized according to their main purpose: exploratory, descriptive, or explanatory.

> An *exploratory* case study (whether based on single case or multiple cases) is aimed at defining the questions and hypotheses of a subsequent (not necessarily a case) study or at determining the feasibility of the desired research procedures. A *descriptive* case study presents a complete description of a phenomenon within its context. An *explanatory* case study presents data bearing on cause-effect relationships—explaining how events happened. (p. 5)

A case study may therefore be designed to explore and describe phenomena using various constructs, to test theory, to build theory or explanations, to generate hypotheses, to test hypotheses, or to illustrate theoretical insights by way of case vignettes (Merriam, 1988, 1998).

Johnson (1992) writes that "the purpose [of case study] is to understand the complexity and dynamic nature of the particular entity, and to discover systematic connections among experiences, behaviors, and relevant features of the context" (p. 84). This emphasis on *complexity* and of a holistic understanding of the individual's knowledge or performance is foregrounded in recent reviews of the philosophy of science (e.g., Larsen-Freeman, 1997; van Lier, 1997, 2004), as alluded to earlier, which point out that "in complex nonlinear systems [as in SLA], the behavior of the whole emerges out of the interaction of its parts. Studying the parts in isolation one by one will tell us about each part, but not how they interact" (Larsen-Freeman, 1997, p. 157).

The definitions of case study I presented above emphasized that a case is a bounded entity (or instance). Although groups, organizations, and countries may be the focus of case studies, those investigating issues of a psychological or linguistic nature typically undertake the detailed description and analysis of an individual subject (i.e., research participant) from whom observations, interviews, and family or life histories and other narratives provide the primary database (Dobson *et al.*, 1981; Shaughnessy & Zechmeister, 1985).

Regardless of the focus or nature of the case, however, the methodological principles and priorities are basically the same. The individual case is usually selected for study on the basis of specific psychological, biological, sociocultural, institutional, or linguistic attributes, representing a particular age group, a combination of first and second languages, an ability level (e.g., basic or advanced), a skill area such as writing, a linguistic domain such as morphology and syntax, or a mode or medium of learning such as an online computer-mediated environment.

Although generally associated with *qualitative* research, cases may be analyzed *quantitatively* as well. For example, they may be part of an experimental single-case time series design in which research participants' baseline data (over time, without intervention or treatment) constitute a control context against which the effects of new interventions such as tutorials may be measured through time series statistics (e.g., Gall *et al.*, 2003; Mellow, Reeder, & Forster, 1996; Neuman & McCormick, 1995). Mellow's (1996) study, for example, followed a number of Japanese learners of ESL and tracked their production of articles on several tasks. Some of the learners had received intense instruction on article usage and others had not. For each research participant in the study, baseline data established developmental trends in their article use prior to the experimental instructional treatment. Alternatively, the case study may be a qualitative component in a larger, primarily quantitative study, such as a program evaluation (e.g., Antonek, Donato, & Tucker, 2000).

As I noted earlier with respect to qualitative research, case study methodologists come from many philosophical persuasions that could be situated on a continuum that includes, at one end, relatively conservative positivists and postpositivists (e.g., Yin, 2003a, 2003b) seeking to find external truths and ultimately be able to make predictions; interpretive or constructivist scholars (e.g., Merriam, 1998) somewhere in the middle of the continuum, who seek to understand the how and why of phenomena from a holistic, participant-informed perspective; and critical standpoint theorists, at the far end of the continuum, who seek to understand the social, political, and economic (material) conditions (e.g., related to race, gender, power, class, age, immigrant status) that they assume may systematically disadvantage certain people, such as immigrant language learners, people with disabilities, females, transgendered or "queer" people, the working poor, people whose languages or whose futures are constrained by the dominance of another language such as English, and other minorities (Pennycook, 2001).

The examination of cases that comprise more than individual participants—and look, instead, at other types of bounded social entities, such as cities, social groups, communities, institutions, or organizations—is commonplace in applied linguistics, just as in sociology, anthropology, education, political science, and business. In L2 research (e.g., Johnson, 1992), individual groups (e.g., a class of students), organizations (e.g., an intensive language program), or events (e.g., a Japanese language tutorial or a seminar in medicine) may also constitute cases, because any of these contexts could provide a "particular concrete instance" (Lewin, 1979, p. 286) of a phenomenon, where researchers might conceivably find relationships among variables or factors of interest.

2.7 Case Study versus Ethnography

At the risk of oversimplifying differences between two commonly used approaches to qualitative research in applied linguistics, one main difference between *case study* and *ethnography* is that, whereas the former focuses on the behaviors or attributes of individual learners or other individuals/entities, the latter aims to understand and interpret the behaviors, values, and structures of collectivities or social groups with particular reference to the *cultural* basis for those behaviors and values (Duff, 1995, 2002b; Johnson, 1992; Nunan, 1992). Confusion may arise because ethnographies represent a particular kind of anthropological case study—where the case is a defined cultural group or community—and, to confuse matters more, the ethnography may include focal participants who are members of a culture to illustrate features of the whole. In other words, they are case studies within a particular culturally oriented larger case study. Thus, my ethnographic case study of the implementation of bilingual education in Hungary (the country being one level of case) involved three schools (another level, with three cases), several focal teachers (another level, with as many as eight cases), and one or two particular types of speech events across those contexts (e.g., recitation activities and student presentations), as the units of analysis (e.g., Duff, 1993c). As in many case studies of individuals and institutions whose emphasis is not primarily cultural processes and patterns, ethnographies involve extended observation, interviewing, triangulation, and (often) document analysis.

Unfortunately, some discussions of research paradigms in applied linguistics and other fields tend to treat ethnography and qualitative research as synonymous and then contrast this "qualitative research" with all kinds of quantitative research (see Lazaraton, 2003). Readers may find it useful to consult guidelines and standards for several types of qualitative research, including, but not limited to, case study and ethnography (e.g., Chapelle & Duff, 2003; Johnson, 1992) to differentiate the two.

2.8 Case Study in Applied Linguistics

Case studies in applied linguistics, as in most other fields, are now usually associated with interpretive qualitative research. Originally influenced by psychology and linguistics, the "case" in applied linguistics has usually been the individual language learner, teacher, speaker, or writer. The study of individuals and their attributes, knowledge, development, and performance has always been a very important component of applied linguistics research, particularly in SLA. Studies of people learning languages or attempting to integrate into new communities, as we saw in Chapter 1, have generated very detailed accounts of the processes, outcomes, and factors associated with language learning, use, or attrition. The "subjects"[1] of these studies have been infants, young children in monolingual home environments, children in bilingual or multilingual home and school environments, adolescent immigrants, adult migrant workers, college-level foreign language learners, study-abroad students, adults learning an additional language for professional or recreational purposes, or adults losing their languages because of aging, injury, disability, or language shift. Besides the wide range of learners in terms of age, L1, migration history, prior learning, and context, the issues and domains addressed have been far ranging as well, including, for example, lexis, syntax, morphology, phonology, discourse-level features, pragmatics, narrative structure, reading and writing processes, content-based language learning, social and linguistic identities, attitudes and motivation, learning strategies, and anxiety.

Let us consider two case studies, a single-case study of a French learner and a multiple-case study of ESL students in mainstream university courses. Singleton (1987), in the first instance, studied the French of his case study subject, Philip, to determine possible transfer effects from the other languages Philip knew. These errors were then classified and interpreted on the basis of principles of psychotypological distance, or the perceived linguistic distance and differences between English and French.

Case studies of learners may also involve more than one subject or participant, and many have four to six such focal participants, which increases the sense of representativeness of, or variation among, cases (Chalhoub-Deville, Chapelle, & Duff, 2006; Duff, 2006). These are sometimes called multiple-case studies or collective case studies (Stake, 2005). Morita (2002), for example, conducted a longitudinal multiple-case study of six Japanese women's academic discourse socialization into graduate and senior-level undergraduate courses at a Canadian university. With an understanding of the experiences of these six, Morita (2004) focused on three of the cases to illustrate issues connected with their variable participation (including silence) in class discussions. She also provided interpretations and explanations for the observed levels and types of participation (in part from her own observations of their in-class interactions, but also based on in-depth interviews with

---

1   The terms *subject* and *participant* are often used synonymously in case studies, although *participant* is the preferred usage currently in the social sciences. Some accounts of case study still use the earlier term *subject* because the research participant is the main subject of the study. *Informant* is still used in some anthropological research, although it is falling out of favor.

them), and then observed changes in their participation patterns over time and across different courses within the same semester. She found that many factors influenced the way they "performed" these identities in course contexts differently: their status as English teachers, non-native English speakers, non-Canadians, older versus younger Japanese nationals, women, and so on; their positioning by teachers and classmates in particular ways (e.g., ascribed identities, as "outsiders"); and their negotiation of these positionings and their sense of agency (e.g., asserting their rights).

Single- and multiple-case studies have also been conducted of teachers (e.g., Duff & Uchida, 1997), particular types of programs (e.g., Duff, 1993c), immigrant workers' language use and workplace socialization (Li, 2000), individual families' language maintenance strategies (e.g., Guardado, 2002), and countries' language policies and planning (Hornberger & Ricento, 1996).

The case study approach to applied linguistics research has been very productive and influential. Many of the prevailing models and hypotheses in SLA were founded on a small number of well-documented studies from the first wave of case studies of language learners in the 1970s and 1980s: children and adults who were known by such names as Nigel, Hildegard, Paul, Tomiko, Igor, Uguisu, Alberto, Wes, Marta, Homer, Nora, and Ge (see e.g., Hatch, 1978a; van Lier, 2005). Of these, Schmidt's (1983) longitudinal case study of "Wes", although now more than 20 years old, is still the most frequently cited in methodological overviews of case study research in L2 learning (e.g., Brown & Rodgers, 2002; Mackey & Gass, 2005; Nunan, 1992; van Lier, 2005). Other cases may be less widely recognizable by their names or pseudonyms but may have nonetheless made an important contribution to applied linguistics.

Many of the early case study participants were either the researchers themselves or their friends and relatives, and the tradition of conducting diary studies, memoirs, autobiographies, or reflective essays begun in the 1970s in applied linguistics continues to this day (e.g., Belcher & Connor, 2001; Pavlenko & Lantolf, 2000; Schmidt & Frota, 1986; Schumann, 1997; see Chapter 3). The resulting publications have generally been very concrete, detailed profiles of L1 and L2 learners/users, which have stimulated further research, such as additional single- or multiple-case studies, analyses of aggregated case studies, studies of a more experimental nature, and studies using a combination of qualitative and quantitative designs to pursue similar sorts of research questions.

SLA involves linguistic, cognitive, affective, and social processes. That is, it is an ongoing interplay of individual mental processes, meanings, and actions as well as social interactions that occur within a particular time and place, and learning history. SLA case study research such as my study of Jim in the past tended to focus more on the cognitive, linguistic, or social-psychological characteristics of learning than on the macrosociological. Yet a growing number of scholars argue for a greater focus on the contextual basis of performance and the ecology of learning and performance more generally (see Coughlan & Duff, 1994; Kramsch, 2002; Larsen-Freeman, 1997; Leather & van Dam, 2003; van Lier, 1997). Many also argue for a much more explicitly sociocultural orientation as well (Lantolf, 2000; Lantolf & Thorne, 2006), although not all sociocultural research is contextualized well.

What constitutes *context* in case study? A "systems perspective" (Patton, 1990, p. 78) of observable phenomena, which is used in case studies of organizations, recognizes that each human case is complex, operating within a constellation of linguistic, sociolinguistic, sociological, and other systems, and the whole may be greater than—or different from—the sum of its parts. This kind of "synthetic thinking" (Patton, 1990, p. 79) distinguishes some current qualitative research, including case studies that examine language learning and use both macroscopically and microscopically, from previous studies that focused on just one element within a speaker's linguistic system.

Sometimes the analysis of an individual's knowledge system and performance within a classroom context or within a particular activity setting provides sufficient background information to interpret influences on L2 comprehension, production, or task accomplishment, for example. Other times, the analysis is enhanced by looking at the home, school, community, or workplace environment and by looking at the individual within a social network of family members, peers, teachers, and others. The socially situated and constructed nature of cognition and performance is emphasized (e.g., Lave & Wenger, 1991). It is therefore important to consider what level of context is relevant and necessary to gain a fuller, more ecological understanding of the individual's abilities, traits, behaviors, and knowledge.[1]

While early L2 case studies such as Huebner's (1983) addressed the issue of linguistic ecology in terms of a "dynamic paradigm" with interconnected linguistic subsystems, current theorizing also capitalizes upon developments

---

1   van Lier (2005) offers three contextual or ecological models for case studies that he has applied in his own recent work.

within science related to chaos and complexity theory (Patton, 1990; Larsen-Freeman, 1997). For example, a question of relevance to qualitative researchers in applied linguistics is: "How do we observe and describe dynamic, constantly changing phenomena without imposing a static structure by the very boundaries we impose in seeking to define and understand?" (Larsen-Freeman, 1997, p. 83).

2.9 Previous Scholarship on Case Study Methodology in Applied Linguistics

Despite the prominence of case studies in applied linguistics and the widespread theorizing about language learning, use, and loss based on them, discussions of case study methodology were almost nonexistent in research methods textbooks for applied linguistics prior to the 1990s. The majority of these texts were written with an explicitly quantitative orientation (e.g., Brown, 1988; Hatch & Farhady, 1982; Hatch & Lazaraton, 1991) and did not include qualitative approaches such as case study and ethnography; other textbooks with titles suggesting a broader survey of methods focused instead on areas such as conversation analysis and interlanguage pragmatics (e.g., Tarone, Gass, & Cohen, 1994).

However, some of the same researchers producing quantitative research methods textbooks have also championed the cause of qualitative research or combined methods. Hatch (1978a), for example, made a substantial contribution to the field by publishing her landmark collection of SLA case studies, many of which were conducted by her graduate students and colleagues (see Chapter 3). But for the next two decades, comprehensive thematic applied linguistics textbooks had relatively little discussion of research methodology, particularly of qualitative methods. What discussion there was of qualitative research tended to suggest that it was a fledgling precursor to more robust quantitative methods, akin to the stereotypical "weak sibling" in social science research, as described by Yin (2003a, p. xiii), or "a method of last resort" (Yin, 1993, p. 40). Richards (2003) is one of the first volumes dedicated to qualitative research methods in TESOL.[1]

Several L2 research textbooks (e.g., Brown & Rodgers, 2002; Johnson, 1992; Nunan, 1992) dedicate a chapter to case study research in language learning. They also provide concrete examples and analyses of case studies.

---

1   TESOL = The field of Teaching English to Speakers of Other Languages.

For example, Johnson analyzed Hudelson's (1989) study of two Spanish-speaking children's development as L2 writers; Nunan analyzed Schmidt's (1983) research of one Japanese adult learner's (Wes's) oral ESL development; and Brown and Rodgers examined Helen Keller's L1 (not L2) development as reflected in her written letters. Seliger and Shohamy (1989) devote just a few pages to a discussion of qualitative and then descriptive research (as separate types of research), with one paragraph about case study under the latter and then some mention of it later in the chapter. Mackey and Gass (2005) and Richards (2003) also devote a couple of pages each to case study. Other, more encyclopedic volumes on language education also include chapters on case study (e.g., Faltis, 1997; van Lier, 2005).

A large proportion of theses, dissertations, and published studies continue to use case study design, as an electronic library search of publications using the terms *language* and *case study* reveals. However, a review of the results of such searches reveals that writers often mean very different things by the phrase *case study*, such as a vignette, a one-shot study, an example, or a thorough examination of one case. Thus, some terminological clarity is needed.

2.10 Longitudinal Case Studies

Traditionally, cases in applied linguistics research have been language learners or users in either instructional or noninstructional settings. Besides conducting research that documents learners' knowledge, abilities, or performance at one point in time, researchers can analyze their behavior synchronically (at one time) and then compare it with behavior observed at one or more subsequent or previous points in time (diachronically). A *longitudinal case study*, such as my study of Jim (Chapter 1), and many others described in Chapter 3, examines development and performance over time. It yields multiple observations or data sets, as information is collected at regular intervals, usually over the course of a year or longer (Saldaña, 2003). As Ortega and Iberri-Shea (2005) point out in their useful review of recent longitudinal research in SLA, the length of the study depends on the number of participants (sample size), the frequency, spacing, and comparability of observations or measurements, the influences of biological or institutional timescales or other relevant "social and developmental chronologies" (p. 38), the intended temporal analytic focus, and the "grain size of the phenomenon under investigation" (p. 39)— the level of analytic detail sought or required. They note that a definitive study of fossilization, for example, might require a very long timescale. Life history research would also normally entail reflections on a long temporal period (e.g., across decades), reflecting a longitudinal perspective, but data collection itself might be restricted to just a few interviews, especially in life histories. Research on intergenerational language shift might be conducted cross-sectionally (examining the linguistic knowledge and behaviors of people of different ages or developmental stages at one point in time, with the goal of drawing longitudinal inferences), or it might examine in a more truly longitudinal design how young people shift from one dominant language to another within a generation (e.g., a 15-year period) or over a shorter or longer period, depending on how rapidly the shift occurs.

Except in (positivist) single-case quantitative (experimental) research, referred to above, the researcher usually does not provide experimental *treatments* or interventions that might modify the normal process of change. Rather, the data reflect natural changes in the learner's behavior and knowledge, influenced by numerous possible factors, such as the environment, physical maturation, cognitive development, and schooling, which the researcher therefore must also take into account in order to arrive at valid conclusions concerning learning processes and outcomes. Because the observed changes are essentially undirected or uncontrolled by the researcher and are associated with these various factors, longitudinal studies often preclude the testing of specific hypotheses or predictions about outcomes prior to the completion of the study. Longitudinal analyses, where there is a basis for comparison (e.g., behavior at Time 1 vs. Time 2 vs. Time 3), lend themselves to some quantitative discussion or data reduction, usually with descriptive statistics. The behaviors, knowledge, or other attributes of cases may be analyzed with coding, counting, and statistical analyses of patterns or developmental differences, or qualitatively, using narrative or detailed linguistic accounts and examples, or some combination of the two.

In the past, some erroneous assumptions were made about case studies: for example, Larsen-Freeman and Long (1991) seemed to equate longitudinal approaches with case study research of oral language development. They also asserted, as many others do, that case studies are categorically ungeneralizable because of the small numbers of subjects involved:

> A longitudinal approach (often called a case study in the SLA field) typically involves observing the development of linguistic performance, usually the spontaneous speech of one subject, when the speech data are collected at periodic intervals over a span of

time... The longitudinal approach could easily be characterized by at least three of the qualitative paradigm attributes: naturalistic (use of spontaneous speech), process-oriented (it takes place over time) and ungeneralizable (very few subjects). (Larsen-Freeman & Long, 1991, pp. 11–12)

However, larger-scale studies that do not involve case study (e.g., multi-year program evaluations, or tracking studies) may also be longitudinal; thus, the two terms should not be conflated. (For a more thorough discussion of longitudinal qualitative research, see Saldaña, 2003.)

Furthermore, whereas issues of generalizability arise almost predictably with case study research, they are less often reflected upon in quantitative research, regardless of the particular contexts in which studies are conducted, the small number of subjects involved, their unique combinations of L1 and L2, and so forth (Chalhoub-Deville, Chapelle, & Duff, 2006; Duff, 2006). The results of many quantitative studies are therefore often referred to as general facts in the absence of compelling evidence of their generality.

A final point is that it is a widely held view that many more careful, longitudinal case studies need to be conducted in a variety of L2 learning contexts.[1]

2.11 Advantages and Disadvantages of Case Study

Case study methodology is often contrasted, negatively, with large-scale experimental methods, especially in psychology or the natural sciences. The strengths of one approach tend to be the weaknesses of the other. As Lewin (1979) puts it, "there must be a trade off between the study of one or two variables in many cases and the study of many variables in one or two cases" (p. 286). This does not mean that every case study focuses on many variables, but that is common practice. According to Shaughnessy and Zechmeister (1985), the goals, methods, and types of information obtained from the two approaches are simply different. Because of their complementarity and the value in combining approaches in some kinds of research, many research methodologists now suggest that researchers move beyond the dichotomy of qualitative versus quantitative research and an allegiance to one over the other. However, studies that effectively combine methods are rather few and far

---

1   At a 2007 symposium on social and cognitive aspects of second language learning and teaching in Auckland, New Zealand, that was also the clear consensus of the invited participants.

between in applied linguistics (Lazaraton, 2000), and there is a need for more, and better, mixed-method studies in the field (see, e.g., Caracelli & Greene, 1993; Tashakkori & Teddlie, 1998, for models).

Although space does not permit a complete review of the quantitative/qualitative research "paradigm debates" (or wars) here and the politics of methodology, they continue to influence descriptions and evaluations of qualitative research and theory building in many fields (Creswell, 1994; Duff, 2002a; Duff & Early, 1996; Gall, Borg, & Gall, 1996; George & Bennett, 2005; Palys, 1997). Authors in Eisner and Peshkin's (1990) edited volume, *Qualitative Inquiry in Education: The Continuing Debate*, address recurring themes in debates about the strengths, weaknesses, and validity of different approaches to research and problems with imposing quantitative constructs on qualitative studies, or asserting that quantitative research is necessarily objective, generalizable, reliable, and so on.

As with most approaches, case studies have their own inherent strengths and weaknesses, which are described below. As long as one is aware of both the potential and limitations of case study methods, however, and presents one's claims accordingly, researchers can carry out robust, rigorous, informative, and significant studies.

2.11.1 Some Advantages of Case Study

Case studies have a number of characteristics that make them attractive. When done well, they have a high degree of completeness, depth of analysis, and readability. In addition, the cases may generate new hypotheses, models, and understandings about the nature of language learning or other processes. Such knowledge generation is possible by capitalizing on either unique or typical cases in theorizing about particular phenomena that challenge current beliefs. In addition, longitudinal case study research helps to confirm stages or transformations proposed on the basis of larger (e.g., cross-sectional) studies and provides developmental evidence that can otherwise only be inferred. These several advantages of case study research are discussed in turn below and then elaborated on in later chapters.

2.11.1.1 Thick Description and Triangulation

By concentrating on the behavior of one individual or a small number of individuals (or characteristics of sites), it is possible to conduct a very thorough analysis (a "thick" or "rich" description) of the case and to include triangulated perspectives from other participants or observers. Detailed case histories, including family background, previous education, and language learning, may be much more feasible for one person than for a large number of individuals. In studies with many participants, case studies may be provided to personalize or illustrate profiles of particular members within a studied group.

Related to this depth of description and the layers of triangulation, case study may involve considerable primary data, such as interview transcripts, transcribed task-related or classroom/workplace discourse, writing samples, and participants' and researchers' journal notes. These large quantities of data must be meaningfully condensed, presented, and interpreted (e.g., Miles & Huberman, 1994). They enable readers to get to know the cases well and to consider corroborating cases or counter-examples.

2.11.1.2 Exploratory, Innovative Potential and Role in Theory Building

Because case studies are often exploratory, they can open up new areas for future research, by isolating variables and interactions among factors that have not previously been identified for their possible influence on the behavior under investigation. They may also reveal new perspectives of processes or experiences from participants themselves. Case studies therefore can generate hypotheses or models that can be tested later, using the same or other research designs, such as a larger cross-sectional design, experimentation, meta-analyses or meta-synthesis, computer modeling, or additional case studies. Reviews of the accumulated findings reported in many different case studies can also be very illuminating (e.g., Andersen & Shirai, 1994; Norris & Ortega, 2006). The case study approach is, for this reason, sometimes referred to as data-driven, or hermeneutic, interpretive research, which attempts to develop hypotheses, models, and ultimately theories on the basis of the findings from data. This orientation is often contrasted with theory-driven (positivist) research, where an existing theory or model is tested and the standard quantitative (experimental, quasi-experimental) procedures of random sampling, pretesting, assigning groups randomly to treatments, posttesting, and so on, may be employed. As I noted earlier, though, some case studies may be designed to test theory; therefore, such stark dichotomies may be unhelpful. Furthermore, much case study research aims to be more descriptive and explanatory than simply exploratory, and exploratory research itself should not be construed as atheoretical. The researcher must articulate the theoretical framework guiding the study, the relationship between the study and other published research, the chain of reasoning underlying the study, and the theoretical contributions the study makes.

An often-cited illustration of data-driven research from a case study is that of Alberto, from whom Schumann developed many ideas concerning fossilization, acculturation, and pidginization, some of which were developed into well-known models of SLA (Schumann, 1978). An example from outside of applied linguistics, in the neurosciences, comes from Diamond, Scheibel, Murphy, and Harvey (1985), whose careful postmortem analysis of Einstein's brain revealed extensive growth of dendritic spines on neurons, thought to be correlated with higher-level cognitive functioning. This finding then generated larger cross-sectional studies of human brains comparing the dendritic growth and density across individuals of different ages and intellectual attributes. This research, in turn, was seen to have potential relevance to SLA (Jacobs, 1988).

A related advantage of case studies is that they can sometimes provide counter-evidence to existing theoretical claims. As most scientific research is aimed at eventually constructing theories or models to account for observed phenomena, counter-evidence must also be taken into account. For example, if a model of SLA claims that acculturation is a crucial causal variable in L2 mastery, yet there is evidence from a case study of an apparently highly acculturated individual who did not master L2 target forms (other conditions, such as input and interaction being equal; Schmidt, 1983), the model must be questioned, at least in its strong form (Schumann, 1993). In the same way, if we claim that all learners necessarily traverse and acquire an invariantly ordered set of morphemes or other developmental stages in English, although there are sound cases where subjects violate or bypass this order (Hakuta, 1976; Tarone & Liu, 1995), we must somehow modify our earlier claim or seek another explanation for the disparities across cases.

2.11.1.3 Unique or Atypical Cases

Related to its being a potentially innovative, inductive approach to research, an added strength of case study is that individuals whose behavior or background appears to be atypical but theoretically interesting can be fruitfully studied, as in the investigation of Einstein's brain referred to above. These cases often advance the field's knowledge considerably. Carefully selecting cases along a continuum of experience, as extreme cases, critical cases, or typical cases, enables researchers to explore the range of human (e.g., linguistic) possibilities in a particular domain.

One well-documented and highly unique language acquisition case study was that of Genie, a girl raised in California and studied extensively in the 1970s (e.g., Curtiss, 1977; Rymer, 1993). Because of extreme neglect and abuse in her upbringing, Genie had been deprived of a normal childhood and opportunities to acquire and use English, her L1, for most of her first 13 years of life. After her abusive situation was discovered, an interdisciplinary team of researchers set out to study and help her. Because Genie was considered to be a test case for the critical period hypothesis, evidence that she could learn language (her L1) successfully even after the onset of puberty, it was asserted, might discredit the critical period hypothesis for language acquisition. There was also a fundamentally important connection between Genie's case and the field of SLA, which has engaged in an ongoing debate for or against such a sensitive or critical period, in order to account for varying ultimate levels of attainment in an L2 compared to an L1, especially for adult learners (Ioup, 2005). Therefore, Curtiss's important and provocative case study of Genie, a highly abnormal case, following on earlier newsworthy cases of children who had spent periods of their childhood deprived of normal access to human language, helped applied linguists and psychologists understand the relationship between maturation and cognitive and linguistic development. However, because of her unique history and context, the findings in Genie's case were rather ambiguous, and this is one of the disadvantages of using atypical cases, a point we return to below.

Other sorts of atypical cases have been of highly successful (or talented) and highly unsuccessful language learners (e.g., Ioup, 1989; Ioup, Boustagui, El Tigi, & Moselle, 1994; Ioup, 2005; see Chapter 3). The latter category includes two case studies of deaf individuals with a history of linguistic isolation, a female (Chelsea) and a male (E. M.), who obtained hearing aids after puberty (in adulthood and in adolescence, respectively) and then, like Genie, displayed only limited language development (Curtiss, 1994; Grimshaw, Adelstein, Bryden, & MacKinnon, 1998).

2.11.1.4 Longitudinal Research

Another advantage of case studies is that by undertaking an in-depth study of just one or a few cases, it is more feasible to examine change using a longitudinal design (e.g., in children's cognitive or linguistic development; see examples in Ortega & Iberri-Shea, 2005). Stages can only be inferred when doing cross-sectional analyses. For example, in a cross-sectional study of 600 Chinese learners of English as a foreign language (EFL) across several grade levels (Duff, 1988), I observed the following progression across learners, in terms of their production of English existentials (NP = noun phrase; PP = prepositional phrase):

{NP/locative/PP} *have* NP → *There BE* (*is/are*) NP {locative/PP}

On hill *have* many people → *There are* many people on the hill

From this simple developmental scheme, or based on a more elaborate one with intervening stages (e.g., an ungrammatical stage *There have*)
or concurrent stages (e.g., shifting from minimal subject suppliance and
no subject-verb agreement to greater suppliance), we might speculate that
lower-proficiency learners will at a future time produce the more target-
like structures. We could also chart the first signs of *There is/are* in students'
production (e.g., a short-lived teaching effect among students in the first year)
that give way to an interlanguage form with *has/have* and then a more target-
like existential form as their grammar is restructured.

A longitudinal case study of a subset of the learners showing that they do
indeed proceed in this manner would verify this assumption based on cross-
sectional patterns (looking at students across different grade levels). My
longitudinal study of Jim (Duff, 1993a; see Chapter 1) found that he produced
many constructions like the one on the left side of the arrows, but did not
make full progress toward the structure on the right and exhibited some added
interim stages (e.g., *'S many people*).

2.11.2 Some (Claimed) Disadvantages of Case Study

In spite of the benefits of pioneering, in-depth case study research described
above, several features often considered weaknesses or limitations should be
noted. These include (1) concerns about generalizability, (2) use of "abnormal"
cases to construct a model of "normal" behavior, (3) issues connected with
thick description and triangulation, (4) objectivity versus subjectivity in
research, (5) the data-driven rather than theory-driven approach, (6) attrition,
(7) constraints on quantitative analysis of small-sample (nonparametric) data,
and (8) ethics, especially difficulties protecting the anonymity and privacy of
case study participants. Listing more disadvantages than advantages does not
mean that case study has more going against it than for it. Rather, my goal is to
alert researchers to some of the criticisms and challenges they might encounter
and help them anticipate how to address them accordingly.

2.11.2.1 Generalizability

The first and most pronounced of these disadvantages is related to generalizability. Because this point is so crucial and controversial in understanding the value of case studies, this section deals with it in some depth. Generalizability is a very important concept in positivist (generally quantitative) experimental research. It aims to establish the relevance, significance, and external validity of findings for situations or people beyond the immediate research project. That is, it is part of the process of establishing the nature of inferences that can be made about the findings and their applicability to the larger population and to different environmental conditions, and to theory more universally (Duff, 2006).

Some scholars argue that it is unwise or indeed impossible to generalize from a hand-picked "convenience sample" of one (n = 1). According to Dobson *et al.* (1981), for example, a case study "is not so much a sample of one, but rather a population of one: the study is descriptive and valid only for its subject" (pp. 32–33). That is because, compared to experimental studies, case study lacks control over extraneous variables. With n = 1, it is virtually impossible to disentangle the possible role of a number of factors that might have influenced learning outcomes or performance, e.g., L1 transfer, overgeneralization, idiosyncratic language use, trauma, learning disorders or disabilities, and so on.

According to Merriam (1998), "a single case or nonrandom sample is selected precisely *because* the researcher wishes to understand the particular in depth, not to find out what is generally true of the many" (p. 208). Similarly, Stake (2000) observes that "the search for particularity [in a case, or a biography] competes with the search for generalizability" (p. 439).

Stake (2005) differentiates between more *intrinsic* and more *instrumental* case studies and their claims to generality, a distinction that many other methodologists have found useful. He also concedes that studies may lean more toward one or the other purpose but share some properties of both.

> I call a study an *intrinsic case study* if it is undertaken because, first and last, one wants better understanding of this particular case. It is not undertaken primarily because the case represents other cases or because it illustrates a particular trait or problem, but because, in all its peculiarity *and* ordinariness, this case itself is of interest... The purpose is not to come to understand some abstract construct or generic phenomenon, such as literacy or teenage drug use or what a

school principal does. The purpose is not theory building—although at other times the researcher may do just that.

... I use the term *instrumental case study* if a particular case is examined mainly to provide insight into an issue or to redraw a generalization. The case is of secondary interest, it plays a supporting role, and it facilitates our understanding of something else. The case is still looked at in depth, its contexts scrutinized, and its ordinary activities detailed, but all because this helps us pursue the external interest. The case may be seen as typical of other cases or not. (Stake, 2005, p. 445)

The notion of instrumental case study is related to the concept of analytic generalization. Stake suggests that "even intrinsic case study can be seen as a small step toward grand generalization ..., especially in a case that runs counter to a rule" (p. 448). A good example of this is Schmidt's (1983) aforementioned analysis of Wes, a Japanese artist living in Hawaii whose English did not develop very well despite his high degree of acculturation in the local English-speaking American community. Schmidt used this case as a way of refuting (if not "falsifying") Schumann's (1978) acculturation model; the model, based largely on Schumann's case study of a Costa Rican immigrant to America named "Alberto", posited that acculturation is a major causal factor in successful SLA.

In Stake's (2005) view, multiple-case studies (which he also calls a collective case study) are instrumental in nature: "They may be similar or dissimilar, with redundancy and variety each important. They are chosen because it is believed that understanding them will lead to better understanding, and perhaps better theorizing, about a still larger collection of cases" (p. 446).

Analytic generalization is made not to populations but to theoretical models, often captured in simple diagrams, which also take into account the complexity of L2 learning or other phenomena and the multiple possible outcomes or relationships that exist among factors. However, Bromley (1986) notes that even producing diagrams capturing processes, which is a form of data or theme reduction and representation, provides a level of abstraction and generality beyond the details of the local cases. Such models and heuristics must be backed up with logical reasoning and evidence that warrant the inferences that are drawn by the researcher or may be drawn by others (Bromley, 1986).

This first limitation of case study reflects a historic rift in the philosophy of science. In one camp are the proponents of nomothetic or logico-positivist research, who seek to make broad generalizations from which to formulate general laws or principles; in the other are the proponents of interpretive research, whose focus may be the individual—that which is unique, rather than that which is common.[1] However, there are wide differences of opinion about the issue of generalizability in case study. Gall *et al.* (2003) suggest that a suitably thick description of research participants and sites allows "readers of a case study report [to] determine the generalizability of findings to their particular situation or to other situations" (p. 466). The aim is to understand and accurately represent people's experiences and the meanings they have constructed, whether as learners, immigrants, teachers, administrators, or members of a particular culture. Yin (2003b) states that theory in case studies can help in "generalizing the results to other cases" (p. 5).

For many qualitative researchers, the term generalizability itself is considered a throwback to another era, paradigm, ethos, and discourse in research. Schofield (1990) stated it as follows: "The major factor contributing to the disregard of the issue of generalizability in the qualitative methodological literature appears to be a widely shared view that it is unimportant, unachievable, or both" (p. 202). She attributes this lack of interest in generalizability to cutural anthropology, the source of much (ethnographic) qualitative research. Anthropologists, after all, study other cultures for their intrinsic value—for revealing the multiple but highly localized ways in which humans live.

Similarly, Cronbach (1975) suggested that social science research (and not just qualitative research) should not seek generalizability anyway: "When we give proper weight to local conditions, any generalization is a working hypothesis, not a conclusion" (cited in Merriam, 1998, p. 209). Note that the association of the replacement term *working hypothesis* for *generalization* by some qualitative researchers is not universally accepted, though, because it downplays the affective, interactive, emergent nature of perspective sharing in qualitative research and again uses terminology associated with quantitative research (Merriam, 1998).

Instead, the assumption is that a thorough exploration of a phenomenon in one or more carefully described contexts—of naturalistic or instructed L2 learners with various attributes, classrooms implementing a new educational

---

1   See Allport (1961), a narrative psychologist and one of the most vocal early defendants of the latter approach and the "science of biography"; Dobson *et al.* (1981), who compare "historical science" and "generalizing (natural) science"; and Shaughnessy and Zechmeister (1985).

approach, or diverse learners integrated within one learning community—will be of interest to others who may conduct research of a similar nature elsewhere. Other readers may simply seek the vicarious experience and insights gleaned from gaining access to individuals and sites they might otherwise not have access to, and Stake (2000 and elsewhere) refers to the learning and enrichment that proceeds in this way as "naturalistic generalization"—learning from others' experiences.

A term that is commonly substituted for generalizability in the qualitative literature is *transferability*—of hypotheses, principles, or findings (Lincoln & Guba, 1985). Transferability, which is sometimes also referred to as comparability, assigns the responsibility to readers to determine whether there is a congruence, fit, or connection between one study context, in all its richness, and their own context, rather than have the original researchers make that assumption for them. Stake (2005) describes the complex and sometimes precarious process of "knowledge transfer, from researcher to reader" as follows:

> As reading [the case study] begins, the case slowly joins the company of cases previously known to the reader. Conceptually for the reader, the new case can not be but some variation of cases already known. A new case without commonality cannot be understood, yet a new case without distinction will not be noticed.... [Researchers] seek ways to protect and substantiate the transfer of knowledge. (p. 455)

Still, some qualitative researchers find the concept of transferability to be too similar in focus to generalizability to be a useful departure from traditional views, and it makes too much of the need for similarity or congruence of studies (e.g., Donmoyer, 1990). They feel that difference, in addition to similarity, helps sharpen and enrich people's understandings of how general principles operate within a field beyond what the notion of transferability suggests. Also, rather than seeking "the correct interpretation", they would aim to broaden the repertoire of possible interpretations and narratives of human experience. Qualitative research, in this view, provides access to rich data about others' experience that can facilitate understandings of one's own as well as others' contexts and lives, through both similarities and differences across settings or cases.

Because of lingering issues and debates connected with generalizability in case study, researchers often express caution about generalizing from the findings in unwarranted ways. At the end of their case study of Schmidt's learning of Portuguese, for example, Schmidt and Frota (1986) wrote:

> We remain aware of the problems inherent in the self-report data ...
> as well as the general limitations of case studies for both proposing
> and evaluating general theories and models [of SLA]. Each learner's
> biography is not only unique but also complex, so that the relative
> importance of variables hypothesized to be important in language
> learning can not be completely unraveled. (p. 307)

Yet despite such disclaimers and cautionary notes, the theoretical findings from groundbreaking early case studies (e.g., those in the 1970s and
1980s by Schumann, Schmidt, Hatch, and colleagues; e.g., Hatch, 1978a), as
well as more recent influential studies examining gender, race/ethnicity, and
identity in L2 learning (e.g., Norton, 1997, 2000; Norton & Toohey, 2001),
have nevertheless achieved fairly wide generalization within the field (especially analytic or theoretical generalization), giving rise to important new
understandings of L2 learning and use. For example, general claims have been
made about the acculturation model (for and against) in relation to SLA, the
impact of noticing gaps on language learning, fossilization, language loss,
and the role of identity, power, and motivation/investment in SLA. We must
remember, though, that some of these generalizations and models have originated from just a small handful of case studies, some but not all of which have
been followed by larger-scale research or corroborating case studies.[1]

In part, this extension of findings in the absence of widespread evidence is a symptom of a young field that may seek originality or novelty
in studies, more so than the robustness, durability, replicability, or transferability of findings with different pools of subjects/participants and in
different contexts. This latter tendency is probably linked to the notion that "it
becomes necessary to build theory when there is none available to explain a
particular phenomenon or when existing theory does not provide an adequate

---

1   This kind of theoretical (over)generalization from cases sampled by convenience has not only
    occurred in hallmark qualitative studies. Because of the lack of replication in many kinds
    of quantitative SLA or classroom-oriented studies as well, findings from small (e.g., quasi-
    experimental or otherwise) one-off studies or even larger studies conducted with a particular
    population are similarly taken as proof that, for example, gender (or task familiarity, partner
    familiarity, ethnicity, same L1 status, etc.) does or does not make a difference in language
    learning or use, that learners do not generally learn from one another's errors, and so on; or,
    in more abstract terms, that variable x has such and such effect on variable or population y (or,
    when generalized, to possibly all language learners) (Duff, 2006).

49

or appropriate explanation" (Merriam, 1988, p. 59).

There has seldom been a critical mass of case studies using similar methods investigating the same phenomenon in applied linguistics (e.g., form-function analyses or the development of information structure or even identity). Some exceptions are the series of case studies inspired by several scholars' work in the 1970s and 1980s, referred to earlier:

- Hatch (1978a) and her students' and colleagues' studies of children, adolescent, and adult learners of English, or bilinguals
- Klein and Perdue (1992) and the European Science Foundation study of adult migrant workers
- Pienemann (1998) and his colleagues' studies of the learnability of German and English, based on processing constraints
- Case studies of tense-aspect acquisition by Roger Andersen and his students and colleagues (e.g., Andersen & Shirai, 1994)

Norris and Ortega (2006) provide a persuasive argument for, and examples of, the value of research that systematically synthesizes existing research, including qualitative studies. Postpositivist approaches to synthesis include qualitative comparative analysis (e.g., Ragin, Shulman, Weinberg, & Gran, 2003). Interpretive approaches might examine emergent themes across studies using the constant comparative method espoused by Glaser and Strauss (1967) or a meta-synthesis/meta-ethnography approach (Noblit & Hare, 1988) that uses "the nature of interpretive explanation to guide the synthesis of ethnographies or other qualitative, interpretive studies" (Noblit & Hare, 1988, p. 25).

2.11.2.2 Abnormal, Atypical, or Deviant Cases

Another issue, related to generalizability, concerns the use of "abnormal", "deviant", or "extreme" cases as the primary data source for the construction of a theory (or model) of "normal" behavior. Some cases are targeted for research precisely because of their atypicality, uniqueness, resilience, or even pathology. They are purposefully or opportunistically selected because of the insights they are expected to generate about the possibilities of language learning and use, for example. Generalizing from studies of aphasics to the neurolinguistic or neurobiological functioning of "normal" individuals must be done with great caution. Likewise, it may be difficult or unwise to develop models of optimal L2 teaching or learning strategies based on just a few studies of exceptionally successful or exceptionally unsuccessful language learners (see Obler, 1989).

In the unusual case study of Genie presented in Section 2.11.1.3, it was asserted that evidence that Genie could learn language (English, her L1) successfully even after the onset of puberty might discredit the critical period hypothesis (CPH) for language acquisition. However, Genie's language development (e.g., morphology and syntax) after several years of intervention was quite modest, and her lack of target-like proficiency in English was difficult to explain, precisely because of her extreme atypicality. One explanation, of course, was that she had exceeded the critical period for language acquisition. However, any inferences drawn about Genie in connection with the CPH were perhaps not completely warranted, especially considering her highly atypical social-psychological history, which included far more than just the presence or absence of language learning opportunities. She had also been deprived of normal human attachments, basic opportunities for cognitive stimulation and development, nutrition, and physical exercise. Yet, if Genie had been able to achieve something approximating "normal" native proficiency in English despite her early deprivation, the inferences and generalizations drawn from the study would have been far more powerful and remarkable. It can thus be difficult to interpret the findings in such pathological or atypical case studies.

2.11.2.3 Thick Description and Triangulation

Whereas conducting an in-depth, holistic, multiperspective analysis is potentially a very positive feature of case studies, the amount of data from different sources to be analyzed and synthesized can be daunting. The researcher needs to be organized and methodical about managing, sorting, analyzing, and interpreting the data, and reporting the findings (see Chapters 4 to 6). There must be a balance struck between presenting information about individual participants (cases) in sufficient depth and the need to elaborate on emergent themes and consider theoretical implications. Space limitations in journals may not permit the inclusion of extensive examples, fieldnotes, quotations, and extracts. Thus, thick description and triangulation present both opportunities and challenges to researchers when analyzing and presenting results.

2.11.2.4 Objectivity versus Subjectivity

Another criticism sometimes leveled against the case study method is that it lacks objectivity—that researchers might have preconceived notions or biases when undertaking research or that they might identify too closely with their case participants and lose all perspective. The researcher is indeed likely to be very close to the case and data, by virtue of being the principal "research instrument" in naturalistic studies: selecting the study participants (or sites), conducting interviews and observations and filtering them through their own worldviews, values, and perspectives (Merriam, 1998), analyzing the data, then sampling from a large corpus of data to select representative examples, and imposing an interpretation on the findings. Similarly, it could be argued that research participants (cases), when asked to provide introspective or retrospective accounts of their experiences or perceptions, are themselves highly subjective as well. The claim of subjectivity is true to some extent, but could also be leveled against much research of all types. Using personal judgment in making research decisions, framing studies based on earlier research, and drawing interpretations and conclusions are involved in all research, although some research may have more procedures in place to establish reliability, for example, in the consistency of ratings or other judgments, or to establish the replicability or consistency of observations. Stake (1995) concedes that "the intent of qualitative researchers to promote a subjective research paradigm is a given. Subjectivity is not seen as a failing needing to be eliminated but as an essential element of understanding" (p. 45). However, he also explains that "subjective misunderstandings" (p. 45) must be put to the test by making efforts to try to disconfirm one's own interpretations. Hesse-Biber and Leavy (2006) concur, observing that "most qualitative paradigms agree on the importance of the subjective meanings individuals bring to the research process and acknowledge the importance of the social construction of reality" (p. 79). Standpoint epistemologies (e.g., feminist, critical) are especially unapologetic about the nature of subjective experience or judgments.

Therefore, most qualitative researchers, especially poststructuralists, do not see subjectivity as a major issue, as something that can or should be eliminated. Rather, they see it as an inevitable engagement with the world in which meanings and realities are constructed (not just discovered) and in which the researcher is very much present.[1] Many interpretive/post-structural qualitative researchers question whether researchers can be truly objective in the human and social sciences. They suggest, rather, that being candid and reflective about one's own subjectivities, biases (ideologies), and engagement with research participants and with the research itself is invaluable. Furthermore, providing sufficient detail about decision making, coding or analysis, chains of reasoning, and data sampling can allay concerns about unprincipled subjectivity. Coming from a more positivist tradition, Yin (2003a) suggests that researchers' unacknowledged biases might be tested by seeing how open they are to findings that contradict their own assumptions, a strategy that interpretive researchers find helpful as well. Miles and Huberman (1994), who also approach research from a positivist orientation, advise that readers' confidence in findings will be increased if researchers use a set of "tactics for testing or confirming findings" (p. 262), such as checking for representativeness of data, checking for researcher effects, triangulating data sources and methods, checking the meaning of outliers, using extreme cases, following up on surprises, looking for negative evidence, ruling out spurious relations, replicating findings, checking out rival explanations, and getting feedback from participants (p. 263). Above all, the research needs to be credible and trustworthy, and those traits must be apparent.

2.11.2.5 The Role of Theory

Another criticism sometimes leveled against case study research is that it is unguided, unplanned, and unmotivated theoretically, or that it does not in turn yield theoretical insights. Earlier, the data-driven versus theory-driven dichotomy in theory construction was mentioned. Certain risks must be taken in data-driven or grounded research. First, it may be difficult to predict what the outcome of the case study will be. In Huebner's (1983) study of Ge's English language development, for example, when the study was first undertaken, the goal was to analyze the development of the tense-aspect system in Ge's evolving English. However, there was really no such development as it turned out. Therefore, Huebner abandoned his original focus and found another productive area to study instead (e.g., the interaction between a shift toward greater subject prominence and more sophisticated

---

1   Also, many early models of L2 learning were inspired at least in part by researchers' own subjective experiences of learning and using languages in different ways and with different degrees of success.

article usage). However, it is unfair to assert that case study is necessarily atheoretical, unfocused, and completely emergent in design. His analysis and theoretical framework were rooted in current/emerging linguistic and acquisition theory.

Much case study research is embedded within a relevant theoretical literature and is motivated by the researcher's interest in the case and how it addresses existing knowledge or contributes new knowledge to current debates or issues. Researchers should carefully present their results and enduring lessons learned from the study, including theoretical insights, without at the same time overstating them or overgeneralizing. Research committees, funders, and ethical review committees will not approve research projects that are aimless, theoretically unmotivated, and have not given due consideration to design, data collection, and analysis. In some cases, though, studies do evolve from the investigator's original intentions for a variety of reasons.

2.11.2.6 Attrition

In any research, it is important that the subjects participate in all aspects of the study and for its duration, as planned. However, another disadvantage of case study, even in research that is not necessarily longitudinal, is possible attrition or "mortality". Attrition means that, for some reason, one or more participants have dropped out—they have become too busy to continue, have moved away, or have lost interest in the study. When the study involves just one person (or site) or a small number of focal participants (or sites), the study may be greatly compromised if anything happens to one of them. When just one person is tracked intensively and longitudinally, attrition is even more serious. In Brown's (1973) seminal study of the acquisition of English (L1) by three children, attrition was a factor; after a year, one of his three subjects, Eve, moved away to Canada from the United States.

Attrition is not uncommon in longitudinal research with immigrant families because they tend to be a very mobile population until they find satisfactory and stable employment, schools, social networks, and housing. Some populations that applied linguists study, such as migrant workers, are by definition migratory. Recall that Jim, my case study participant, started out in one Canadian city and ended up in another and along the way nearly died because of a stroke. Even while he was still in the city where we first met, he lived in many different kinds of housing and in various parts of the city, near and far.

2.11.2.7 Statistical Analysis

Although many case studies do not include the quantification of observations or may just include straightforward descriptive statistics (e.g., of frequencies), studies that plan to describe relationships in the data using more sophisticated statistics must proceed with caution. Because a case study typically involves the analysis of one person's (or just a few individuals') behavior across tasks or observations/times, or examines the production of different linguistic or discursive structures at one time, this research design violates some of the basic assumptions, such as independence of observations, underlying the use of common statistics (e.g., the Chi-square statistic (Hatch & Lazaraton, 1991), which compares the frequency of observations across different categories). When in doubt about the appropriate use of statistics, consult a statistician who really understands the kind of data you are working with. This advice also applies to small-n studies that are not case studies.

2.11.2.8 Research Ethics

The principles of ethical research apply to case studies just as they do in other types of research (see Chapter 4). However, one of the challenges in conducting case studies that include considerable detail and contextualization about the person, site, or event featured is that the identity of the participants may become difficult to protect, even when pseudonyms are used. As a result, researchers may sometimes change or withhold information that might compromise the confidentiality of the case in order to honor agreements about participants' right to privacy.

2.12 Summary

This chapter has provided a brief overview of the definitions, origins, features, advantages, and disadvantages of case study research. The richness of description and detailed contextualization possible with the study of just one case or a small number of cases is clearly the primary advantage of this approach for researchers as well as for consumers of research. Issues connected with the inferences that can be drawn from findings from small sample sizes in case study, including generalizability, or from abnormal, deviant, or extreme cases, concerns about statistical analysis and ethics, and the role of case studies in theory building were also addressed. To offset some of the perceived disadvantages of case study, researchers are advised to carefully consider the representativeness or uniqueness of the cases they study, their own positionality (subjectivities or biases) as researchers, and the chains of reasoning and inference used in the analysis and interpretation of findings. In addition, any alternative or rival explanations that might also account for their findings should be considered.

CHAPTER 3

Examples of Case Studies in Applied Linguistics

3.1 An Overview of Themes and Trends over the Past Three Decades

Case studies of language development and use have focused on a variety of questions and have used many kinds of methods. In this chapter, I provide a synopsis of case studies that have generated interest over the past several decades across bilingual, multilingual/multicultural, and other L2 learning contexts. I also note some current research trends that reflect expanding research agendas beyond traditional (postpositivist) L2 studies. The studies collectively reveal some, but certainly not all, developmental trends in the field of L2 learning and in applied linguistics. Because of the growing number of case studies from which I could have sampled to produce examples and themes for this chapter, there are also obvious omissions across geographical, cross-linguistic and theoretical domains. I have simply tried to find representative examples within the designated thematic areas.

A comparison of case studies conducted "then and now" reveals that many of those conducted in the 1970s and 1980s addressed linguistic and social-psychological questions of the sort shown in Table 3.1.

Unlike earlier, first-wave (or first-generation) SLA studies, often with uninstructed (naturalistic), lower-proficiency-level immigrant children and

Table 3.1 Research Questions in Traditional SLA Case Studies

1.	How do bilingual children learn and manage two linguistic systems when most children are struggling to master one?
2.	Why do some learners fossilize or plateau prematurely in some (but not necessarily all) areas of language development, while others continue to progress?
3.	How important is it for learners to notice gaps in their linguistic knowledge or notice new forms in the input for them to acquire these new forms?
4.	How do language forms and functions (or meanings) map onto each other in early stages of L2 development?
5.	What is the profile of the prototypical "good", "successful", or "talented" language learner?
6.	Is there a critical period for language learning? What is the optimal age to learn another language?
7.	What processes or strategies do effective second-language readers, writers, speakers, or listeners use? And what is the relationship between L1 adeptness in these skill areas and L2 performance?
8.	How do students learn to understand and perform certain speech acts, such as requests, in a second language? What role does L1 transfer play in L2 pragmatics or other aspects of language production?
9.	What is the relationship between acculturation and L2 learning?
10.	How do learners' attitudes, motivation, and aptitude affect their second-language acquisition?

adults learning an L2 that examined their stage-by-stage development in tense/ aspect and other morphology, for example, contemporary case studies focus to a greater extent on poststructural, as opposed to structural, aspects of language learning, use, and loss, and do so using more interpretive and critical analytic practices. They explore bilingual, multilingual and other L2 learners' identities, how these learners are represented or positioned by themselves and by others in social encounters, learners' variable access to target-language communities and speakers, their agency in language learning, and their linguistic socialization into and through various L2 (or multilingual) activities. The studies draw increasingly on anthropological, sociocultural, and phenomenological/ narrative approaches to linguistic and literacy development and activity (see Table 3.2). More of the learners studied are quite advanced in L2 proficiency or are functionally bilingual or multilingual with varying degrees of literacy in those languages. With this emerging research trend, social categories and issues related to race, gender, community membership, postcolonialism, and marginality are foregrounded, analyzed, and theorized differently

Table 3.2 Recent Research Questions in Studies of Language Learning, Bilingualism, Multilingualism, and Education

---

1. What is the relationship between L2 learning and L1 loss (or attrition)? What are the consequences of language loss for learners and their communities?

2. What is the relationship between learners' social identities (e.g., gender, class, race, ethnicity, immigrant status) and their L2 learning experiences? How does social identity affect access to language learning opportunities or increased integration into L2-mediated communities of practice, and vice versa?

3. What is the effect of participating in computer-mediated communication, online instruction, electronic bulletin boards, or other electronic media on language/literacy acquisition and use? How are the target linguistic/literacy genres themselves evolving?

4. How are misunderstandings negotiated and repaired in classrooms, informal encounters, or workplaces?

5. How does emotion mediate language learning and memory? How do personal narratives or life histories of learners capture the influence of affective factors?

6. How do newcomers to a culture or group learn to participate in and gain competence in new language/literacy practices in ways that are expected? How and why do some newcomers resist those same practices and expectations?

7. What are the histories, experiences, hopes, and desires of heritage-language (HL) learners?
    How do HL developmental patterns and ultimate levels of attainment differ from those of non-HL learners of the same target language or proficient L1 users of the target language?

8. How does the acquisition of L2 literacy (e.g., academic and nonacademic writing) affect one's L1 literacy practices? What is the connection between orality and literacy?

9. What are the greatest linguistic and nonlinguistic challenges for L2 learners who have been mainstreamed into academic L2 content courses?

10. How does L2 learning affect L3 (or even L1) learning? In what ways are the sociolinguistic experiences and psycholinguistic processes of trilinguals in contemporary societies different from those of monolinguals and bilinguals?

---

than in earlier applied linguistic research. The linguistic and cultural practices and communities one is able to participate in are often given more attention than is just tacit knowledge (competence) and its development within an individual learner. Earlier questions and research methods have certainly not been abandoned, however, so the newer approaches should be seen as complementary to earlier ones, but clearly seeking answers to very different sorts of questions.

In what follows, I present examples of case studies in applied linguistics in different categories. Many of the early studies, reviewed first below, were longitudinal. They were groundbreaking and innovative when first conducted and are still instructive today. Some of the studies are presented in more detail than others to provide readers, to the extent possible, a survey and discussion of both topics and methods.

3.2 Early Studies of Child Language Acquisition, Bilingualism, and Language Loss

Hatch's (1978a) edited volume lays the foundation for subsequent research on L2 development and bilingualism, particularly in the United States. It includes 17 case studies (some of them reprints) of children's, adolescents' and adults' bilingual/L2 or L3 acquisition in natural environments outside of classrooms. One of Hatch's (1978b) observations when previewing the studies of children's development is that "learning a second language is not as easy and effortless either psychologically or linguistically for some children as folklore would have us believe. Nevertheless, the skill that many children display as second language learners is truly dazzling" (p. 14). She also includes an annotated bibliography of prior case study research on simultaneous and sequential bilingualism, some of which was published in French in the early 20th century by parents investigating their children's linguistic development. The writers examined the development of phonology, lexis, semantics, and syntax, and some also noted the psychological impact of language development (or loss) on the children.

Kenyeres (1938), for example, studied her six-year-old daughter Eva's acquisition of French, her L3, through immersion at a school in Switzerland, and then observed Eva's return to Hungary later, where the girl found that her Hungarian was no longer like that of her peers. (Eva's L1 was Hungarian and L2 was German.) Ronjat (1913) studied his son's incipient bilingualism in French and German in his household, where both languages were spoken (a different one by each parent). By a young age, the boy had apparently developed great facility and metalinguistic flare in both languages and an ability to switch dialects and languages effectively. Pavlovitch (1920) also studied his son's simultaneous bilingual development, in this case in French and Serbian, but only up to two years of age.

Hatch was particularly impressed by Leopold's (1939, 1947, 1949a, 1949b, 1954/1978) careful, longitudinal, four-volume study of his daughter Hildegard's acquisition of English and German during her first six or so years. For that reason, her volume also includes a short piece summarizing some of that research (Leopold, 1954/1978). As with some of the other early case studies of children, Hildegard's rejection of one or the other (or both) languages at different points and her metalinguistic awareness of the two languages was observed as she moved between the United States and Germany and between English and German speakers.[1]

As one might expect, many of these early investigations were exploratory, and many originated as dissertations or theses about the researchers' own young children, since acquisition research too was still in its infancy then. For the purposes of standardized educational testing and curriculum development, early (L1) case studies gave rise to larger cross-sectional studies from about 1940 to 1960, to determine, among other things, normal levels of vocabulary acquisition for children at various ages (Lightbown & White, 1987). Later, with the advent of Chomskyan linguistics, portable tape recorders, and methodological developments in field linguistics and sociolinguistics, applied linguists had new means to achieve their research objectives, which had also shifted considerably. Technology enabled researchers to study more children and more complex language. Case studies were therefore not as common or necessary in psycholinguistic experiments, many of which were designed to examine the correlation between transformational (syntactic) complexity and processing time.

Hatch (1983) also reported on several intriguing case studies documenting the effects of aphasia due to a lesion in the left or right hemisphere of the brain resulting from injuries or disease. Although monolinguals' linguistic functioning is thought to take place to a greater extent in the left hemisphere of the brain than the right, bilinguals' or L2 learners' language processing shows a greater involvement of the right hemisphere. The question was whether, and how, injuries to the right or left hemisphere would affect bilingual and multilingual speakers' subsequent comprehension and production or recovery of the different languages they previously knew, including their L1. For example, if language ability is impaired because of a brain lesion in the right hemisphere, is it the last-learned or first-learned language that is recovered first? The hypothesis was that it would be the later-learned languages most affected. Second, will left-hemisphere lesions result in less impairment or more impairment to L2 and L3 than to L1? The hypothesis was that there would

---

1   Brown (1973) later drew upon Leopold's study of Hildegard's first two years of development to compare the orders of acquisition of morphemes for his three cases (children) and for Hildegard. However, this goal proved slightly problematic since Hildegard displayed a "floor effect" (low levels of criterion performance) because of Brown's high criterion of 90% suppliance in obligatory contexts to indicate that morphemes had been acquired.

be more L1 impairment and less impairment of L2 or L3. Hatch summarized studies reported by Galloway (1981), Paradis (1977), and Whitaker (1976) that revealed a range of results. For example, among Galloway's (1981) five case studies involving left-brain lesions were the following:

1. A German male who had at one time learned French but could at first only speak French during the aphasic phase
2. A German female who had briefly studied Italian and French, who first recovered Italian, then French, but as her French reappeared, her Italian weakened and she answered questions in German in French. Then after two weeks, her German reappeared and her French receded
3. A Russian (L1), French (L2), Serbian (L3) male suffering from syphilis who first recovered Serbian, and then Russian with a Serbian accent

The review of related studies showed a great deal of variability across people suffering brain-related language loss and recovery. In the intervening three decades, numerous other neurolinguistic studies have been conducted, using more sophisticated imaging and testing techniques.

One final, rather unusual, line of research during this same time period, bridging anthropology and linguistics, had chimps, not humans, as the subjects of case studies. Researchers attempted to discover the extent to which higher primates known as Washoe, Sarah, and, more recently, Kanzi could learn, understand, and productively use human language (Savage-Rumbaugh, Shanker, & Taylor, 1998). This research program continues today.

3.3 Natural-Order Studies and Performance Analysis (1960s to 1980s)

In the late 1960s and early 1970s, several very important case studies were conducted by child L1 acquisition researchers. Brown's (1973) case study research on three children named Adam, Eve, and Sarah helped generate a new research agenda for other language acquisition researchers. Researchers were also conducting longitudinal studies of children's acquisition of languages other than English: Finnish, Samoan, Swedish, Spanish, Luo, and German (Brown, 1973). Many of the contributors to Slobin's (1985) later volume on L1 acquisition of Japanese, German, Hebrew, Kaluli, and six other languages drew heavily on parents' longitudinal diary/case studies of children's development in the various languages.

Pioneering research often shifts from case studies to larger, more experimental studies to allow for potentially greater generalization from findings. For this reason, many cross-sectional studies were subsequently conducted on the "remarkably invariant order" Brown (1973, p. 57) had found in the acquisition of 14 English morphemes (e.g., *-ing*, plural *-s*, third-person singular *-s*) in the three children he studied. SLA researchers, in turn, undertook parallel research (see Ellis, 1994; Gass & Selinker, 2001, for reviews). SLA had by then become a legitimate subfield of (applied) linguistics, and the new "focus on the learner" in the 1970s generated both case studies and cross-sectional studies of learners' errors, classified by types or error source. This analytic approach, in retrospect, was more descriptive than explanatory or theory generating.

Because of the research agenda and methodology inherited from the L1 morpheme-order studies, many interesting developments in learners' L2 linguistic or communicative systems were ignored (Larsen-Freeman & Long, 1991). Researchers soon began to examine not only what learners did wrong—their "errors" or performance in relation to a fixed set of morphemes—but also their highly innovative and systematic uses of L2. This approach came to be known as performance analysis (Long & Sato, 1984), and it was in that context and spirit that many of the case studies in Hatch (1978a) were undertaken. Morphological forms, such as possessive *-'s* and regular past tense verb endings, were no longer SLA researchers' sole focus, although Hakuta's (1976) case study attracted attention because his subject, Uguisu, acquired morphemes in a different order than the established norm.

Research from the mid-1970s to the early 1990s began to take into account more idiosyncratic, creative, functional aspects of SLA than before.[1] The relationship between the appearance of linguistic forms and the ways in which they were used (their functions or meanings) was reconsidered as case study data suggested that the two did not necessarily correspond and, on the contrary, often had no systematic relationship whatsoever. Wagner-Gough's (1978) discussion of a young Persian boy's overextended use of the progressive morpheme *-ing* in various nonprogressive linguistic contexts such as imperatives (e.g., *Sitting down like that* instead of *Sit down*) helped raise awareness of this mismatch. Therefore, it was a hallmark in the

---

1   By functional linguistics or functional analysis, I mean work that considers carefully the semantic and pragmatic properties and uses of morphemes, words, phrases, or other linguistic structures. For a review of functional approaches used in child L1 studies, see Budwig (1995) and Mitchell and Miles (2004).

genesis of form-to-function analysis (Larsen-Freeman & Long, 1991). Various functional-linguistic approaches to describing natural language systems were incorporated in these studies (e.g., Givón, 1979), although Hallidayan systemic-functional linguistics (SFL) (e.g., Halliday, 1975) in that period perhaps had less impact on L1 and L2 studies in Canada and the United States than in Australia. However, interestingly, Halliday's conceptualization of the development of language as a semiotic system that unfolds through social interaction was heavily influenced by his case study of the L1 development and meaning making of his own young son, Nigel, in his first three years. (A recently edited collection of Halliday's influential and prolific writing includes a volume on Nigel's development and a CD of the "Nigel transcripts" (Webster, 2003).)

Another important study from that era was the functional analysis of certain forms in the evolving language of Ge, Huebner's (1983) English (L2) case study participant (see Chapter 1). A Hmong immigrant in Hawaii, Ge used the forms *da* ("the") and *isa* (an invented topic marker) in creative ways, and over the initial one-year study the use of these forms changed quantitatively and qualitatively. Whereas *da* came to be used in more environments (it "flooded"), such as with definite subjects, *isa* was used less (it "trickled") as a topic marker and sometimes-copula, to a copula function mainly. Thus, the scope and semantic features of the two forms under investigation changed. Huebner's was also one of the first such case studies in SLA to include a quantitative (nonstatistical) analysis of change and a microanalysis of the semantics of article use. This study, therefore, reaffirmed the need to examine learners' language as a dynamic, ever-changing system and also echoed Wagner-Gough's (1978) call for more attention to disparities between language forms and functions.

At the same time that fine-tuned, narrowly focused microanalyses of learners' evolving grammars were under way, the focus in SLA case studies was also broadening. The deficiencies of early performance analysis research (morpheme-order studies), coupled with its lack of explanatory power, led to a growing interest in sociolinguistics and conversation analysis and other kinds of discourse analysis in relation to language development through interactional encounters. The examination of grammar as a natural outcome of conversational interactions became a new trend, and descriptive methods derived from conversation analysis were adopted and are still widely used (see Markee, 2000, 2006). Although syntax continued to be the major focus of attention in SLA, pragmatics (e.g., speech acts such as apologies and requests) and other aspects of linguistic competence and use also grew in popularity.

In Huang's study of his son Paul (Huang & Hatch, 1978), for example, the relationship between input structures and output structures in his discourse was analyzed, suggesting that through imitation of what he was hearing at his English nursery school, Paul was producing yet unanalyzed, chunked phrases without knowing quite what they or their component parts meant (e.g., *Get out of here!* and *It's time to eat and drink!* p. 121). Eventually these would become analyzed. Several years later, Peters (1983) also examined the way children acquire their L1 in a gestalt versus analytical manner, from either the top down (chunks) or the bottom up (words), depending on the child. Her case study of Minh showed how a child comes to analyze previously chunked expressions or units (e.g., *Look at that!*), again highlighting the observation that language is not simply analyzed and acquired in a word-by-word, structure-by-structure manner. Scollon's (1976) book, based on his dissertation, was a case study of a young relative named Brenda. He discussed the relationship between the production first of "vertical" constructions, which were strings of related but separate one-word utterances, and then "horizontal" constructions, fluent multiword utterances under one intonation contour. By stringing together the vertical pieces syntactically through conversation, caregivers could help learners internalize complete, grammatical (horizontal) utterances. This scaffolding of discourse by more competent speakers was also thought to play a causal role in language acquisition universally (Peck, 1978; Hatch, 1978c), a viewpoint that was later contested based on new evidence from different cultures in which caregivers did not engage in scaffolding in this manner (Schieffelin & Ochs, 1986).

The observation that children do not acquire their L1 or L2 in the same fashion—even if certain morphemes seem to develop in a similar order—and that all children do not use the same strategies emerged in other studies too (e.g., Wong-Fillmore, 1979). Itoh and Hatch (1978) noted, for example, how a young Japanese child in the United States coped with living in her new linguistic environment, with a long rejection phase initially, followed by a repetition stage, and lastly a spontaneous production phase. In this general approach, target forms produced to a predetermined criterion level were not of central importance; rather, the way learners used what (limited) linguistic means or forms they had was of great interest, and so too was silence or resistance to learning. The actual mechanisms of learning and a holistic theory of grammar were not always evident, however.

A new set of function-form studies investigated changes in negation and question formation (Cancino, Rosansky, & Schumann, 1978), representing new "natural orders", but based on observed ungrammatical interim stages as well as grammatical ones in final stages. Thus, an interest in target-like forms in SLA was complemented by an interest in process or transitional stages encountered by learners before mastering target forms. Many of these insights were gleaned from seminal case studies such as the one by Cancino *et al.* (1978). The negation continuum generated by that project was based on the findings of a longitudinal study of six Spanish-speaking learners of English who acquired negation and question formation by traversing essentially similar stages. However, one learner, Alberto, never mastered these structures, and his atypicality became the subject of much subsequent research and discussion. Alberto, a Costa Rican learner in the United States, appeared to have stopped progressing in English at a very low level (Schumann, 1978).

As we saw in Chapter 2, exceptional cases are often very productive for theory construction, as they tend to challenge widely held assumptions about behavior. Schumann posited that the lack of acculturation, a social-psychological variable, was the chief causal factor accounting for Alberto's lack of success in English (e.g., in negation, question formation, use of auxiliaries, and provision of subjects). Even when Schumann tried to give Alberto intensive instruction in negation, there was no lasting effect in Alberto's spontaneous speech. The explanation was that he was simply not integrated sufficiently well into the U.S. English-speaking culture, demonstrating a social-psychological distance from it instead, which is why his English seemed unalterably fossilized.

Based on his case study and supporting research from sociolinguistics, Schumann (1978) proposed that early language development represented a kind of pidginization process, reflecting many of the simplified features of attested pidgins in various countries. However, his causal claims about acculturation became controversial, and counter-examples appeared as evidence against the strong form of Schumann's acculturation model or hypothesis. One such study was carried out by Schmidt (1983) on his acquaintance Wes, a Japanese artist in Hawaii. Wes satisfied all the criteria for being well motivated, acculturated, exposed to ample English input and interaction in Hawaii, and so on, but nonetheless did not seem to acquire target-like morphology and syntax. Schmidt's study revealed that learners may be very competent communicators in their L2 without having acquired many of the fundamental linguistic structures in the language. Moreover, the interest in conversational ability and pragmatics illustrated in Schmidt's study was an indication of the broadening scope of SLA at that time.

3.4 Individual Differences: Exceptionality, Talented and Untalented Learners

Individual differences in language learning, effective learning strategies, and variable success have been important areas of SLA research since the late 1970s, again reflecting the shift in attention from uniform stages of development (e.g., in morphemes) to differentiated learning processes and outcomes (e.g., Gass, Madden, Preston, & Selinker, 1989; Skehan, 1989). Research on individual differences has examined successful or unsuccessful learning strategies (and learners) as ascertained by language tests, interviews, contextualized observation, and, in some cases, extensive testing of learners' aptitudes, intelligence (IQ), and family histories. One aim was to determine profiles associated with L2 success, especially among adults, in whom the greatest variation in L2 outcomes is found.

In a well-known study of several children learning English in California, Wong-Fillmore (1979) found considerable individual differences among the children's behaviors and also in their progress in English. One of her participants, Nora, was much more socially aggressive and cognitively strategic in her language learning than the others, and ultimately more successful as well. Nora was particularly invested in her L2 learning and in her identity as an English speaker and was a precocious learner, especially in comparison with another one of the participants, a boy named Juan, who was far less outgoing or successful. Nora used to join groups quickly and pretend she could understand English even when she could not, and then would rely on friends to assist her. She was also willing to produce English even when she had quite limited linguistic means at her disposal in the L2, and formulaic or chunked expressions (unanalyzed) facilitated this.

Another case study of learner strategies involved two Spanish students in an intensive English program (Abraham & Vann, 1987). The two learners were selected from clusters of 15 students in three groups: very successful, moderately successful, and unsuccessful. One learner was judged to be very successful and the other unsuccessful based on research tasks and an interview. The authors then examined the two learners' different learning contexts and philosophies that seemed to influence their use of more or less productive or successful strategies, and considered how "poor", unsystematic strategy users might be trained to be more effective strategy users.

A very different approach to research examining variation investigated possible neuropsychological correlates to exceptionally efficient L2 learning. Normal children, in spite of individual strategies, learning styles, and minor differences among them, appear to acquire their (oral) L1 reasonably well, and many also acquire an L2 or L3. Adults often fare much less well in learning an L2, or their success is less predictable. An understanding of the relationship between the neural or neurobiological substrate and linguistic behavior, it was thought, might account for some of the individual differences in SLA that otherwise could not be easily explained.

Studies of talented individuals, musical and mathematical geniuses, individuals with photographic memories, and child protégés have been done, in some cases with postmortem analysis of the subject's brain (see discussion of Einstein in Chapter 2; Obler, 1989; Obler & Fein, 1988[1]; A. Scheibel, personal communication, 1988). But aside from large-scale "good language learner" studies in the 1970s (e.g., Naiman, Frohlich, Spada, & Todesco, 1978), there had not been comparable investigations of talented language learners from the perspective of neuropsychology or neurolinguistics, looking at brain-behavior linkages, until Obler's work (Obler, 1989; Novoa, Fein, & Obler, 1988). Her research participant, CJ, was a 29-year-old Caucasian-American male graduate student whose L1 was English and who grew up in a mostly monolingual environment. From the age of 15 (past the onset of puberty), he had studied the following languages in succession: French, German, Spanish, Latin, Moroccan Arabic, and Italian, some of which he learned at school in the United States, and others he "picked up" quickly abroad. He was recruited by Obler through campus notices seeking exceptional language learners. The native speakers of languages CJ spoke judged his ability, including his pronunciation, as native-like. Obler also sought details about CJ's personal history, related to the "Geschwind cluster" (Geschwind & Galaburda, 1985, cited in Obler, 1989), which are factors apparently linked to fetal hormonal levels, believed to have behavioral correlates connected, possibly, to enhanced right-hemisphere development. For CJ these factors included the following: he was left-handed, homosexual, had allergies and hives, and had a twin brother and a schizophrenic grandfather (a presumably infrequent combination of factors). The battery of psychological tests CJ was given revealed that his musical and visuospatial aptitudes were only average (contrary to views about the

---

1 See Norton and Toohey's (2001) critique of these "good language learner" studies.

correlation between musical and linguistic ability), his IQ— including verbal IQ—was normal, and his language aptitude as judged by the Modern Language Aptitude Test (MLAT) was average on most sections. However, on the IQ test (Weschler Adult Intelligent Scale–Revised), CJ did particularly well on the vocabulary and code-learning and retention subtests. He also obtained superior scores on cognitive subtests related to pattern matching and decoding. Finally, on the MLAT, he again excelled on subtests related to learning new codes, and also did very well on guessing a word when only the consonants were given. His verbal memory (but not other types of memory) was outstanding and thought to be closely linked to his highly successful L2 learning profile. Thus, the case study of CJ established a neuropsychological profile for an exceptional adult L2 learner (a kind of analytic generalization) with an intriguing combination of psychological/cognitive attributes and fetal-hormonal history.

Working within the same general research domain, Schneiderman and Desmarais (1988a, 1988b) differentiated between talent and aptitude for L2 learning. They referred to talent as "an exceptional ability to achieve native-like competence in a second language after puberty" (1988b, p. 91). Their case study participants were two English learners of French, by then in their 20s and 30s, who had started L2 learning after the age of 11. Both had native-like French proficiency, excellent memory and decoding skills, and evidence of greater than usual right-hemisphere involvement in both French and English tasks. The researchers hypothesized—and found—that highly talented adult L2 learners have greater neurocognitive flexibility, and that the right hemisphere of their brains plays a greater role in language processing than in their "untalented" counterparts. In other words, their language functions were not restricted to the left side of the brain primarily. Like the earlier studies of exceptional learners, the two learners in this study also displayed characteristics from the Geschwind cluster, such as family left-handedness, eczema, allergies, albinism, and schizophrenia, and both subjects were fluent in languages other than French as well (all learned as young adults or adults).

Ioup, Boustagui, El Tigi, and Moselle (1994) also explored exceptionality in adult language learning by demonstrating, through extensive testing, the native-like proficiency attained by a British naturalistic learner of Egyptian Arabic. Julie, the case study participant, had immigrated to Cairo at age 21 when she married her Egyptian husband. She had since then lived in the country for 26 years and used Arabic at home with her children and other family members. Within 2.5 years of her arrival in Egypt, Julie passed as a native speaker and had, in the meantime, mastered the intricate discourse structure of the language as well as all aspects of syntax and phonology in her oral production and intuitions of grammaticality. She was also able to distinguish among various other varieties of Arabic and could discriminate among Egyptian dialects (e.g., Cairene).

Another participant in the study, Laura, also performed very well (native-like) but not to the level Julie demonstrated. Julie's success was attributed to basic language learning "talent", or language aptitude, likely based on exceptionally good cortical (brain) organization, flexibility, and functioning that enabled her to perceive linguistically significant contrasts in the L2 input and to organize the new grammar as a system independent of her L1. This case was also cited as evidence against a critical period for L2 learning, since Julie was well past puberty when she began to learn Arabic. Ioup (2005) also notes that Julie's and Laura's relative success in language learning was not simply because they were exceptionally well motivated or were professional language teachers, because other equally motivated participants in the study with similar life histories and jobs in Egypt had achieved L2 fluency but were much less native-like in Arabic.

Smith and Tsimpli's (1991) case study also featured a highly talented language learner, a so-called "savant linguist" named Christopher, who had apparently achieved varying degrees of proficiency in 16 languages despite other mental challenges that left him institutionalized. The analysis involved generative grammar parameters such as the "pro-drop" parameter, related to obligatory versus optional subject suppliance in languages. It focused on Christopher's ability to translate to and from English the various languages, and in particular examined his proficiency in modern Greek. The authors concluded that Christopher's L2 learning was not subsumed under his general cognitive processes. Rather, the L2 was some how modularized and governed by "specific neural architecture" encapsulating language (p. 327), allowing him to translate quite masterfully.

Finally, at the opposite extreme on the success continuum are those people who unfortunately experience considerable difficulty and lack of success learning other languages. Examples include:

- Ehrman's (1996) study of a 40-year-old member of the U.S. Foreign Service, a very unanalytic learner who, to his great frustration, progressed very little in his L2 study, despite several tours of duty to regions in which the target language was spoken, and instruction in the U.S. preparing him for that

- Shapira's (1978) study of a Guatemalan immigrant to the United States who progressed very little in English even after three years
- Ioup's (1989) study of unsuccessful adolescent ESL learners who had immigrated to the United States as children and would now be characterized as "Generation 1.5" students. I elaborate on Ioup's study below.

Ioup (1989) focused on a Chinese teenager in New Orleans, Jeanne, considered to be a bright and capable student, especially in courses requiring little writing, but was a very unsuccessful English writer. She was fully proficient in Chinese reading and writing, having attended school in Taiwan Province of China up to age 9, and 10 years later still enjoyed reading both Chinese and English literature. She was also good in music and mathematics. Yet, despite her native-like English pronunciation and her success in high school, Jeanne had to repeat two required nonintensive ESL courses multiple times after she entered university. She produced sentences like *Because of many influences and education are for the making money* (p. 166). Ioup then compared this student to a Vietnamese male student, Minh, who had mastered English as an adult and had only lived in an English-speaking environment for five years. On the basis of a series of linguistic and neuropsychological (cognitive) tests, the major difference that emerged between them was their verbal memory subscores and performance on tests of linguistic knowledge (e.g., semantics) and composition, in which Jeanne obtained much lower scores than Minh. Ioup found the results baffling, especially considering the length of exposure to English Jeanne had enjoyed from childhood in a city without an established Chinese-speaking community outside of the family home. There were no obvious affective or sociolinguistic explanations.

3.5 Diaries, Memoirs, and (Auto)biographies of Linguistic Experiences

Diary studies of language learners themselves or by parents about their children have been conducted for many decades, yielding many important theoretical insights into language learning and use, bilingualism, and language loss or forgetting. Diary studies are usually done on just one individual, unless the goal is to synthesize the findings of many such studies. They can therefore be viewed as a kind of case study. In the late 1970s and early 1980s, a number of applied linguists attempting to learn foreign languages documented their experiences, attesting to the various linguistic processes and social-psychological factors, such as anxiety, operating in adult SLA, and also revealing their variable levels of success (Bailey, 1983; Bailey & Ochsner, 1983).

One of the most comprehensive and analytical case studies in recent years, a variation of diary study, was carried out by Schmidt and Frota (1986). The study describes Schmidt's attempts to learn conversational Portuguese while in Brazil for several months, and the data are analyzed in a triangulated manner from different perspectives, the learner's (Schmidt's) and a Brazilian applied linguist's. Frota interacted with him throughout the study and was instrumental in analyzing the data. Their work is very informative in a review of developments in case study methods for several reasons. One striking feature of the research is the scope of the investigation and the discussion of how it relates to a number of current issues in SLA theory. Unlike many of the case studies examined above, Schmidt and Frota examine Schmidt's linguistic ability in Portuguese in many different areas: conversation, pragmatics, grammar, vocabulary (lexical verbs), and formulaic speech. The analysis is rather ambitious in scope in trying to cover so much, but it is quite comprehensive as a result. The methodological strengths of the study are that it includes both qualitative and quantitative analysis, provides two points of view of the same learning process, as well as actual production data, and includes Schmidt's perceptions of his input/intake and output. Finally, the main theoretical insight that emerged from the study was the "notice the gap" principle accounting for the acquisition of new structures (i.e., learners need to notice or become aware of new target-language forms before they can acquire them). The study also addressed issues connected with the role of instruction, interaction, correction, and formulaic speech in adult L2 learning.

A more recent departure from established case study research methods and reports of the sort reviewed earlier in this chapter are studies of L2 teachers, students, events, and sites using more humanistic narrative inquiry traditions that emphasize personal voice, identity, affect, agency, and lived experience (e.g., Bell, 2002; Granger, 2004; Pavlenko & Lantolf, 2000; Pavlenko, 2002). Hoffman's (1989) autobiography, *Lost in Translation* (unrelated to the movie with the same title), is an often-cited book-length narrative of the author's experiences as a Polish immigrant who came to Canada as a child and then moved to the United States. Hoffman reflects on her English language learning and concomitant loss of crucial aspects of her sense of self (see below).

Other personal narratives of language learners include those by Kaplan

(1993) in *French Lessons*, Mori's (1997) *Polite Lies*, and Lyovich's (1997) *The Multilingual Self*, which Pavlenko and Lantolf (2000) analyze, together with other narratives in this genre, from Vygotskian and Bakhtinian perspectives. Pavlenko and Lantolf's focus is the loss, recovery, and reconstruction of "self" in the lives of bilinguals who "attempt to become native speakers of their second language" (p. 162).

Schumann (1997), a strong proponent of diary-based research in applied linguistics for its social, psychological, and now neuroscientific insights, provides a detailed analysis of these and other autobiographies, biographies, and diary studies in L2 learning in his book on the neurobiology of affect in language learning. For example, he presents numerous excerpts from Kaplan's (1993) narratives of her experiences, desires, and even disappointments studying French in the United States and Europe, and later becoming a professor of French working alongside expatriate French native speaker colleagues. He analyzes Kaplan's "appraisals" of her French learning as extremely positive: identifying completely with the language, the methods of teaching French, the people and culture, and her ongoing socialization into it. He observes:

> What are some of the unique factors that contributed to Alice [Kaplan's] trajectory? She suggests that a French identity allowed her to escape the sadness of her father's death and the awkwardness of her adolescence. Her interest in French Nazis perhaps linked her with her father, a Nuremberg lawyer, but quite remarkably allowed her to find something positive even in the darker side of France. (p. 125)

Hoffman's (1989) language learning was, like Kaplan's, very successful on many levels: she became a doctoral student of English literature at Harvard University, and later an English professor and writer in the United States. Unlike Kaplan though, her appraisals of her experiences were quite negative, at least superficially. In a third case study, Schumann describes Watson (1995), a philosopher whose specialty was Descartes. In anticipation of a conference to be held in France, Watson enrolled in half a year of oral French tutoring. However, unlike both Kaplan and Hoffman, who began their L2 learning as children and became nearly infatuated (if not obsessed) with the target languages, the 55-year-old Watson did not appreciate the sound of French or the methods used to teach it to him and felt humiliated and intimidated by not being able to speak French well. His low appraisal led him to abandon his goal of mastering spoken French, even though he was a highly skilled reader and translator of French.

Schumann provides many other narratives and commentaries on the appraisals of language learners and concludes that "variable success in SLA is the product of the history of one's stimulus appraisals, whose influence on second-language learning is highly variable, and essentially unique for each individual" (p. 188).

Finally, diaries have also been a component in case studies of language teachers as well as learners. Miller (1997) reported that the diarized reflections of an itinerant German L2 teacher in Australia yielded quite different insights, and much more affectively charged ones, than the same teacher's interview comments did in a case study of teachers' beliefs and experiences teaching modern languages at the primary level. The teacher, Joanna, was studied in two classes in different schools, one much more conducive to the teaching and learning of German than the other. In one interview, for example, Joanna remarked relatively calmly: "I end up with one hour 15 minutes contact time because you lose it with the students not being on time" (p. 47). In contrast, a diary entry by the same teacher for the same class was much more critical in tone: "The students are disruptive, unsettled, ratty, distracted, rude and antisocial.... There are some incredibly rude and insolent girls in that class. Nagging and ranting and raving from my side plus at times sheer despair" (p. 48). Miller concluded that teachers' research diaries provide complementary data to interview data alone, and certainly in this study revealed the level of frustration experienced by the itinerant teacher with an extremely uncooperative class.

3.6 Identity, Investment, and Gender in Language Learning

Related to case studies involving diary or other personal accounts that document the many struggles, tensions, and desires of language learners, Norton's (2000) study examines the lives of immigrant women and the conditions under which they are allowed, encouraged, and enabled to speak in English, their L2, or are silenced and suppressed instead. Norton critiques what she refers to as the "SLA canon", and in particular studies and theoretical models that categorize learners as inherently "good" or "bad", as motivated or unmotivated, as users of better or worse cognitive and psycholinguistic strategies, or as acculturated or unacculturated members of society. She explains that "theories of the good language learner have been developed on the premise that language learners can choose under what conditions they will interact with members of the target-language community and that the language learner's access to the target language community is a function of the learner's motivation" (p. 5).

Norton's (2000) compelling multiple-case study of five immigrant women's attempts to learn English in Canada (from Poland, Vietnam, Czechoslovakia, and Peru; see Chapter 4) took place over a 12-month period and used participant observation, a diary study, and interviews with women about their experiences at home, school, and in the workplace. Norton argues for a greater focus on the learners' multiple, shifting subjectivities or social identities; their "investments" in language learning; their often restricted access to target-language speakers and communities; and the "contradictory position" the women in her study faced, needing access to English-speaking social networks to practice English, but also needing adequate proficiency in English to participate in those same networks. In framing her analysis, she offers a critical L2 perspective, foregrounding issues of power, racism, reproduction, hybridity, identity, (cultural) capital, and the complex social histories and desires of learners. In marked contrast to some of the other case studies reviewed in this chapter on language learning (e.g., individual differences), Norton does not present an analysis of her participants' actual linguistic ability or development over time, but rather presents and interprets their experiences and their perceptions of their abilities and opportunities from a critical discursive, social, and feminist perspective. Several subsequent case studies of younger, school-aged immigrant learners have drawn on Norton's conceptualization of identity, investment, and critical social processes as well (e.g., Day, 2002; McKay & Wong, 1996; Miller, 2003; Toohey, 2001).

3.7 Language Learning, Stabilization, and Fossilization

Case studies on fossilization (the cessation of language development in one or more areas) tend to be longitudinal because development or lack thereof must be temporally contextualized. It is difficult to determine, however, just how long in duration a study must be to draw conclusions about fossilization and how to interpret some findings (e.g., Han, 2004).

Lardiere (1998a, 1998b, 2006) conducted a study of an adult Hokkien-/Mandarin Chinese-speaking Indonesian English language learner, Patty, who arrived in the United States at age 22 after having been raised and schooled in Indonesia, Chinese mainland, and Hong Kong SAR. Drawing on current generative grammar principles, Lardiere analyzed Patty's oral language production by means of tape-recorded "conversations" after 10 years of residence in the United States (a 34-minute interview) and again 8.5 years later (two interviews, 34 to 75 minutes each). She also analyzed some short written e-mail messages sent by Patty from 1997 to 2002, after the third interview, and then a final 20-minute oral interview. Despite Patty's high degree of social integration and immersion in English-speaking contexts, formal ESL instruction, marriage to an English speaker for six years, successful completion of university undergraduate and graduate degrees in the United States, and her management position in an American company, her grammar seemed to have fossilized, even in some very basic areas of morphology. For example, in obligatory, nonformulaic contexts for thematic/finite verbs, she consistently undersupplied past tense (about 35% of required cases at both points in time) and third-person singular present -s morphology (less than 5% in the first two interviews): e.g., *M. want to go too; her sister said no; she never come* (Lardiere, 1998a, p. 14). Interestingly, Lardiere argued that Patty had in fact acquired the target grammatical representation for (or knowledge of) these features but was simply unsuccessful at mapping her knowledge morphophonologically. In other words, she had a production problem—her competence far exceeded her performance.

Two additional studies looking at potential fossilization—or at least incomplete development after years of study—were conducted by Han (1998) and Long (2003). Han's (1998) two-year study examined two adult Chinese learners of English and their use of three structures in their written English and their stabilization or apparent fossilization. Long's (2003) case study, with structured oral interview data collected on two occasions, 10 years apart (1985–1995), and then three more times between 1996 and 2000, featured a highly acculturated first-generation Japanese American immigrant woman, Ayako, who exhibited "numerous lexical gaps, little complex syntax, and many persistent morphological errors" (p. 509), and a great deal of variability and "volatility" in her English language production (in terms of accuracy). Yet, she had resided for more than half a century in the country and was acculturated and motivated to learn English.

As a set, these studies raise interesting issues about the relationship between observed stabilization (or, rather, instability and variability) in speakers' production of non-target-like forms and criteria for making well-founded judgments regarding their fossilization. They also beg the question as to why some people's development or production stabilizes (or stops) in particular linguistic areas at certain points while others' does not (Han, 2004), an issue that the individual differences research has also tried to address.

3.8 Language Loss

Although many case studies have been conducted of L2 development, fewer have looked at either L1 or L2 attrition/loss. Kouritzen's (1999) retrospective life history study includes innovative narrative reconstructions of five individuals' experiences in Canada. The five were language-loss case study participants she recruited by an advertisement in a city-wide newspaper. One participant was a third-generation Chinese Canadian (an ESL teacher), who had been assimilated ("Canadianized", in her words) to the point of losing the Cantonese that she had grown up with and had spoken until age 4. The woman, Ariana, resented new Chinese Canadians for their foreignness but regretted having lost her own language and culture, and felt bitter about the era in which she was raised, for that reason.

Another case dealt with L1 loss and relearning much later. Richard was an Aboriginal (Cree) man who had endured the humiliation of residential schools in Canada, where Cree speakers had been outnumbered by speakers of other First Nations (Native) languages. In the process of being schooled outside of his home culture, he lost his Cree at about age 8 or 9, only to recover it many years later when he returned to the Cree community at about age 30. He then spent five years trying to relearn it, which he likened to waking up from a deep sleep. He recalled: "I became a Cree speaker again because everybody around me was a Cree person; everybody spoke Cree.… English is nothing anymore. English is something that you use at work to communicate in the form of the written page again" (p. 70). Reflecting on his earlier experience of English-medium schooling and socialization ("the politics of destruction", p. 65), he mused:

> It was not easy to admit that you had become an uncultured, uncivilized person. It was not easy to admit that you had lost the most precious thing you ever had, which is your Cree tongue, your Cree soul, your Cree language, your culture.… So you deal with it by speaking English, and that way you don't have to face the hurt of the loss … you hide behind the language of the dominant society for a while. (p. 66)

Kouritzen's other cases were Finnish, Korean, and Hungarian Canadians, who had different histories but had all experienced L1 loss. In addition to her in-depth analyses of these five cases, Kouritzen presented short descriptions of 16 others, representing various heritage languages and cultures, who participated in her study but were not focal or key participants. Her final chapter then explores themes that emerged from across all 21 in relation to language loss: (1) family relationships, (2) self-image and cultural identity, (3) school relationships, (4) school performance, and (5) the meaning of "loss".

3.9 Pragmatic and Sociolinguistic Development

Most early case studies of L2 development focused on phonological and grammatical development, particularly of word order, morphology, question formation, and negation in English or German (e.g., Ellis, 1994). Studies of L2 pragmatics during the same period employed quantitative methods for the most part, often using Discourse Completion Tasks or other survey questionnaires of people's intuitions about their production of L1 and L2 speech acts, such as apologies, requests, and complaints. (Ellis's (1992) study of two boys' classroom requesting behaviors was more contextualized.) However, a number of recent qualitative case studies have focused on pragmatic, sociolinguistic, and sociocultural processes in language learning (e.g., Belz & Kinginger, 2002, featuring two American students' acquisition of appropriate address forms in either L2 German or French; and Li, 2000; Siegal, 1996).

Siegal's (1994, 1996) research stands out for several reasons: it examines sociolinguistic and pragmatic aspects of the L2 development and use of Japanese rather than English or another European language; it provides broader ethnographic contextualization regarding the teaching and learning of Japanese in Japan; and it involves a multiple-case study of "the sociolinguistic competency of white women in Japan studying Japanese" (Siegal, 1996, p. 359). Instead of providing only a (socio)linguistic analysis of language use either at one particular time or longitudinally, Siegal (1994) discusses Japanese societal norms related to gendered and hierarchically differentiated language use. The social status of foreign women in Japan and its implications for their Japanese language development are also discussed. Fieldwork for the study included data collection over an 18-month period with four focal participants, all "white Western upper-middle-class women between the ages of 21 and 45 of intermediate to advanced Japanese language proficiency studying Japanese" (Siegal, 1996, p. 359). Data collection included language learning journals, learner interviews (42 hours), field observations, audiotapes of the participants' interactions in Japanese (116 hours), formal interviews with each one at the beginning and end of the study, interviews with native Japanese speakers about the participants' interactions, and an examination of articles about non-Japanese residents in Japan. Thus, the study draws on naturally occurring interactions and triangulates the perspectives of the research participants, researcher, interlocutors, and other sources.

One of the English learners of Japanese in her mid-40s, Mary, was a Japanese language teacher from New Zealand conducting research in Japan as a temporary resident and also studying Japanese. Framed by a discussion of identity and subjectivity in language learning, particularly as informed by poststructural feminist theory and interactional sociolinguistics, Siegal's (1996) data included one conversation between Mary and her professor, drawing on broader information about Mary's and other women's experiences learning and using Japanese throughout the analysis (e.g., referring to foreign women as "racialized 'others'" within Japanese society). Although Mary apparently wanted to appear polite, inoffensive, and sociolinguistically competent when using Japanese as a female speaker, she had adopted some pragmatically inappropriate politeness strategies (e.g., overuse of the modal verb *deshoo* ("I wonder"), lack of honorifics, and irregular use of the utterance-final tag/ particle *ne*). Siegal suggests that some Japanese language programs, with their low expectations of Japanese L2 acquisition and acculturation, contribute to such sociolinguistic aberrations by not teaching the full range of honorific/ polite language. However, not all the women in her study actually aspired to emulating the highly feminized, hierarchical, honorific language usage that was called for, partly because it violated their Western sensibilities as empow- ered women (Siegal, 1994). They therefore resisted such practices in their own speech.

A second case study of L2 pragmatics, conducted by Li (1998, 2000), examined the linguistic socialization of Chinese immigrant women learning English and clerical skills in the Chinatown of a large city in the United States. Li (1998) presented detailed case studies of four Chinese American women and their experiences before and after coming to the training program, against the backdrop of a set of 16 others who participated more peripherally in the study. The focus of Li's (2000) case study of one Chinese immigrant, Ming, was her English L2 requesting behaviors in naturally occurring situations, with particular reference to differences between indirectness and directness in Chinese and English. Li studied Ming longitudinally as she completed her English and clerical training, sought employment, and learned to negotiate with her new colleagues using English increasingly in pragmatically effective ways. However, since some of Ming's native English-speaking interlocutors themselves engaged in inappropriate (rude) sociolinguistic practices with Ming, Li cautions that so-called L2 models and experts are not always effective linguistic/pragmatic socializers for newcomers.

3.10 Families as Cases: Studies of Bilingual Language Socialization and Maintenance

Families have been prominent in sociological and anthropological case studies since the 19th century (Hamel *et al.*, 1993). They also constitute useful and valid cases in applied linguistics research, especially in research on family literacies, family dinnertime interactions and other socializing activities in the home, and cross-generational language shift (Duff & Hornberger, in press). Much research drawing on linguistic anthropology has examined family socialization patterns involving young children across a range of cultures (e.g., Schieffelin & Ochs, 1986). Another strand of research examines families as crucial social networks and sites for socialization into both monolingual and bilingual/multilingual language and literacy practices, such as those observed around the family dinner table (e.g., Blum-Kulka, 1997).

One example is de la Piedra and Romo's (2003) case study of a Mexican immigrant family, with two working parents and five female children, who had lived in Texas for over a decade. The analysis, part of a larger project, focused on the role of older siblings in the family as "literacy mediators" or bilingual socializing agents assisting family members (the toddlers or mother) to participate in various interactional and literacy activities. Data collection included participant observation, interviews with the mother, an interview with the oldest daughter, and naturally occurring interactions recorded in the family home setting.

The longitudinal ethnographic study conducted by Schecter and Bayley (1997, 2002) represents another, more extensive, multiple-case study of bilingual family socialization involving Spanish-speaking Mexican-descent families in Texas and California. Forty families participated in the larger study, from which four families were singled out for intensive analysis, two in each state. The family and societal ideologies connected with Spanish maintenance, revival, and use within the home and community were examined and illustrated using narrative content analysis, linguistic analysis, and cross-case analysis. In each family, or case, there was a focal elementary school-aged child in grade 4, 5, or 6. The study examined communication in the home, language choice, and discursive elements of talk and literacy (e.g., code-switching).

Data for each of the four families included 25 hours of recorded observations during home visits at different times during the day and week, two interviews with caregivers, two interviews with each focal child, samples of the child's writing in English and Spanish, and narrative data elicited by picture books (to establish children's levels of proficiency in the two languages).

Underlying the analysis was a keen interest in issues of linguistic and cultural identity, and the "acts of identity" performed by families linking language and culture, language maintenance and shift. The results revealed that, far from being a monolithic population despite their common origins and languages and the misguided tendency by the public to essentialize such populations and cultures, the Texas and California families represented quite different sociocultural ecologies in terms of their orientation toward the use of Spanish to affirm their cultural identities as people of Mexican heritage. The intergenerational transmission of Spanish and the role of the school in helping them maintain it also differed across the family groups. Whereas the two Texas families used much more English within the home, the California families favored Spanish in parent-child interactions instead. Thus, only two of the families used "aggressive home [L1] maintenance strategies" (p. 513), though all four were committed to preserving their heritage culture. The discussion provides explanations for the differences and implications for policy, schooling, and research.

3.11 Mainstreamed ESL Students: Identity, Representation, and Positioning

Many of the case studies in this category, as in the previous one, are ethnographic. They examine the educational cultures and conditions for immigrants learning through the medium of English at a given school by focusing on four to six students (cases). For example, Harklau (1994a) examined differences in learning environments for immigrant secondary school students in ESL versus mainstream courses at a California high school. Her longitudinal ethnographic study tracked four newcomers from ethnic Chinese backgrounds in their transition from ESL classes to mainstream courses over as many as seven semesters. She contrasted the kinds of linguistic interaction taking place in one or the other curricular context (ESL or mainstream content areas) and also differences between lowtrack and hightrack mainstream classroom discourse (Harklau, 1994b), in terms of language use, literacy practices, and intellectual rigor. Later, she examined the students' school-to-college transitions and the contradictory ways in which the students were represented in college (negatively) compared with high school (positively) (Harklau, 1999, 2000).

Several other studies deal with the same themes of mainstreaming, participation, linguistic socialization, and students' in-class experiences. First, Willett's (1995) one-year study in a mainstreamed grade 1 class in the northeast United States focused on three ESL girls, friends seated together who collaborated very effectively, and a boy, the only male ESL student, who was unhappily seated with a different set of girls. Willett examined the ESL learners' gendered interaction patterns (with the children strongly favoring the segregation of boys and girls) and ideologies connected with phonics seat work that particularly disadvantaged the little boy. With little chance to gain approval or assistance from other boys in the class (even some fluent in his L1, Spanish), the boy resisted the way he was positioned by the teachers as a "needy ESL child", but he was nonetheless unable to access help from his seat neighbors (girls) to display his competence. Willett called for more research looking at classroom routines and activities, seating arrangements, and ideologies (such as gendered participation) that help some children, like the three focal girls in the study, but inadvertently hurt others.

Second, Hunter's (1997) two-year study of a Portuguese English bilingual child's writing activities, language development, and representation in grade 4 and 5 classrooms in Canada was similar to Willett's in some respects. In both studies, the focal boys wanted desperately to be validated by their male peers but had difficulty accessing their male peer social networks or winning their approval, because of their ESL language skills, the negative assessment of those skills by teachers, and their own dispositions. In Hunter's study, the boy was considered too quiet by the other boys and too "good", writing about tame family-oriented stories while they wrote pop culture-inspired fantasy action narratives (though the following year he joined them).

Third, McKay and Wong's (1996) two-year study of four Mandarin speakers in grades 7 and 8 in California investigated the multiple discourses (identities, expectations) they negotiated at school, such as a colonial/racial discourse, model minority discourse, Chinese cultural nationalist discourse, school discourse, and gender ideologies or discourses.

Last in this section, Toohey (2000) conducted a three-year sociocultural (ethnographic) study of six English language learners from kindergarten to grade 2 and their home/school identities, social relations, and classroom practices that reinforced particular ideologies, such as individual ownership of physical resources, ideas, and language (as in Willett, 1995). She conducted interviews with parents and teachers, did home visits, and collected data through regular classroom observations. Her unit of analysis was private *disputes* that occurred among the children and the implications or consequences of children's variable participation in these peer disputes for their subsequent language learning and self-esteem. Toohey contrasted the linguistic backgrounds and current experiences of two Canadian-born children from her larger sample of focal students: Julie, a Polish girl who, despite having had limited proficiency in English upon entering kindergarten, had made rapid and effective progress in English and was considered an "average student" by her teacher; and Surjeet, a Punjabi girl who, despite living in a bilingual Punjabi- and English-speaking home and having become English dominant by age 5, "by the end of Grade 2 had acquired a school identity as an ESL learner with learning disabilities" (p. 264).

Thus, the studies in this section all addressed the construction of multiple identities by—and for—students from different ethnic and linguistic backgrounds, identities that the most vulnerable students struggled with (or against).

3.12 Second-Language Writing and Academic Discourse Socialization

One of the subdisciplines of applied linguistics in which perhaps the most case studies are currently being conducted is L2 writing and academic discourse socialization. However, important case studies of L1 and L2 composition have been done for several decades, involving think-aloud verbal reports of planning, writing, or revising processes; comparisons of more skilled and less skilled writers and their strategies; or the examination of international or immigrant university students' L2 longitudinal writing development, while negotiating thesis or dissertation writing, for example. In this section, I highlight several noteworthy studies. A more complete overview of case studies in literacy/writing is found in Casanave (2002). Again, as in the previous section, many of them are ethnographic, with attention paid to the sociocultural ecologies in which the writing occurs.

Leki (1995) examined the challenges faced by three graduate and two undergraduate international students from Europe and Asia in their first semester at a U.S. university. Of interest were the English writing requirements in students' content courses across the curriculum and their coping strategies as newcomers to the local academic culture. She looked at the students' approaches to completing their writing assignments based on interview narratives of their academic discourse socialization. Data included weekly interviews with students, document analysis (e.g., students' writing), students' journals about their academic experiences, and interviews with some of the students' professors. Leki presented a profile of each of the five students in terms of their backgrounds and the challenging writing requirements in certain courses.

For example, one student, Ling, had to write an essay for a course in behavioral geography that presupposed considerable tacit knowledge of American popular culture[1]. Leki described how Ling overcame her difficulties by appealing to classmates or professors for help, incorporating more information about Taiwan Province of China or Chinese mainland in her essays (even when this was not what the instructor wanted), or comparing Chinese and American cultures. In some situations, Ling displayed resistance toward a professor's demands or requirements. Another student, Yang, described his dilemmas writing critical reviews of articles on international relations: he felt that he did not yet have the expertise to make authoritative, critical comments about published articles. Leki then discussed themes from her inductive analysis of the data, including 10 different strategies that students employed, but that the professors were sometimes oblivious to, such as resistance strategies. She also suggests how university-level ESL instructors should prepare students for the intellectually and rhetorically complex tasks in mainstream courses.

Other significant case studies of academic writing in the university mainstream were conducted by Spack (1997) and Casanave (2002) and their colleagues. Spack's (1997) 60-page journal article dealt with a Japanese student's literacy development before and during her time in an American liberal arts college program. As in other qualitative studies, data came from multiple sources: taped interviews with the student (Yuko) and with two of her content-area professors, Yuko's writing conferences with Spack (her ESL teacher at the outset), classroom observations, texts from 10 of Yuko's courses,

---

1 The culturally loaded task was as follows: to place a hypothetical group of people into fictional neighborhoods by determining in broad terms their socioeconomic class through an examination of certain personal characteristics, whether, for example, they drink Budweiser or Heineken, read *GQ* magazine or *Track and Field*, drive a Dodge or a Saab (Leki, 1995, p. 241).

and other relevant written documents (e.g., marked assignments, quizzes). The study had initially been planned for one year, but it continued for another two years, by which time Yuko had finally achieved academic success. The study focuses on the many tensions, frustrations, and breakthroughs in Yuko's experiences of reading, writing, and speaking in American courses.

Casanave's (2002) collection focuses on multicultural case studies of academic and professional writing socialization at the undergraduate, graduate, and postgraduate or professional academic levels. Her own bias against the "academic writing games" that many students and scholars must engage in is clear from the title. Ambivalent about the term *case study* because of its clinical and impersonal connotations, she favors *narrative* and *portraiture* instead. Dozens of key case studies in the field of L2 writing are reviewed, both those conducted by her (e.g., Casanave, 1992, 1998; Casanave & Schecter, 1997) and those by others (e.g., Ivani , 1998; Prior, 1998). The studies deal with such topics as plagiarism, agency, authority, authorship, authenticity in writing, doctoral student mentoring, article-revising strategies, silence, power and (textual) identities, voice, disciplinary enculturation, experiences of multilingual writers, and resistance. The changing cultures and practices within and across disciplines such as sociology are also examined.

The last set of case studies in this section appear in an edited volume by Belcher and Connor (2001) with narratives by 18 scholars, many of whom are known for their research on L2 literacy/writing (e.g., Miyuki Sasaki, Suresh Canagarajah). They each have chapters in which they reflect on their own formative bilingual or L2 literacy experiences and their current "multiliterate lives", as professors in North America, Asia, Israel, or Scandinavia, for example. They describe their experiences of publishing and moving back and forth across languages and literacies, and negotiating different textual expectations along the way. Although the cases are quite interesting first-person accounts of navigating through different literacy practices and expectations, the volume unfortunately lacks an overarching analysis of the different studies, in search of commonalities, differences, and major themes.

3.13 Online Language Development and Use: Socialization into Virtual Communities

With the increasing use of computers and the Internet for teaching and learning and for all kinds of communication, case studies of new digital discourse contexts and communities are also emerging. Here I summarize three such studies, two by Lam and one by Yim. Lam's (2000, 2004) case studies of online language use examine both the construction and transformation of "textual identities" of ethnically Chinese high school students in a west coast American city. Lam (2000) focuses on one teenaged boy's synchronous (chat) and asynchronous (e-mail) correspondence with Japanese, Chinese, and other transnational peers over a six-month period from around the time he entered junior college. She also studied a personal Web site the young man, Almon, had constructed based on Japanese pop culture. From her inductive analysis of his texts, observations of his computing activities, and interviews with him, Lam identified "the discursive strategies that he uses to articulate and position himself in written texts (and other semiotic media) as he negotiates diverse discourses on the Internet" (p. 461). She also contrasted the difficulties Almon previously had negotiating oral or written English at high school the year before and the apparent freedom he now had producing English online:

> Whereas classroom English appeared to contribute to Almon's sense of exclusion or marginalization (his inability to speak like a native), which paradoxically contradicts the school's mandate to prepare students for the workplace and civic involvement, the English he controlled on the Internet enabled him to develop a sense of belonging and connectedness to a global English-speaking community. Almon was learning not only more English but also more relevant and appropriate English for the World Wide Web community he sought to become part of. (p. 473)

In her second, related study, Lam (2004) examined a bilingual Cantonese English chat room and observed new forms of language socialization among immigrant youth in modern virtual communities. The case study participants were two teenaged Cantonese-speaking cousins living in the United States who, like Almon, felt marginalized from their English peer groups at school but highly affiliated with virtually dispersed communities. The two girls, who struggled with ESL, sought refuge in a Hong Kong SAR (China) chat room where a mixture of English and Cantonese (both romanized and character based) and other symbols (e.g., emoticons) were used, allowing them to express their hybrid identities spontaneously and creatively. Their Cantonese-laced English marked them as bilingual Chinese emigrants in a global network of others like themselves. An unexpected consequence of their online textual practices was that the girls reported being able to speak English more freely and with greater confidence even at school after some time.

Finally, Yim (2005) examined international and domestic graduate students' experiences in mixed-mode courses at a Canadian university that had both face-to-face and online, out-of-class required components. The latter involved threaded discussions related to seminar topics on electronic bulletin boards. Although she provided some details about her 12 participants (6 native speakers and 6 nonnative), the more meaningful cases in her study were the two contrasting graduate courses and instructors, and the different cultures of academic discourse into which the students were socialized in their respective courses. Like Lam, Yim noticed how learners' identities and writing evolved on the basis of their ongoing experience participating in the electronic communities, and from their observations of how others constructed messages, responded to earlier postings, and presented their perspectives on academic matters. In one course, where the instructor promoted a more casual, interpersonal register in postings and responses to messages, the students attended very consciously to one another's pragmatics, register, manner of citing earlier postings, language use, and argumentation, and made choices about their own discourse practices accordingly. In another course, where the instructor required postings to be in a very formal academic register, there was relatively little uptake of one another's postings and both native and nonnative speakers of English in the course felt intimidated and disinclined to participate more than absolutely necessary. One conclusion of this study was that with new technologies, such as Web-CT (Course Tools), the writer's L1 or L2 status can be a less robust indicator of course participation levels and satisfaction than the openness of instructors to different styles of writing online and to the building of trust and relationships within instructional communities.

3.14 Bilingualism and Biculturalism: Immigrant, Sojourner, and "Returnee" Identities

At the beginning of this chapter, a number of mid- to late-20th-century studies of bilingualism conducted by researchers of their own children were described. More recently, Kanno (2003) studied four Japanese "returnee" children who had learned English as a second language while in Canada and she then followed up on them two years later, after they had returned to Japan. She described their experiences over the three-year period (one chapter per case) in terms of their "identity narratives". Other returnee-type narratives of bilinguals include professional applied linguists' reflections of their own academic language use in English versus their L1 after returning to their home countries, such as China (Shi, 2003). Questions addressed include whether, and how, their L2 literacy socialization influences their L1 writing in that context.

Marx (2002) provides an interesting retrospective account of her own experiences of negotiating membership in multiple linguistic, national, and cultural communities and being a "continual border-crosser" (p. 278). Like Kanno's students, Marx moved back and forth between cultures for several years, never intending to settle permanently abroad. A Canadian native speaker of English, French was Marx's L2 and German her L3. She describes the linguistic and cultural phases of her entry into German culture as an exchange student in Germany and her return to Canada (and the United States) three years later. One area in which she indexed her identity, apparently quite self-consciously, was in her adoption of different accents in not only her L3 but also her L1. Upon moving to Germany, she reported initial feelings of displacement and loss of aspects of her own cultural and linguistic identity, and attempted to actively differentiate herself from being perceived as "American" by affecting a French accent in German and dressing in particular ways. Later, she tried to appropriate a more German accent (and dress code) in order to pass as a German. However, over time she began to encounter difficulties expressing herself in her L1 (though she was teaching English). She found herself incorporating elements of British English and German pronunciation in her English, in part to distinguish herself from her prior self. Finally, after returning to North America, she studied in the United States and eventually reconciled herself to her Canadian identity but, interestingly, returned to work in Germany after just five months. Reflecting on her own experiences and those of other migrants, she wonders:

> How often can an individual be displaced, in how many different cultures, and is a full unification of identities within the self possible under such conditions? Perhaps such a shift is not possible, and we become multicompetent but "imperfect" speakers of both the L1 and L2 [or L3], displaying foreign accents in both languages which reflect the omnipresent foreign aspects of our selves and our identities. (p. 278)

Marx's account differs from some of the diary studies described earlier because there is no direct documentary evidence or data (e.g., diary excerpts or language samples) of her language production or feelings of acculturation while it was taking place; rather, she attempts to theorize the experiences reported in this memoir.

3.15 Teachers as Agents of Linguistic and Cultural Socialization

Many case studies have been conducted on language (or content) teachers' questioning or feedback patterns or their beliefs and decision making related to grammar instruction, use of students' L1 in class, and ways of representing L2 cultures (e.g., Borg, 1998; Duff, 1995, 2002b; Duff & Li, 2004; Duff & Uchida, 1997). Borg (1998), for example, did an exploratory interpretive case study of an experienced L2 teacher in Malta in an English as a foreign language (EFL) class for European adults. His research goal was to ascertain "how teachers approach grammar in their work and an understanding, from their perspective, of the factors behind their instructional decisions" (p. 11). He did so by recording observations of the teacher (15 hours) over a two-week period, transcribing and coding the data for critical incidents or grammar-related episodes, and also analyzing transcripts from three interviews with the teacher and deriving salient themes about "behavioural and psychological dimensions of grammar teaching" (pp. 31–32). The teacher in Borg's study was not only an agent of linguistic socialization for his own students, but had himself been socialized into particular beliefs, pedagogical orientations, and practices by means of prior experience, in-service training, and institutional and other contextual factors. Duff and Li (2004) identified similar factors at play in the decision making of a university-level teacher of L2 Mandarin Chinese (Jin), although the duration of their study and Jin's prior training were much more extended. Another more recent case study of this type (Rankin & Becker, 2006) examined one relatively inexperienced teacher (one of the co-authors, Florian, a doctoral student and German teaching assistant) as he tried to interpret current SLA research findings on different types of corrective feedback and then apply them in his own German L2 teaching at an American university.

Studies have also investigated the explicit and implicit treatment of culture. Duff and Uchida (1997) undertook a six-month-long multiple-case study of four English teachers in Japan, two Japanese nationals and two Americans, each of whom, regardless of nationality, was oriented differently to the teaching of culture. For example, one of the American teachers resisted her students' desire that she teach about American (e.g., Hollywood) culture and create a playful class atmosphere, whereas the other American teacher relished his role as a David Letterman-like talk show host entertaining his (female) classes and bringing in pop culture texts from American television shows or movies on a regular basis. The Japanese teachers, in contrast, felt that the teaching of culture was best left to the native English-speaking teachers and that they should focus on language teaching, not culture teaching. The study examined the contextual and historical basis for these stances and ideologies, and the manner in which the teachers' sociocultural identities and practices were coconstructed, negotiated, and transformed in class. Data included teacher questionnaires, videotaped class observations, weekly retrospective journals by teachers, fieldnotes, research journals, and other documents (e.g., instructional materials).

3.16 Summary

While certainly not exhaustive, the sampling of case studies in this chapter provides a kaleidoscope of research in language learning and education over the past century—and especially the past three decades—in different domains. The trends in case study methods and topics in different periods reflect the evolution of the field of applied linguistics itself. The chapter also outlined some current directions in research on learners, teachers, and users of language in times of globalization, with its attendant new literacies and technologies, new understandings of culture and identity, and increasing transnationalism and mobility. Research agendas and publications once dominated by highly focused analyses of formal or functional linguistic structures now often include poststructural analyses of *identity*, *discourse*, *text*, and *culture*. The concepts of discourse *community* and *participation* (or interaction), long established in applied linguistics, have been reconceptualized somewhat to better understand 21st-century online and diasporic or transnational groups and their sociolinguistic networks and practices.

Learners in applied linguistics case studies increasingly are portrayed as multidimensional individuals with histories, hopes, and desires, who may learn, lose, and relearn languages while other aspects of their identities and knowledge also evolve. Skill-based case studies, to which I referred mainly for some of the prominent work on writing, continue to examine topics such as *strategies*, but they are contextualized better within the social institutions in which they are inculcated, practiced, resisted, or transformed. The chapter admittedly has inevitable gaps in its depth and breadth of coverage, such as case studies on trilingualism or multilingualism or multiliteracies in the European context or elsewhere (e.g., Dagenais & Day, 1999). However, in many such case studies the methods, theoretical arguments, and trends parallel those reviewed here.

CHAPTER 4

How to Conduct Case Studies (Part 1)

Research Design, Data Collection, and Ethics

4.1 Introduction

This chapter examines key methodological components of case studies and procedures for conducting them. We consider ways of framing questions, designing studies, and selecting cases. These principles are illustrated with published studies in applied linguistics, some of which were introduced in previous chapters. The last major section of the chapter is devoted to important ethical considerations in case study and other research. Chapter 5 then explores in greater detail issues of data analysis, interpretation, and criteria for evaluating case study research, and Chapter 6 discusses how to report the research findings.

Figure 4.1 provides a visual display of the overall process of how to conduct case studies and other forms of qualitative research. Note that arrows move between and across components, in both directions, so that theory informs research practice and research, in turn, informs theory; data collection and analysis inform interpretation, and interpretations, in turn, may warrant further data collection; and the writing up of research (another form of analysis and interpretation, as well as representation) and presentation of results to others may also feed back into subsequent refinement of data analysis, interpretations, conclusions, and future research. Invisible chains of reasoning

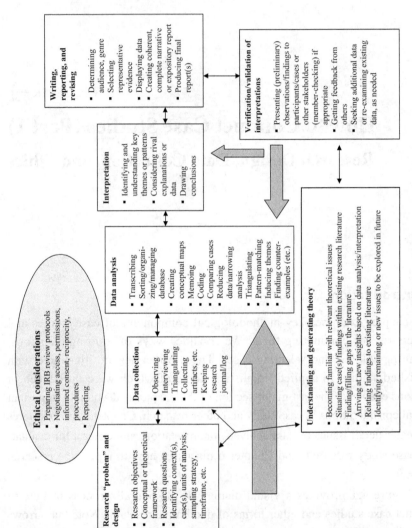

Figure 4.1 How to conduct a case study: crucial components, steps, and interactions.

or narrative should tie what appear to be separate components of the research enterprise into a cohesive and coherent whole.

In this chapter, we consider components on the left side of this figure, and the following chapters examine the center and right side. However, the various components are crucially and dynamically interrelated.

4.2 Research Objectives

The reasons for undertaking case studies and the research problems or issues to be addressed affect other decisions that are made in designing the studies, collecting, analyzing, and interpreting data, and writing up the results. Therefore, it is important to know in advance what one's overarching goals are, what issues are to be addressed, what other recent research has been conducted on similar issues, and how the issues in the cases to be analyzed are likely to relate to other existing theoretical models or debates, even if the goal is to generate new insights. Describing a case for its own sake (*intrinsic case study*, according to Stake, 2005), because it is inherently interesting, is not normally an adequate reason to conduct research in higher education.

Case studies may be primarily *exploratory* (to formulate new research questions), *descriptive* (answering "What?" questions), *relational* (examining how variables are related to one another), *explanatory* (answering "How?" or "Why?" questions), *evaluative* (e.g., Which learner, program, or interlocutor is more effective?), *confirmatory* (Does this study confirm existing findings or understandings?), or some combination of these (Gall *et al.*, 2003; Miles & Huberman, 1994; Yin, 2003a). Case studies that are primarily relational/ explanatory go beyond pure description to find causal or relational patterns among observations or yield explanations about phenomena. Whether it is descriptive, explanatory, or evaluative, important new constructs, hypotheses, theoretical understandings, themes, models, or principles may emerge from the case study. Examples of theoretically interesting outcomes of case studies that have led to subsequent theory building are the "notice the gap principle" in language learning (Schmidt & Frota, 1986), the acculturation model in SLA (Schmidt, 1983; Schumann, 1978), and investment and identity in language learning (Norton, 2000), described in Chapter 3.

Some research has explicit political objectives related to achieving social justice, such as changing the status quo in favor of greater equity or access to employment, services, or education for disadvantaged groups. Lather (1991) talks about the potential of a study to catalyze change (its "catalytic validity") as an important objective of certain types of research. Casanave (2003) suggests that more "sociopolitically-oriented case study research" needs to be done in the area of L2 writing, in terms of the factors and contexts that affect writers and the assessment of their writing. This increasingly critical, activist, or emancipatory stance taken by many researchers has been highlighted in recent applied linguistics theory and research (e.g., Pennycook, 2001).

Besides delimiting the objectives of research and the type of case to be analyzed, researchers must also decide on the exact phenomenon to be examined and the unit of analysis. Is the phenomenon of interest an individual's or group's actions, their linguistic intuitions or development, their code-switching, or their identity construction? Or, is it patterns of silence in classroom interaction, a teacher's questioning behaviors, group project work, scaffolded actions, curriculum reform efforts, or literacy activities? When the case is not a person but an institution, the type of recurring event examined might be parent-teacher meetings, job interviews, or training workshops. In other kinds of applied linguistics research, the case might be a country's language policies or reforms as enacted in law or embodied in official curriculum documents (e.g., the unit of analysis).

A larger-scale study's original broad research objectives and those pursued in published articles about the study may vary, however. Individual articles based on a larger study may each present a different issue or theme explored in the larger study.

One criticism of case study research discussed in Chapter 2 (Section 2.11.2.5) is that it can appear to be—and may in fact be—anecdotal, unguided, or atheoretical. Sometimes the problem is that the description and analysis are simply too superficial. Or the research is not situated within a broader scholarly context, drawing on "substantive theory" (Hatch, 2002) or a "conceptual framework" (Miles & Huberman, 1994) to make it relevant, interesting, and informative to others. In order to make an original contribution, it is important to know one's field, to be aware of other related research—quantitative, qualitative, or mixed method, and any other case studies that might be comparable—so that existing work is not unwittingly duplicated, unless replication or corroboration is the intention. In this respect, conducting a case study is no different from other types of research (see Mackey & Gass, 2005). The goal is to bring empirical data and insights to bear on timely topics. Reading and finding gaps in existing literature is therefore the first necessary step in conceptualizing one's own research, even when the researcher already has a case in mind (Marshall & Rossman, 1995).

Valdés (1998) states the purpose of her case study of two English language learners as follows:

> The purpose of my article is to try to bring to you not only a notion of what some of the distances between homes and schools, countries and cultures involve but what it means for youngsters to arrive at school without knowing English. I will describe two middle school students—Lilian and Elisa—who arrived in this country in the summer of 1991 and enrolled in a school in the greater Bay area. I will talk about who they were and what they expected when they came to school, and I will describe the school climate that they encountered. I will describe their English class and their subject matter classes and tell you about their successes, their frustrations, and their failures. I will also talk about the community in which these girls lived, about their homes, and most especially about their mothers. Finally, I will use their lives and their experiences as a lens through which I will examine both the policy and the instructional dilemmas that now surround the education of immigrant children in this country. (p. 4)

In this introduction (which bears some stylistic or register traces from the original oral presentation), Valdés provides helpful contextual information that she later elaborates on: the geographical location, the number of cases (two), the girls' level at school and their level of English upon arrival, their arrival date, and the larger community they live in. Based on the stated objectives, the reader can anticipate learning about positive and negative aspects of their experiences and how their experiences can be interpreted in light of language and educational policies and instructional practices.

In my original case study of Jim (Duff, 1993a), my purpose was stated as follows:

> This paper attempts to account for Possessive/Existential (P/E) overlap in second language acquisition (SLA). First, I will present an overview of language typological literature demonstrating that coalescence of form and function in this way is both natural and common. Then, using SLA data from several sources, and longitudinal data collected from the speaker ..., I explore in greater detail the notion that language learners are likely to adopt one form in their early syntactic development to accomplish both P and E —even when the interlanguage (IL) construction is ungrammatical

(or at least marked) in the target language. I will then argue that attributing IL production in this domain to language transfer alone is inadequate; otherwise, it would be equally predictable, for example, for learners with a first language (L1) like English to encode P and E with distinct morphology in an undifferentiating language such as Chinese as a second language (L2), which apparently does not happen. Rather, the preference for P/E overlap promotes L1 transfer in a predictable direction, resulting in convergence, especially in untutored and low-level instructed SLA. (p. 2)

The purpose of my study—to examine particular kinds of syntactic development in SLA—is stated, and the general claims to be made based on the study, and even speculative predictions, are foreshadowed, together with the reasoning behind them. Of course, because article introductions are normally written after a study has been conducted, there is usually more clarity about the research outcomes than when the researcher first embarks on the study.

4.3 Research Questions

When designing a study, researchers must identify the research "problem" and consider the research questions to be addressed. Besides being clear, specific, and answerable, the research questions should be meaningfully interconnected and "substantively relevant"—that is, "interesting and worthwhile questions for the investment of research effort", according to Punch (1998, p. 254).

Valdés's (1998) research question in the study presented above was: "Why is it that so many non-English-background students fail to learn English well enough to succeed in school?" (p. 4). The framing of her question suggests that the study will be interpretive and possibly critical (of educational or public policy), answering the question "Why?".

Spack (1997) began her case study of the literacy development of her subject Yuko, a Japanese learner of English at a U.S. university, with the four exploratory (descriptive) framing questions (p. 5) shown on the left side of Figure 4.2, in which I capture Spack's research question development. Within three weeks, however, she produced two more focused questions, as shown on the right side of the figure (p. 6).

In effect, the first set of questions sought fairly basic background information, based on Yuko's history of Japanese and English education in Japan, and also related to what Spack hoped to learn upon first meeting her case study participant. The second set of questions were broader and more conceptual, although the questions still needed a bit more sharpening. They did not specify that the focus was reading and writing activities, and success with them specifically, nor were the terms *success* or *manage* defined. Typically, operational definitions or an explanation of key terms would be included in the methodology section of the study if not in the immediate vicinity of the stated questions. One reason for the evolution of questions in this case is that the study began without a clear purpose; it was more curiosity driven, opportunistic, and exploratory. However, the research problem is evident: that there are barriers to international students' academic success related not only to their own personal backgrounds and prior education, but also to the way courses are taught.

Ioup *et al.*'s (1994) research questions regarding "talented" L2 learners in Egypt were more straightforward and carefully conceived. It appears that the questions were formulated after the researchers came to know about the participants' exceptional Arabic proficiency, since there was no mention of formal recruitment for this study. The research questions outlined, respectively, the intended comparisons of (1) Arabic–L2 learners' competence compared with native Egyptian Arabic speakers, and (2) the grammatical proficiency of tutored (or instructed) versus untutored L2 learners of Arabic:

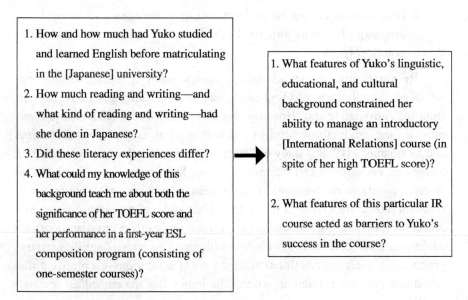

1. How and how much had Yuko studied and learned English before matriculating in the [Japanese] university?
2. How much reading and writing—and what kind of reading and writing—had she done in Japanese?
3. Did these literacy experiences differ?
4. What could my knowledge of this background teach me about both the significance of her TOEFL score and her performance in a first-year ESL composition program (consisting of one-semester courses)?

1. What features of Yuko's linguistic, educational, and cultural background constrained her ability to manage an introductory [International Relations] course (in spite of her high TOEFL score)?

2. What features of this particular IR course acted as barriers to Yuko's success in the course?

Figure 4.2 Spack's research question development.

1. How does the linguistic competence of a talented untutored adult L2 learner compare with that of native speakers?

2. Do tutored and untutored L2 learners who achieve near-native levels of proficiency exhibit similar achievement in the various domains of grammar? (p. 77)

Norton (2000), in her multiple-case study of adult immigrant women learning ESL in Canada, collapsed her research questions into two sets. The first has implicit embedded theoretical assumptions related to the relationship between interaction and acquisition, the importance of social structures (possibly hierarchical power relations, race, class, gender, etc.) in interaction, and the learners' own agency. This set also introduces the constructs of *investment* and *identity*. The second set of questions has theory-building and pedagogical implications as its primary objectives.

1. Since interaction with target language speakers is a desirable condition for adult SLA, what opportunities for interaction exist outside the classroom? How is this interaction socially structured? How do learners act upon these structures to create, use or resist opportunities to speak? To what extent should their actions be understood with reference to their investment in the target language and their changing identities across time and space?

2. How can an enhanced understanding of identity and natural language learning inform both SLA theory and classroom practice? (p. 22)

Research committees and other readers, such as journal manuscript reviewers, usually expect to find easily identified research questions set apart from the surrounding text. However, not all published case studies in journals present their guiding questions in this fashion. For example, Schneiderman and Desmarais's (1988b) study of "talented" learners' behaviors begins with a theoretical background and then presents four hypotheses to be tested. Yet no research questions are presented. Other studies (e.g., Lam, 2004) may proceed from the literature review directly to a discussion of research context and procedures, or pose their questions a bit more indirectly. Lam's study of two adolescent girls' development of hybrid bilingual Cantonese English discourse practices in their transnational Internet communications exemplifies this less direct and less explicit approach. The italics flag the embedded research questions:

For US-based ESL learners who are participating through English
in the social world of the Internet, the question arises as to *what
language practices and social relations they are developing through English, and
how these practices on the Internet relate to their experiences with English in the
US.* A related question of particular interest to educators is *how their
participation in the networked environments affects their processes of English
learning.* (Lam, 2004, p. 5, italics added)

Thus, different writers and editorial boards may have preferences about
how the main questions to be addressed in case studies are presented (see
Chapter 6). Their stylistic choices may also be related to the purpose of the
case under examination and the audience.

4.4 Research Design

4.4.1 Defining and Operationalizing Constructs

After formulating the research questions, how does one design a study?
Case study itself can be considered a type of research design. Careful case
selection and sampling are required, processes that are described in depth
in this chapter. Designing research involves the identification of *constructs*
or theoretical concepts likely to be of greatest interest (e.g., critical period,
motivation/investment, identity, language loss, aptitude/talent, language
policy, subjacency, topic prominence). Research design also (usually) involves
a careful consideration of reliability and validity, terms that in qualitative
research are often referred to as consistency, dependability, and trustworthiness
of the research process and interpretations (see the discussion of reliability
and validity in Chapter 5). Since different scholars may use the same terms in
different ways, it is important that readers understand not only what is meant
by a term, but also how it will be identified and measured (if applicable),
and perhaps how the term is used in comparison with other recent work. For
example, "Generation 1.5 learner" or "heritage-language (HL) learner", two
different types of learners, are operationalized by scholars in different ways.
For the *Generation 1.5 learner*, the points of variance are related to the age at
which the person immigrated (e.g., between 5 and 12 years of age, as opposed
to having been born in the immigrant-receiving country), and how many
years of schooling have taken place in the L2. For *heritage-language learner*,
definitional fuzziness is related to differences in the following: (1) the age at
which language shift occurred from HL/L1 to L2, (2) whether the HL was ever
the student's L1 (it may have just been a parent's or grandparent's L1), and

(3) whether the family/ancestral HL was the same dialect as is currently being learned (Li & Duff, in press). Thus, in research on these topics, a working definition is important for both theoretical reasons and practical purposes, such as the recruitment of appropriate participants.

To give another example of construct definition based on a multiple-case study, Kouritzen (1999) defines her principal construct, *language loss*, drawing on some existing definitions, but with particular reference to her target population of immigrants who have lost their first language:

> Language loss occurs "... when [a] minority group member can not do the things with the minority language that he [*sic*] used to be able to do... Some of the proficiency he [*sic*] used to have is no longer accessible" (Fase, Jaspaert, & Kroon, 1992, p. 8). It may also refer to incomplete or imperfect learning of a language spoken in childhood. (Kouritzen, 1999, p. 12)

She then provides definitions of other terms related to or used synonymously with *language loss* in some contexts, such as *language shift*, *language attrition* or *language regression*, *subtractive bilingualism*, *language death* or *obsolescence*, and *language change*. The operationalization of the construct for her research purposes became clear in her recruitment and sampling/selection of subjects (see Section 4.5.2).

4.4.2 Establishing Chains of Evidence

Like most research, regardless of paradigm, case study research design entails establishing clear, credible, coherent, and strong "chains of evidence" (Gall, Gall & Borg, 2005; Krathwohl, 1993; Yin, 1994) or an "audit trail". Yin (2003a) uses the phrase "the logic of design" to refer to this process of linking research questions and data as part of "a comprehensive research strategy" (p. 14). Decisions about research design—how many cases, which kinds of cases, contexts for cases, types of analyses foreseen or intended—are based on the kinds of evidence needed to speak to an issue with any authority (Bachman, 2004). Readers, in turn, can assess the strength of arguments and interpretations by seeing clear connections among the research questions, raw data, analyses of data, and conclusions (Gall *et al.*, 2005).

Denzin (1994) discusses issues of *representation* and *legitimation*. Representation refers to how we represent or position our participants, data, and interpretations, and also, perhaps indirectly, how we position ourselves as researchers in relation to those studied. Legitimation is the basis for the *warrants* or claims we make about our data and the authority of our reports (see Edge & Richards, 1998).

A concept related to warrants is the need to provide an audit trail (Gall *et al.*, 2003, 2005; Merriam, 1998). This involves keeping records of relevant documentation for decisions made, data collection strategies, the development of instruments or protocols, and examples of analysis procedures. These records might be included in an abbreviated form in an appendix or, if not published, might constitute a paper trail of what was done and why, should questions arise later. Journal reviewers, dissertation committee members, or scholars wishing to replicate the study or follow similar steps may seek further information, but it can be difficult to recall the basis for decisions several years after having made them without keeping good notes or records.

4.4.3 Mixed-Method Designs

Case study is increasingly used in mixed-method studies such as program evaluations. Here I will provide some details about one such study in the context of a Japanese Foreign Language in the Elementary Schools (FLES) program in the United States. Antonek *et al.* (2000) reported on their evaluation of the program in its fourth year, which they had been investigating since its inception. Using a stratified random sample of 32 qualified students, they conducted oral proficiency interviews and a word recall assessment exercise with each one. They then described a typical day in the Japanese program and proceeded with a multiple-case study of students' achievement, linguistic growth, and attitudes toward learning Japanese in the program:

> We have conducted a case study of six upper-elementary learners to provide a more in-depth view of the older FLES learner. Their profiles enable us to document and examine more closely differential linguistic development and differential engagement with the Japanese FLES program of older learners who have had an uninterrupted sequence of instruction.... Having identified students who had relatively homogeneous Japanese learning experiences, we selected three students who had received Pro-I [oral proficiency interview] ratings in the novice range and three students with intermediate range ratings. (p. 330)

They then reported on not only the proficiency measures for these students, but also the results of a learner questionnaire, an interview with a classroom teacher, and with the FLES (Japanese) teacher specifically, and examined the students' Japanese homework. Next, they conducted a cross-case analysis of the six children, first describing each student in some detail and then building a composite picture of all six students in terms of their achievement and attitudinal data. They concluded that multiple measures in the assessment of language learning by children are very important because the learners demonstrated the "multifaceted, developmental nature of language learning" (p. 344). Citing one of the students, Lilly, as an example of a learner who had made "dramatic improvement" in oral proficiency despite not having a "completely positive attitude profile", they observed:

> Labels alone do not tell us all that we need to know about a student's proficiency level. Knowing the optimal conditions under which Lilly was learning Japanese provided an understanding of her dramatic proficiency gains that would not have been possible if only numbers had been collected. Lilly's case demonstrates the importance of interviewing both FLS learners and their parents. (p. 347)

Besides mixed-method program evaluation, another common design is to conduct a survey (e.g., involving questionnaires) and then to follow up with a small number of respondents who indicate a willingness to take part in additional research and who represent important sectors or types of cases within the larger survey. The survey then also allows the researcher to establish the representativeness of the cases presented. Alternatively, the larger study might be (quasi-)experimental, with case studies included to provide a more concrete or more vivid description of the phenomenon explored in the larger study. Another approach is to conduct a larger qualitative study, of multiple institutions, for example, and then to concretize the analysis by including case studies of individual institutions and their ecology of teachers/employees, administrators, or students/clients to illustrate general trends or differences among the sites. Other options for mixed-method study designs are described further by Caracelli and Greene (1993) and Tashakkori and Teddlie (1998). Qualitative and quantitative analyses may be conducted concurrently or sequentially (with either one preceding the other type), but with a synthesis of results at the end.

4.4.4 Single-Case versus Multiple-Case Designs

Yin (2003a) presents four types of case study research design in a 2   2 matrix (see Figure 4.3); along the horizontal axis (top) are single- versus multiple-case designs, and along the vertical axis (left side) are holistic versus embedded units of analysis. In this way, he differentiates contexts, cases, and units of analysis but concedes that "the boundaries between the case and the context are not likely to be sharp" (p. 39). Holistic analyses would involve a more global and possibly more abstract consideration of one or more cases, such as organizations, programs, or participants.

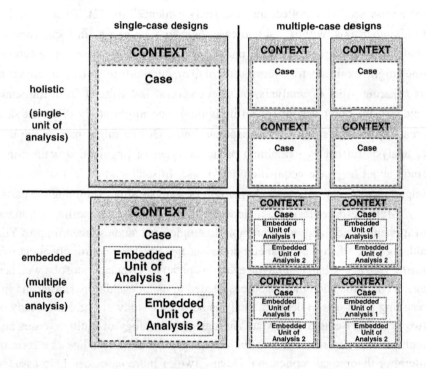

Figure 4.3 Types of case study design. (From Yin, R. K., *Case Study Research*, 3rd ed., Sage, Thousand Oaks, CA, 2003, p. 40.) Copyright 2003 by Sage Publications. Reprinted with permission of Sage Publications.

Yin suggests that a single-case design is appropriate—and even "eminently justifiable" (p. 45)—when studying "critical" or "revelatory" cases (e.g., Schmidt's (1983) study of Wes). In such instances, "the single case can represent a significant contribution to knowledge and theory building" (p. 40). It is also appropriate when studying extreme cases, either unique or representative/typical cases, longitudinal cases, or pilot cases in a planned multiple-case study. He cites Whyte's (1943/1993) *Street Corner Society* as an example of a revelatory case, "previously inaccessible to scientific investigation" (p. 42). However, Yin cautions readers that single-case designs may be unpredictable, and they "therefore require careful investigation of the potential case to minimize the chances of misrepresentation and to maximize the access needed to collect the case study evidence" (p. 42). Then, returning to his other axis, within a single case there may be one main focus (unit of analysis) or multiple embedded units. For example, if the case was a school, one might examine teachers, students, or curriculum policy documents as separate units of analysis, or select several individuals from the same category for comparison; for an individual, one might study different skill areas (speaking vs. writing) as separate units. Or one might narrow the unit of analysis further by examining particular types of linguistic structures in a study about language acquisition and/or use. In such studies, Yin stresses the importance of returning to the larger unit of analysis after examining the parts.

Multiple-case designs, if done well, can provide compelling evidence of a phenomenon and are preferable to single-case studies, according to Yin, although not all case study methodologists agree or feel so strongly about this matter (see also Chapter 2). However, this putative advantage must be weighed against the time and other resources needed to include additional cases and the resulting trade-offs in depth of analysis between a study of one and a study of two or more. Being a positivist, Yin makes the analogy of multiple cases and multiple experiments, and sees the advantage of multiple studies as a form of literal or theoretical replication. Having two or more cases can help assuage concerns that cases are unique in unforeseen ways.

4.4.5 Closed or Flexible Case Study Design

A final design feature is whether the study is closed (predetermined and inflexible) or flexible, evolving throughout the research process (Hatch, 2002; Yin, 2003a). Most qualitative researchers recognize the importance of being accountable to the unfolding data and situation and view flexibility as a strength of interpretive research. That does not mean that the studies should be unstructured or without focus, though. Research participants, supervisors, and institutional ethical review boards normally require that researchers plan their studies carefully and be as explicit as possible about the study's goals and intended methods in advance. Besides allowing others to judge the soundness of the design and methods, for research ethics purposes it enables the researcher to be very clear about what the expectations are for potential participants, in terms of both the time and the activities they will engage in. They also need to know the focus (to the extent one can reveal all of the specifics in advance without influencing behaviors unduly), the procedures, the benefits or risks to the participants, and the total duration of the study (see Section 4.14). A significant change in design, such as the inclusion of new types of subjects or new instruments, may require the submission of amendments to the original ethical review application or the submission of a new application.

4.5 Case Selection and Sampling

Case selection and sampling are among the most crucial considerations in case study research, and for that reason, I devote several pages to that topic here and provide many examples of current practice. The first decision in case selection, referred to earlier, is what entity will constitute the case, whether it is about a school, a program, an intervention, a workplace, a country, a city, a neighborhood, a policy, a language, or, as is often the case in applied linguistics, a language teacher, language learner, or language user. Second, what phenomenon within the case will be investigated? Is it the evolving tense-aspect system, measures of advanced proficiency, social distance and enclosure from target-language cultures, interactional competence, or trilingual literacy development? What does the researcher want to find out? Once the type of case has been narrowed down, crucial decisions about case selection and sampling follow.

Sampling and case selection are discussed in detail in many qualitative methodology textbooks. For example, Patton (1990) and Miles and Huberman (1994) and others differentiate the selection of cases according to the strategies shown in Table 4.1.

4.5.1 Sampling in Single-Case Studies

In much single-case study research in applied linguistics, the selection of cases

105

Table 4.1 Case Selection Strategies (Sampling)

Selection of Cases with Particular Characteristics

- Extreme or deviant case sampling
- Intensity sampling (information-rich cases but not extreme)
- Within-case sampling (sampling behaviors or attributes of individual cases)
- Multiple-case sampling (similar or contrasting cases)
- Maximum variation sampling (e.g., in a multiple-case study)
- Comprehensive sampling (examining *every* case or element)
- Homogeneous sampling (to describe a particular subgroup well)
- Typical case sampling (average or typical exemplars)
- Stratified sampling (with predefined points of variation or subgroups)
- Purposeful sampling (random sampling from an accessible population)

Conceptual Rationale

- Critical case sampling (test cases)
- Theory-based or operational construct sampling (manifesting important constructs)
- Confirming and disconfirming cases (vis-à-vis other case studies; seeking exceptions, variation)
- Purposeful random sampling (sampling from larger sample of eligible cases)
- Criterion sampling (cases meet predetermined criteria)
- Dimensional sampling (sampling across variables for contrasts, finding exemplars)
- Quota selection (taking cases from major subgroups)
- Sampling politically important cases
- Reputational case selection (on the recommendation of key participants or experts)

Emergent Strategies

- Opportunistic sampling (taking advantage of opportunities that arise)
- Snowball or chain sampling (finding cases by recommendation, referral, or association with others)

Strategy Lacking Rationale

- Convenience sampling (available cases)

---

is primarily based on opportunistic convenience sampling, the last category shown above: people in one's own social network, such as one's children. This was a trend established in the 1960s and 1970s but still continues for obvious, practical reasons. A recent example is Achiba's (2003) book about her child's English L2 requesting behaviors over a 17-month period while the Japanese researcher and her child resided in Australia (while Achiba, the mother, did her graduate studies). However, it might be argued that this sampling is actually *purposeful* (or purposive, as some call it) and that the children or learners selected are considered either typical or special in some respects, points that of course should be demonstrated or verified. The advantage of studying people with whom one is already familiar is that access and informed consent are easier to obtain. In addition, it may be possible to observe or interact with familiar participants or sites for a more extended or intensive period, and as a result, the researcher may obtain more useful data about the case. Finally, there is likely to be a greater understanding of the context based on prior knowledge.

Another strategy has been to use existing databases of case studies (e.g., the online CHILDES[1] database) in order to examine transcribed, sometimes even precoded, data for different features and to sample purposefully according to L1, for example. Hilles (1991) reexamined data from an earlier multiple-case study of six Spanish learners of English (two children, two adolescents, two adults) first reported in Cazden, Cancino, Rosansky, and Schumann (1975). One of the adults was Alberto, whom Schumann (1978) had previously studied. In contrast to the goals of the earlier analyses, Hilles examined the issue of whether universal grammar (UG) principles (in particular, a principle involving the suppliance of pronominal subjects and agreement inflection in English, a point that differentiates English and Spanish) were upheld by L2 learners in the same way they were exhibited in data from L1 learners. In that study, having participants with the same L1, Spanish, and also having different age groups was crucial in making the case—that one adolescent and both adults exhibited limited (or no) access to UG but the two children and one adolescent did.

When researchers seek volunteer research participants for case studies through public recruitment advertisements, they often do not have a great deal of choice over who will respond to the notices or will agree to participate, despite attempts to delimit the selection criteria in advance. Choice is possible when more potential subjects than necessary respond. In less deliberate

---

1   CHILDES stands for the Child Language Data Exchange System developed by Brian MacWhinney at Carnegie-Mellon University (http://childes.psy.cmu.edu/). It is a corpus of interactional child and adult L1 and L2 data that can be freely accessed, together with coding and analysis schemes, topics in language acquisition, bibliographies, and other resources.

recruitment, focal participants may simply emerge or present themselves to the researcher by referral or through existing social networks, because they are "interesting" in some theoretically relevant way: more silent, more outspoken, more proficient, more resistant, more metalinguistically aware, and so on. Snowball sampling is one approach by which researchers get to know potential participants by means of others' referrals or by word of mouth because of their reputation for being adept language learners, for example.

Such a serendipitous scenario is reflected in Singleton's (1987) account of the selection of his subject, Philip, a native speaker of English who had only limited experiences of learning French, but who apparently transferred knowledge from Spanish (but not Irish or Latin, other languages he knew) to French when he did not know the appropriate French term. This enabled him to communicate reasonably well in French. Singleton explained:

> The study reported here was sparked off by something of a mystery.
> The subject ... had never been taught French at school ... and had
> picked up most of the French he knew during three brief visits to
> France, none of which lasted more than two weeks. And yet informal
> observation suggested that he was able to function in French—at
> least at a general conversational level—with a very high degree of
> communicative efficiency.... [This] led me to look in detail at the
> kind of French he was producing. (p. 329)

Although not an applied linguist, Wolcott also originally described as "serendipity" his selection of "Brad", a high school dropout, who became the subject of his well-known educational case study. Brad had turned up, literally, in Wolcott's own backyard:

> Brad was not part of a systematic research effort on my behalf to
> collect life histories in order to examine alternatives to school and
> work as young people in similar straits perceive them. To the contrary,
> I can not imagine that I would have written this account had I
> not happened to encounter Brad, for my own everyday existence
> comprises the very world of school and world of work.... Nor do I
> write about Brad because he is "typical" or "average".... Brad is not
> typical or average at all. Nevertheless, there are many like him; if he
> is not typical, neither is he one of a kind.... I think his story is worth
> relating, because its implications extend far beyond the case of one
> seemingly "screwed-up" kid. (Wolcott, 1994, pp. 227–228)

And:

> [Brad's] uninvited presence on my 20-acre sanctuary, in search of
> sanctuary himself, brought me into contact with a type of youth I
> do not meet as a college professor. He piqued my anthropological
> interest with a worldview in many ways strikingly similar to mine but
> a set of coping strategies strikingly different. (p. 99)

In studies of diaries, memoirs, or (auto)biographies, the choice of one-
self or others as research subjects can be rationalized because we presumably
have better access to our own thoughts and experiences than someone else
does or than we have access to another's thoughts and experiences. Moreover,
if we are applied linguists, we also have access to a level of metalinguistic
reflection that nonspecialists likely do not have, though we are not typical of
the general population for that very reason.

Sometimes case selection can be rationalized after the fact. Schmidt's
(1983) study of Wes was, in effect, a *disconfirming* case analysis (Gall *et al.*,
2005) because Wes's attributes in terms of acculturation in the United States
and his English development and communicative competence provided an
important counter-example to an earlier generalization or claim about the role
of acculturation in SLA (e.g., Schumann, 1978). But his lack of significant
progress after three years was probably not anticipated by Schmidt at the
outset of the study, just as Jim's limited development (Chapter 1) was not
anticipated by me. Wes appeared to have been initially selected as a case
because Schmidt knew him well and already had a sense of his communicative
competence in English. Wes in turn agreed to participate in a longitudinal
study of his language development and use. Only at the end of the three-
year study was it apparent just how acculturated Wes had become in Hawaii
(he had by then become a permanent resident of the United States) and that
he had become a disconfirming case: in spite of his low social distance from
other Americans and his high degree of acculturation to U.S. culture, he still
failed to develop in many areas of L2 grammar, yet communicated reasonably
effectively regardless.

Unfortunately, many case study authors, particularly in short articles, do
not mention how or why a particular case was selected or what the relationship
or history was between researcher and researched, and what bearing that relationship had on the research process or interpretations.

Butterworth and Hatch (1978), for example, describe in detail an adolescent Colombian student's development of English along several syntactic

dimensions commonly studied then and now (negation, question formation, verb phrases, tense-aspect marking, pronouns), but nowhere explained how Ricardo came to participate in the study—whether he was Butterworth's student (data were recorded at a school) or a previously unknown volunteer selected because of his age or underdeveloped L2 syntax, his simplification of L2 utterances (e.g., *Me go Dana Point tomorrow*, p. 245), or his apparent lack of development over a three-month period. Since it is often said that case study researchers are themselves instruments of data collection because of their intense involvement in a study, such information is an important piece of the larger research context.

4.5.2 Sampling in Multiple-Case Studies

In research with multiple cases, case selection presents many more possibilities and dilemmas. Should you sample very similar cases (e.g., two extremely talented learners of Egyptian Arabic as in Ioup *et al.*'s (1994) study) or cases representing a range of attributes, with differences in terms of the following sorts of variables: L1, years of residence in the target-language setting, age, gender, immigration history, level of attainment in L2? There needs to be a rationale for sampling intensively within a narrower band versus sampling widely across variables or attributes. Generally, sampling widely is done in an exploratory study so as not to prematurely rule out particular variables or factors. Another alternative is to select two or three clearly contrasting cases.

Research by de Courcy (2002), for example, compared two distinct cases of second-language immersion programs in Australia, in Chinese and in French, to see if students' experiences of learning in the two classroom contexts were different. French immersion had been widely studied, but there was much less research on Chinese immersion, so choosing immersion in that language provided an interesting contrast case.

Duff (1993c) selected three schools, or cases, in three very different geographical and sociocultural contexts in Hungary: in the capital city, a small resort town, and a distant provincial capital. The purpose was to study the implementation and impact of dual-language education on classroom discourse in post-Soviet times in three very different parts of the country.

Morita's (2002, 2004) study of Japanese women's variable participation and silence in Canadian university courses featured six female participants (three pairs). She had originally included one male participant as well, but ended up not analyzing or including his data in those works. The reason was that, in addition to his being male, he was unlike the other six in other ways too: he was a doctoral student, and had a different professional status in Japan, having worked there as an associate professor of Industrial Sociology and Economics for several years. Thus, Morita used a more homogeneous sampling strategy, in terms of L1, years of study in Canada, gender, and student status, but did acknowledge some variation within the group regardless, in both the students' biographies and observed behaviors. As a Japanese graduate student herself, Morita had earlier made the decision to sample from among Japanese international students exclusively—but only after researching the demographics of international graduate students from different home countries at the university and considering the implications of including a cross-section of ethnolinguistic backgrounds. She did not impose gender as a selection strategy at first, but in the end most of her volunteers were female, perhaps not surprising in the fields of language and education. As a fellow Japanese graduate student, she had the added advantage of being considered a peer to them, an "insider" who also shared their language and many of their experiences. This common background enabled her to carry out the study more easily than it might have been for someone from a different gender, L1/ethnic background, age group, or professional status.

She explains her sampling as follows:

> The primary participants were six female, first-year master's degree students from Japan in three different departments (language education, educational studies, and Asian studies). All had agreed to participate by responding to a letter sent to all incoming graduate students from Japan in eight departments. They were all born in Japan, considered Japanese their first language (the language they were most comfortable with), and therefore could all be characterized as *international students from Japan* or *Asian female students* in the Canadian classroom. However, they in fact came from a variety of backgrounds that affected how they participated in the classroom. (p. 578)

Although Morita did an in-depth analysis of all six cases in her dissertation, discussing them in pairs in each of three chapters (Morita, 2002), her article based on the same study (Morita, 2004) presented only three of the women in detail because of space limitations.

In another full-length study of silence among language learners in classroom discussions, but with a focus on the relationship between silence and gender, Losey (1997) selected five focal students for her study, all Mexican

Americans aged 18 to 37, of whom two were males and three were females studying English in a community college outreach program in California.

Kouritzen (1999), on the other hand, in her life history narrative study of first-language loss, deliberately selected five focal participants (cases) from among a much larger and quite diverse volunteer pool (21 in total, including her five cases); the larger pool was used for cross-case analysis. She devoted two chapters (an introductory metanarrative and then a first-person narrative) to each focal participant, and then in a later chapter provided a profile of additional participants before proceeding with a cross-case thematic analysis. In an appendix, Kouritzen provided the criteria for her selection of cases:

1. Eliminating outliers (with either very negative or completely "untroubled" views vis-à-vis L1 loss)
2. Including two of five people with oral L1 traditions
3. Eliminating people who had lost their L1 through adoption or other complicating factors
4. Including families that supported bilingual development
5. Choosing cases representing five different languages—with two from Asian language backgrounds, two European, and one Indigenous
6. Choosing cases that would provide data to address a range of themes
7. Choosing speakers across different age groups
8. Choosing speakers across the spectrum of both L1 and L2 proficiency (low or none to high)
9. Including a mix of females (n = 3) and males (n = 2), reflecting the larger number of female volunteers

Thus, her strategy, quite unlike Morita's, was to seek maximum variation across participants to examine the intersection of language, identity, culture, and marginalization in contexts of L1 loss and L2 learning. Although she had in mind certain selection criteria before doing her recruitment, the characteristics of those who did respond helped her to formulate which combination of cases or experiences might be most compelling for her analysis.

Morita (2004) and Kouritzen (1999) both used a helpful strategy in sampling that I referred to earlier: they conducted a broader survey or sampled widely before selecting focal cases. Surveying may take place through the use of questionnaires, a review of census data, or other preliminary attempts to establish either the representativeness or uniqueness of the cases ultimately selected against the backdrop of the population from which they are drawn. Another alternative is to conduct some kind of survey *after* conducting a (multiple-)case study—as in Harklau's (1994a) study—again to demonstrate the typicality of one's cases and findings, which in turn contributes to claims of generality.

4.5.2.1 Sampling Decisions in Four Studies about Identity and L2 Learning

Four recent studies examining L2 learning and identity in immigrant populations allow us to explore further the sampling and case selection strategies of several L2 education scholars. First, in her book-length study of immigrant youth in Australian schools, Miller (2003) chose four participants with Chinese ethnic backgrounds and one Bosnian participant. She then devoted one chapter each to a discussion of (1) a pair of Hong Kong and Taiwanese students (one male and one female), (2) a Bosnian girl, and (3) a pair of Chinese mainland girls. By pairing up four of the focal participants, Miller was able to look for similarities and differences between their experiences and could foreground particular themes (recall that this pairing of cases in chapters was also done by Morita (2002) and Norton (1995)). Although Miller is not explicit about her reasons for selecting a Bosnian girl, Milena, for a case study with four other Chinese speakers (the logic of the case selection would have helped readers), 9 of 17 students in Milena's class were Bosnian. Thus, it appeared to be a sizable immigrant group reflecting a very distinct history and experience of migration and multilingualism, as well as personal agency, themes taken up by Miller in that chapter. In addition, Milena was very proficient in English, was socially skilled, and was forthcoming in interviews, all generally positive traits for research participants in applied linguistics.

Norton's (2000) selection of her five focal participants, immigrant Canadian women, followed a multistage and multimethod strategy. Her involvement started with co-teaching an ESL course during which she got to know potential participants for her study on identity and language learning. Some months later, she invited former students to participate in a three-part study. The subtasks and the response from volunteers are outlined below:

1. Detailed biographical questionnaires: 14 participated (a mixture of males and females)
2. A personal interview: 12 participated (a mixture of males and females)
3. A two-month diary study (which was subsequently followed by a

final interview and questionnaire six months later): five women participated

Norton conceded that perhaps those final five women as a group were different in various ways from others in the group who had not volunteered to take part in the diary study. For example, they felt comfortable writing about personal topics and had enough time to do so and to meet to discuss their experiences. In the final analysis, Norton (2000) found two natural groupings within the five cases: the two younger, single women (Eva and Mai, from Poland and Vietnam, respectively, both in their early 20s) and the three older married women with children (Katarina, Martina, and Felicia, from Poland, Czechoslovakia, and Peru, respectively, ages 34 to 44). She devoted a chapter to each set in her book, but in at least one journal article examined only a subset of the cases in detail (e.g., Martina, one of the older women, and Eva, one of the younger ones, in Norton Peirce, 1995).

A third example comes from Toohey (2000). The six focal children in her longitudinal ethnographic study were selected from eight English language learners in a class of 19 kindergarten children in Canada. Toohey explained that it was only after three school visits that she selected her focal participants for the three-year study: two children (a boy and a girl for each ethnolinguistic group) from homes in which Punjabi, Chinese, or Polish were spoken. She deliberately included mixed-gender pairs for each ethnicity.

The fourth example comes from Valdés (1998), who selected her two focal participants because they met her age group criteria (middle school), were new Spanish-speaking immigrants, and spoke virtually no English on arrival. However, after seven years, the two girls in the study had demonstrated very different English learning trajectories: one did reasonably well in high school despite the poor ESL program they were both enrolled in, and was hoping to attend a community college; the other learned very little English, joined a gang, had a baby, and did not complete high school. Thus, there was maximum variation between the two despite their common backgrounds.

To summarize, the approach taken by many researchers in applied linguistics case study research is to select two to six cases for in-depth analysis (Duff, 2006). Sometimes three to four focal cases in qualitative research are also analyzed against the backdrop of a larger set of participants and data (e.g., Kouritzen, 1999; Li, 1998). The authors may marshal various kinds of evidence (e.g., excerpts from interviews or classroom interactions) to support their claims.

Most of my own thesis or dissertation students conducting multiple-case studies have selected four to six participants in one or more sites (e.g., Duff & Uchida, 1997; Kobayashi, 2003; Morita, 2004). Choosing six initially means that if there is attrition among participants, several cases will likely remain, providing multiple examples of the phenomenon under investigation. The greater the number of participants, cases, or sites, however, the less possible it is to provide an in-depth description and contextualization (or thesis chapter) of each one, taking fully into account the complexity of interactions, the perspectives of the participants, and so on. Nevertheless, having more than one focal case can provide interesting contrasts or corroboration across cases. Exceptional cases, just like counter-examples to findings, need to be explained, however.

4.6 Contextualization

Contextualization in a case study, as in most social science and education research, is also quite crucial (Duff, 2006; Johnson, 1992). Contextualization may be important to replicate studies, to judge the transferability of findings, to ascertain the various factors impinging on the case, and to understand the sociocultural, political, or psychological situation in which language is researched. There are various kinds of contextualization to be considered: the theoretical contextualization of the research, the methodological contextualization, and finally a description of the actual situation in which the case is embedded and in which the research questions will be addressed. This third type of context may be defined on a number of analytic levels: it may be a linguistic or discursive context, a task or activity context, a social, political, historical, or cultural context, an instructional or institutional context, an interactional context, or a combination of these. The amount of contextualization needed depends on the nature of the study (Miles & Huberman, 1994).

The impact of the research or the researcher's presence on the context, whether inside a classroom, a research office, or workplace, should also be reflected upon. For example, what is the apparent effect of the researcher's observations or recordings on the events or participants? Understanding learning communities as ecologies or organic systems is increasingly being stressed in applied linguistics and other social sciences (Kramsch, 2002; van Lier, 1988, 1997, 2004), as is the importance of local contexts and cultures of language learning and use (Breen, 1985; Duranti & Goodwin, 1992; Holliday,

1994). Even task-based research can be analyzed with a view to understanding the kinds of contexts that are created by tasks and the impact of those contexts on the generation and interpretation of findings over time (Coughlan & Duff, 1994; Duff, 1993b).

In my studies examining educational systems in transition as a result of changing social/linguistic demographics, L2 policies, curricula, and so on, documenting these larger contexts in which more focused observations were situated and trying to understand macro-micro interfaces proved to be very helpful and illuminating (Duff, 1995; Duff & Early, 1996). The larger sociopolitical structure not only influenced the events and interactions in everyday classrooms, but was a product of—or was constituted by—some of those same recurring events and interactions.

Many qualitative case study researchers insist on investigating the phenomenon under scrutiny in its *natural* context, for example, in a class-room instead of a laboratory when looking at how a student participates in or carries out particular pedagogical tasks. Their goal is to maximize the *ecological validity* of the study, or the ability to interpret the results in as natural a context as possible. However, case study research in psychology has often been conducted in research laboratories where the fidelity of recording equipment is greater, where other equipment can be used most effectively, and where the study can proceed without extraneous noise or interruptions. Even within psychology, context is considered important, though. Bromley (1986) considers attention to context one of six basic rules for psychological case studies:

> The person must be seen in an "ecological context"; that is to say, a full account must be given of the objects, persons, and events in his or her physical, social, and symbolic environment. The proper focus of a case-study is not so much a "person" as a "person in situation". (p. 25)

In addition to the immediate physical setting in which research takes place, Altheide and Johnson (1994) suggest that researchers should pay attention to the following aspects of context: history, environment, number of participants, activities, schedules and temporal sequence of activities, division of labor, routines and variations, significant events, participants' perceptions, and social rules and norms. Context in some types of qualitative research, such as conversation analysis, is theorized differently and more locally, however (e.g., Markee, 2000; Silverman, 2004).

Finally, for ethical reasons, researchers should not normally use the real names or provide other obvious identifiers of institutions or participants. In some cases, therefore, it may be necessary to change or withhold some contextual or biographical details in order to protect the privacy of participants and their institutions or social networks.

4.7 Gaining Access to Research Sites

The challenge of negotiating and gaining entry to the research context and access to the case for any length of time, and particularly for a longitudinal study, can not be underestimated. Being familiar with the site and participants, having an "insider" status or having an ally on the inside, being clear about the research objectives and procedures, not placing unreasonable demands on one's research participants, and offering some form of reciprocity all help a great deal when negotiating access and permissions. Reciprocity means that both sides will benefit from the collaboration. Although it is conceivable that participation in research reflecting on linguistic issues has its own inherent rewards, small gifts are often appreciated as well, both as incentives to participate and as expressions of gratitude. These might take the form of a gift certificate, an honorarium or stipend based on the time required to participate, or the offer of meaningful assistance that will not compromise the study's outcomes, such as tutoring.

In schools or workplaces, making sure that principals or employers understand and support a project is very important to help negotiate entry. Similarly, teachers or company co-workers should be "on-side". Often, having one of the staff members become enthusiastic about a project will in turn open many other doors. For research with children, it is essential that parents or guardians understand the goals and procedures and give their informed consent (see Section 4.14). Having supportive, respected school staff members send a message home to parents can also help mediate the process. Informing linguistically diverse parents and other participants effectively may also involve providing information packets or information sessions in their home language. In my recent classroom-based research, however, even with information prepared in students' L1, I found that recently arrived immigrant parents and students were often reluctant to participate in research because they feared it might draw undue attention to the students' difficulties with English (Duff, 2002b). Their reticence was unfortunate because that was the population I was most interested in studying.

Outlining the roles and responsibilities of each party in advance is also

117

good practice (Hatch, 2002). Furthermore, access is something that often has to be negotiated and renegotiated on an ongoing basis during a lengthy study, especially as conditions change (see Duff & Early, 1996).

Finally, in addition to access strategies, exit strategies should also be planned. These are procedures for ending a project, informing participants or stakeholders of findings, and possibly for maintaining relationships with the participants for future research purposes.

4.8 Data Collection: Sources of Evidence

Yin (2003a) lists six sources of evidence commonly used in case studies:

- Documentation
- Archival records
- Interviews
- Direct observations
- Participant observation
- Physical artifacts

Using multiple sources of data allows researchers to "corroborate and augment evidence from other sources" (Yin, 2003a, p. 87). Not all case studies involve all of these sources of data, though. Wolcott (1994) provides the mnemonic of three E's in (ethnographic) qualitative data collection: *experiencing* (participant observation), *enquiring* (interviewing), and *examining* (studying documents).

In applied linguistics, data collection often includes a number of instruments or techniques (see Mackey & Gass, 2005, for examples). Many studies focus on documents, archives, or artifacts (e.g., in policy studies or text studies), or on observation and interview data (e.g., in SLA or classroom studies). Document analysis might involve relevant paperwork and artifacts, such as textbooks, newspaper articles, students' writing samples or assignments, course outlines, and research journals kept by participants or researchers. In addition to the possible data sources already listed are tests, elicited responses in the form of grammaticality judgments, stimulated recall, verbal reports (e.g., introspective or retrospective reports), and questionnaires (especially for surveying a larger group from whom cases are selected).

Data collection is determined by the underlying research questions and the forms of evidence deemed necessary to answer those questions. Data collection decisions also depend on what the researcher plans to do with the data. The study must be feasible or doable, and this consideration should factor into the research design. Collecting masses of data that will never be analyzed or that would take an inordinate amount of time to transcribe, for example, is wasteful in terms of time, energy, other costs, and goodwill, and some would say it is unethical as well.

In the remainder of this section, I provide examples of data collection strategies in some published case studies. I also include relevant data collection information in some of the summaries of studies in Chapter 3.

Table 4.2 Summary of Database

Methods	Data Collection Period (Sept. 1999–April 2000)	Data
Weekly self-reports by students	• Ongoing • 1–3 times per week, per student	• E-mail messages • Audiotaped face-to-face or telephone conversations • Written journals • 283 reports total, about 16 different courses
Interviews with [6] students	• Interview 1: Beginning of academic year • Interview 2: End of Term 1 • Interview 3: End of Term 2	• Audiotaped and transcribed interviews • 18 interviews total • Average 1.7 hours each
Classroom observations	• Ongoing	• Field notes on 59 lessons in 5 courses (151 hours of observation)
Interviews with instructors	• Once with each instructor toward the end of the courses	• Audiotaped and transcribed interviews • 10 interviews total • Average 1.2 hours each
Documents	• Ongoing	• Course outlines • Handouts for presentations • Self-evaluations of class participation

Source: From Morita, N., *TESOL Quarterly*, 38, p. 581, 2004. Published by Teachers of English to Speakers of Other Languages, Inc. This work is protected by copyright and it is being used with the permission of Access Copyright. Any alteration of its content or further copying in any form whatsoever is strictly prohibited.

In Morita's (2004) multiple-case study of six Japanese students' participation and perceptions of their own participation in whole-class and small-group discussions in Canadian university classrooms, data collection and analysis proceeded in the manner shown in Table 4.2, over an eight-month period. She employed a variety of methods: students' self-reports (by e-mail, in journals, etc.), classroom observations with fieldnotes taken, interviews (with the focal students and their instructors, separately), and documents of various types related to courses.

Achiba's (2003) longitudinal single-case SLA study examined the English L2 developmental patterns and requesting strategies of her child. The unit of analysis was a *request*. She collected two types of data: (1) audio- and video-recordings of the child during playtime interactions at 14 different times over a 75-week period, during which the child interacted, in turn, with a peer, a teenager, and an adult; and (2) diary notes of the child's spontaneous use of English with her, primarily. Because Achiba was more concerned than Morita about exact linguistic structures produced (as opposed to more general participation patterns of the type Morita investigated), audio- and video-recordings of language use were important.

Finally, Jarvis's (2003) case study employed a combination of naturalistic and more laboratory-like experimental procedures. He examined the effects of an adult immigrant's acquisition of an L2 (English) on her L1 (Finnish). His "natural use" data included Finnish constructions produced in informal Finnish oral interactions over more than a year, based on which Jarvis detected 15 "unconventional" or "deviant" patterns (primarily lexico-semantics and idiomatic usage). His "clinical elicitation" data collection, on the other hand, included showing short film clips devised to elicit narratives containing the marked structures, eliciting metalinguistic judgments regarding the same set of constructions, and gathering self-report data from a debriefing interview with the Finnish woman about her judgments.

In contrast to the preceding studies, my study of Jim (Chapter 1) involved only structured oral interview data, elicited by several types of tasks during each interview: small talk, picture description, picture sequence narration, and personal or folktale narratives. Thus, in different types of case studies, different types of data will be collected and analyzed, according to the evidentiary needs and traditions of the subdiscipline, and often based on ethical and logistical considerations as well (i.e., whether permissions have been granted).

4.9 The Role of the Researcher

In the earlier section on case selection and sampling in this chapter, I noted that it is very helpful in written reports of case studies for researchers to clarify their role in the research process and their history with the participants or research site without jeopardizing anonymity. For example, knowing that a child studied was not just "any child" but the researcher's own child might lead readers to interpret the researcher's claims differently (e.g., about the "brilliance" of the child, her "excellent upbringing", or "linguistic precociousness", to give hypothetical examples). Or, knowing that the researcher was the instructor of a course in which the teacher's (own) questioning patterns were examined might shed light on claims about "sensitive and skillful questioning" or "inspired classroom management". Providing this kind of information helps contextualize the research and also helps readers understand the researcher's personal investment in the case, or perhaps intimate familiarity with the context or participants, which can work either for or against the researcher. The researcher may be seen as too close to the case to see things differently, that is, to consider alternate explanations, or she may be too removed from the case to understand the fullness of the case and context well. Seeking a balance between subjectivity and objectivity in reporting, or (rather) seeking *rigorous subjectivity* (Wolcott, 1994, p. 354) that can be interpreted with some transparency by others, is important. However, revealing certain kinds of behind-the-scenes information also raises provocative ethical questions. I will illustrate this dilemma with an intriguing account of what might be viewed as an extreme case of personal investment and self-revelation in qualitative research, demonstrated in Wolcott's (1983/1994) seminal ethnographic autobiography of a high school dropout named "Brad".

Wolcott (1994) described Brad as a 19-year-old "alienated youth" at the outset of his two-year study. Brad had become a drifter and a squatter on Wolcott's rural property in Oregon, a situation reported earlier in this chapter in the context of convenience sampling. The original 1983 study examined Brad's dysfunctional family history, how and why he had dropped out of school in his early teens and had ended up in reform school, and then a halfway house, and finally became a homeless young man who survived by shoplifting and other kinds of theft, by being "sneaky", as Brad himself put it. Wolcott noted that he wanted readers to transcend "a specific and circumstantial life story to illustrate the necessity of regarding education as more than just schooling and of pointing out how little we attend to that broader concern" (p. 99).

Only subsequently, however, in a piece on validity and interpretation in qualitative research, did Wolcott (1994) reveal the extent of his relationship with Brad—that prior to and during the two-year study, they had been intimate partners; that Brad was later diagnosed with paranoid schizophrenia; and that several years after their relationship and study had concluded and Brad had moved out of state, Brad was convicted of attempted murder and arson, having assaulted Wolcott and destroyed the researcher's house and all his possessions in a deliberately set fire. In the trial that ensued, ethical and legal issues about the relationship between the two were raised. Brad's confidentiality was lost when Wolcott's original article (Wolcott, 1983) was brought forward as evidence of Wolcott's alleged gullibility and exploitation of Brad sexually and professionally. And, as another blow to Wolcott, he reports that "under oath, Brad's mother insisted [Brad] had made up most of it [Brad's life history]— this, the story I felt I had finally gotten right—simply to impress me" (1994, p. 362). Brad was sentenced to a short jail term regardless.

Wolcott's experience was therefore a very unusual and tragic case study of fallout from a personal and professional relationship with a research subject who also happened to be a deeply troubled individual. The story also illustrates how the fuller, later disclosure of information about the researcher-researched relationship might change one's interpretation of the original research and lead one to question the researcher's judgment (see Section 4.14).

4.10 Interviews

Interviews play an important role in much research in sociolinguistics and applied linguistics/SLA. Not surprisingly, they are very commonly used in case studies (see Section 4.8; Merriam, 1998). Many helpful books and articles deal with research interviewing in the social sciences and humanities (Briggs, 1986; Fontana & Frey, 1994; Holstein & Gubrium, 1997; Kvale, 1996; Miller & Glassner, 1997; Mishler, 1986; Seidman, 2006; Spradley, 1979; Schostak, 2006; Yow, 1994). In applied linguistics, some recent textbooks also devote considerable space to practical approaches to qualitative interviewing (e.g., Chapter 2 in Richards, 2003). In this section, I summarize some of the main points of relevance in qualitative case study research.

There are various ways of categorizing interviews. For example:

- Structured, semistructured, or unstructured interviews
- In-depth interviews (either semistructured or unstructured)
- Focus group or group interviews
- Oral history or life history interviews

The amount of control or structure imposed by researchers on the interview format and resulting speech event varies across studies. Many early—(post)positivist—case studies of L2 learners (e.g., Hatch, 1978a) involved interviews eliciting L2 production through the use of pictures, conversational question-answer segments, personal narratives, and think-aloud protocols in what was construed to be an oral interview (i.e., as distinct from a test or lab experiment). The goal was to learn more about the full extent of language learners' (oral) competence/performance in their first, second, or additional languages. The use of a variety of tasks helped elicit as many types of discourse or targeted structures and as much analyzable language as possible to understand learners' true abilities and systematic language use.

A second approach to linguistic interviewing draws more on Labov's (1966) classic work using personal, sometimes affectively charged, narratives of past events primarily, particularly for studies of phonological variation, tense-aspect systems, narrative structure, and discourse-level phenomena in casual, everyday speech. Again, the focus is primarily structural (formal or functional).

A third approach uses interviews primarily to collect data about the insights or perspectives of research participants, with less attention paid to the actual linguistic or textual features of the discourse. A content or thematic analysis, rather than a linguistic or interactional analysis, is primary.

Phenomenological research is another approach that focuses on people's "lived experiences" with respect to language, culture, education, immigration, and so on, in the humanities, social sciences, and education. This approach places greater emphasis on participants' narrative reconstructions of aspects of their lives and experiences, such as the connection between their affective or emotional states or their identities and their experiences of language learning (e.g., Kouritzen, 1999; Pavlenko, 2002; Schumann, 1997). In content- and narrative-oriented research such as this, it is common to conduct more than one interview with interviewees. In that way, the researcher can follow up on issues or clarify uncertainties emerging from an earlier interview. The purpose is not usually to examine developmental changes in this instance, but to seek clarity and perhaps consistency in accounts as well as an elaboration on significant topics. Life history interviews fall into this category.

Whichever approach to interviewing is taken (and there are others), it is important to recognize that a research interview is a "construction" or joint production by interviewer and interviewee (Briggs, 1986; Coughlan & Duff,

1994; Mishler, 1986). It produces a version of truth, a snapshot of competence or of ideas elicited for a specific purpose in a particular space and time. The data are generated by means of social interaction between interviewer and interviewee and can not necessarily be taken as decontextualized, independent facts or observations. Each interview has, and is, its own discourse context, which also evolves over the course of the interview and from one interview to the next. Even research on oral proficiency interviews in language testing in recent years now acknowledges the highly interactional and contingent nature of interviews (e.g., Young & He, 1998).

As a type of speech event, moreover, interviews may have a different cultural status or discursive form in different societies. In addition to being interactive, cultural, and dynamic, there is often a power differential between interviewer and interviewee as well. In *Learning How to Ask*, Briggs (1986) famously reflected upon his own communicative problems ("blunders") doing ethnographic research interviews with *Mexicano* Spanish speakers in New Mexico, and also in trying to make sense of interview data. He critiques interviewing in social science research on a number of levels, one of which is sociolinguistic:

> By participating in an interview, both parties are implicitly agreeing to abide by certain communicative norms. The interview moves the roles that each normally occupies in life into the background and structures the encounter with respect to the roles of interviewer and interviewee.... Some potential respondents are drawn from communities whose sociolinguistic norms stand in opposition to those embedded in the interview. (pp. 2–3)

Just as some interviewers are better or more adept at interviewing than others, some respondents (interviewees) are better in that role than others. They are more forthcoming, reflective, analytical, proficient, articulate, vivid, or even more interested in the research itself than others might be. The chemistry between the interviewer and interviewee (in addition to context, purpose, history, etc.) may have something to do with why some respondents provide better data. In selecting cases for study (see Section 4.5), it is important to anticipate how well participants will perform in interviews, if they are to be used, and how as an interviewer one might deal with case study participants who are reticent, uncooperative, inarticulate, verbose, or easily sidetracked. Choosing the most articulate candidate interviewees, however, may introduce some skewing of data because they may not be very representative of others in their category. They may have had the most successful experiences learning language or becoming acculturated, for example, or may be more confident or more willing to take risks in unfamiliar social contexts than their peers.

Qualitative research interviews are normally conducted face to face, especially with L2 users, but if it is difficult to arrange meeting time or places, the telephone may provide a useful—albeit imperfect and sometimes challenging—substitute. Audio equipment can be easily found to record the talk, if permission has been granted to do so. Increasingly, e-mail exchanges or threaded discussions can also supplement or take the place of formal interviews, depending on their purpose.

Although one-on-one interviews between researchers and research participants are probably most common in applied linguistics and especially in case studies, in multiple-case studies they could be supplemented with focus group interviews. In focus groups, groups of research participants, for example, six to eight per group, are asked to discuss their perspectives on issues. While perhaps better known in the fields of marketing, sociology, public health, political science, and women's studies, focus group interviews can reveal in a fairly short time frame several people's perspectives on an issue, sometimes referred to as multivocality (Duff, Wong, & Early, 2000; Krueger, 1994; Madriz, 2000). The group interaction itself can prompt others to comment on themes that they might not have thought of or volunteered in one-on-one settings, and participants often find the group format less intimidating than a one-on-one interview. At the same time, sensitive topics are best not broached in such a forum in order to protect the privacy, anonymity, and comfort level of research participants.

Focus group data can be useful either for interpreting case study data against the backdrop of a wider pool of subjects or as a strategy allowing researchers to carefully select possible cases for subsequent study. It is a less effective way of collecting data for the analysis of people's *linguistic* competence (unless interaction during a focus group interview is itself the topic), and it can be difficult to identify speakers during transcription using audiotape recordings alone unless the focus group participants' voices are familiar and do not overlap too much.

Some practical tips for interviewing either individually or in groups are found in Table 4.3.

Table 4.3 Practical Tips for Interviewing

1. Carefully craft the questions to be asked, in terms of both content and form, based on the main focus of the study, and think of the optimal time and location for the interview.
2. Eliminate unnecessary jargon from questions. For example, in seeking insights from immigrant students or workers about their identities, the questions "What is your main ethnolinguistic identity?" or "What are the various identities you negotiate in your daily life?" may draw blank stares (as they have in some UBC research). It is better to paraphrase the concept or exemplify it in terms that people can easily understand.
3. Ask a colleague or nonspecialist to review the questions before the interview or try them out (pilot test) with a nonparticipant to ensure that the language is clear, the questions are not too complicated, and the interview is not too long for the allotted time.
4. Check your recording equipment carefully before each use. Ensure that batteries are fresh, that cassettes (if used) are available and carefully labeled, and that microphones and power supplies are prepared, as needed. Consider bringing and using a backup recording instrument for high-stakes interviews in case the main machine malfunctions. Find a quiet venue for recording.
5. Start the interview with some small talk to put interviewees at ease. Then follow the interview protocol (or set of questions) with whatever strictness or flexibility is necessary or appropriate.

Table 4.4 Types of Questions in Interviews

- Introducing questions (e.g., "Can you tell me about your L2 learning history?")
- Follow-up questions (asking more about the previous utterance or response) e.g., "Could you say more about that?" or "Could you give an example of that?"
- Probing questions (e.g., "Could you say something more about the courses you attended?")
- Specifying questions (e.g., "How did you react?")
- Direct questions (e.g., "Have you ever had trouble being understood?")
- Indirect questions (e.g., "How do you think other students feel about x?")
- Structuring questions (moving onto another topic when off-track or when topic has been covered; e.g., "Now I have a different question/topic/task for you.")
- Silence (to encourage reflection or amplification of responses)
- Interpreting questions (e.g., "You mean that …?")

Source: Adapted from Kvale, S., *InterViews: An Introduction to Qualitative Research Interviewing*. Sage, Thousand Oaks, CA, 1996, pp. 133–135. Adapted with the permission of Sage Publications.

The kinds of questions that might then be asked in an interview are found in Table 4.4.

Ideally, interviewers themselves should demonstrate as many of the attributes found in Table 4.5 as possible (Kvale, 1996).

Normally, interviews are audio-recorded with suitable high-quality tape recorders and microphones in a quiet location. Increasingly, digital recorders are used because the data can easily be uploaded to computers for replay, transcription, analysis, and presentation. The existence of too much background noise will make transcription much more time consuming (and expensive) and onerous; noise is also distracting during an interview. Semistructured or unstructured interviews usually last anywhere between 30 and 90 minutes.

Table 4.5 Desirable Interviewer Attributes

- Knowledgeable, respectful, organized, and clear, both in language use and purpose for the interview
- Aware of how much they themselves are speaking, and for what purpose
- Careful not to ask leading questions that will suggest a certain desired or preferred response or perspective
- Attuned to the level of proficiency or comprehension of the interviewee
- Careful not to interrupt and trained to provide sufficient response time following questions
- Sensitive, attentive, and responsive to answers or questions (in less structured interviews)
- Open to relevant new directions (when appropriate)
- Able to keep discussion on track, but do so gently
- Able to remember what interviewees have already said
- Effective in interpreting interviewees' remarks

The language of interviews (or use of interpreters) and the gender of interviewers in relation to their interviewees may be important considerations in research with culturally and linguistically diverse populations (Goldstein, 1997; Kouritzen, 1999). In some contexts, interviewees might be more forthcoming with an interviewer of the same sex who shares the same L1 and culture. However, in other cases, interviewees might be reluctant to participate in interviews with people from the same backgrounds for fear of judgment or gossip from within that community, or they might find it easier to speak the L2 (e.g., English) with interlocutors from other linguistic groups if their L2 oral proficiency is being analyzed because it would be more natural. If interviewers are closer to research participants in age and status (for example, graduate students interviewing other students), it is often easier to develop rapport and to put the research participant at ease (e.g., Kobayashi, 2003; Morita, 2004). For this reason, in several of my recent studies at the postsecondary level, I have hired research assistants who come from the same linguistic backgrounds as the students they are interviewing. Their in-group status as peers at the same institution has greatly facilitated the data collection process.

Finally, in ethical review applications and in many published reports, the researcher often needs to provide interview guides or protocols in an appendix with sample questions to be asked for reference purposes. Because gaining access to fieldwork sites for direct observation is becoming increasingly complicated for ethical/institutional reasons in some types of research (see Section 4.14), case studies in applied linguistics will probably rely on interviewing and written text analyses to an even greater extent as their principal data collection strategies in the future (see Duff, Wong, & Early, 2000).

4.11 Observation

Many case studies in applied linguistics include the systematic, focused observation of case participants in their natural contexts (classrooms, homes, community centers, workplaces), especially if one of the objectives of the study is to examine people's linguistic performance or interaction in naturally occurring social situations (van Lier, 1988). In classroom-based or workplace studies, for example, observational work can help researchers understand the physical, social/cultural, and linguistic contexts in which language is used, and also collect relevant linguistic and interactional data for later analysis. Although sustained *participant observation* is one of the hallmarks of ethnographic research, it is not always a central feature of case studies. In participant observation, the researcher plays another social role in the research site (e.g., as student, teacher, or co-worker, a co-participant within the local culture).

Nevertheless, the researcher inevitably becomes an unofficial participant in the speech event by his/her mere presence. It is therefore important to consider what effect one's presence has on the unfolding interactions, if any, or whether by being there the very activities or behaviors of greatest interest to the researcher are altered in some way (consciously or not). For example, just by anticipating that a researcher will be videotaping a class or a family dinnertime discussion, the teachers, students, or family members may be on their best behavior, may avoid unpleasant disciplinary actions or outbursts, may be better prepared to participate in discussions than usual, or may avoid certain topics. Only with extended observations does it become clear how typical the observations are. Some researchers arrange to have participants (the teacher or family) record their own interactions without the researcher immediately present, and differences may also emerge from occasions when the researcher is physically (more) present. In any case, it is wise to consult with those who have been observed to get a better sense of how typical or representative the observed behaviors and activities were.

Very often in interpretive case studies, the observations are not guided by a predetermined observational protocol involving the coding of behaviors every 15 seconds, for example, according to the direction, language, or substance of interaction. Spada and Lyster (1997) and van Lier (1997) compare their approaches to L2 classroom observation and analysis, as quantitative and qualitative, respectively. Observational protocols and coding sheets are often used in quantitative studies (e.g., Spada & Lyster, 1997). What one observes and how one observes and records observations are centrally connected with the theoretical framework and traditions of one's work. Having a video camera trained only on a teacher in classroom discourse analysis, while convenient, only shows one side of the interaction, even if students are not speaking. It does not reveal the facial or other nonverbal behaviors of students, the spatial configuration of the class, the times when students raise their hands bidding for turns, and so on. Therefore, it is important to understand the sorts of information or evidence that are relevant and important to one's analysis before undertaking it. Typically in ethnographic fieldwork with focal participants (cases) that is sustained over a period of time, one begins with larger fields of observation and then narrows things down over time, focusing to a greater extent on the cases in question (Duff, 1995). But other research might have a very precise focus from the start (e.g., an examination of doctor-patient or tutor-student interaction, the requesting behaviors of an L2 user) and will focus immediately on the relevant portion.

Observation involves far more than just the mechanical process of zeroing in on and recording observable behaviors (Richards, 2003). However, the mechanics are also important to consider. Audiotaping and videotaping observations, as opposed to fieldnote taking alone, helps preserve the linguistic character of interactions, and videotaping in particular allows researchers to better attend to nonverbal aspects of language interaction, such as gestures, participants' orientation to various media in their environment, eye gaze, and so on.

In my research involving classroom-based observations in which I successfully negotiated the use of videotaping (e.g., Duff, 1993c, 2002b), I normally observed classes on several occasions (sometimes weeks) without any equipment in order for the class to become accustomed to my presence. The classes never entirely forgot about the camera's presence, though, even after many weeks. In one study in which I had received permission to videotape (Duff, 2002b), the teacher eventually asked me, after several weeks, to stop videotaping because some of the teenaged girls in the class seemed to be too distracted by it, directing off-task comments and gossip at the camera microphone from time to time. In addition to a video camera, I typically have one high-quality tape recorder (and sometimes tabletop microphone) on the teacher's front desk. When examining focal participants engaged in group activities, I videotape the group (when possible) and have high-quality small tape recorders for each group being recorded. Markee (2000) discusses other ways of recording multiple individuals within classroom settings, such as outfitting each one with a small tape recorder and microphone, using radio microphones or special directional microphones. In my own classroom research, the most I have ever used was about six small tape recorders in addition to a larger one and a video camera.

I have never managed to use more than one video camera in the same classroom because of the logistics of operating two cameras and also the increased intrusiveness and data management required. In more controlled settings, of one or more cases interacting with a computer in a lab space, for example, it would be advisable to have one video camera focusing on the computer screen and another on participants and the keyboard.

With a single video camera in a classroom, I typically place it on the side of the room (e.g., next to windows to avoid backlighting problems), slightly to the back of the room, and near a power source. There are always trade-offs about where equipment and microphones are placed, how easy it will be to turn tapes over without being disruptive, and how much information can be captured. For observations that are not audio- or video-recorded, the researcher must take detailed fieldnotes, but these records are not really adequate for detailed linguistic analysis. Fieldnote taking may also be done together with recording (if the researcher can manage both or has assistance) to help contextualize the observed behaviors and to note aspects of the observations that merit follow up. Additional comments or classroom configuration comments may also be written immediately after observations either on the fieldnotes or in a research journal. I often sketch the classroom setup. In the classroom in Figure 4.4, I was located on the far right side of the room close to a power outlet, near the "louder local girls"—the same ones whose distracting asides forced me to stop videotaping, unfortunately (Duff, 2002b).

In qualitative case studies, observation is not usually the only data collection technique. It is combined with interviews, to ascertain selected participants' perspectives on their actions or behaviors, and other data collection, such as document analysis. But in some research in which observation is intended, participants may opt for various reasons not to grant permission because of the perceived intrusiveness of having visitors in their midst. This scenario affected data collection in work reported in Duff, Wong,

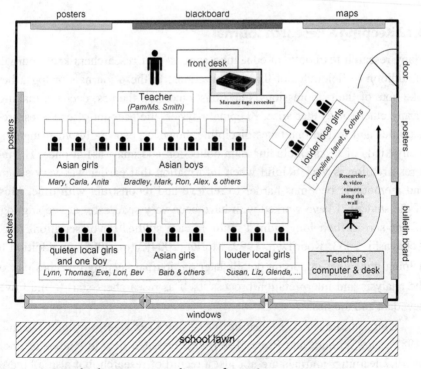

Figure 4.4 Sample classroom recording configuration.

and Early (2000), resulting in an interview-based study instead. In other studies, permission to audiotape but not videotape may be granted (e.g., Duff & Li, 2004).

To summarize, case study researchers conducting observations should consider the following points:

- What their focus will be in the observations, besides the case itself
- How best to record the observed behaviors manually (through notetaking) and mechanically so as to capture key information and avoid mechanical dysfunction (note: have backup equipment and extra batteries)
- What kinds of information will be lost if audio- or videotaping is not permitted
- Over what period of time and what schedule the observations will take place
- How researchers will elucidate participants' perspectives of the observed actions at a later point
- How they will analyze and use the observational data in the study

4.12 Keeping a Research Journal

Many research textbooks in education suggest that researchers keep journals in addition to fieldnotes of their observations. In these journals or logs, they take note of their impressions, questions, emerging themes, decision making, or any other issues that arise. Keeping a systematic account of one's research activities and reflections takes discipline, however, especially when juggling many kinds of tasks (including data collection and analysis) at once. Having a research log is very helpful when information that earlier was very salient and memorable becomes harder to retrieve and reconstruct with time. Most of the students I have worked with have been very successful at keeping logs of this sort in their longitudinal multiple-case studies for dissertations (e.g., Kobayashi, 2003; Kouritzen, 1999; Morita, 2004; Yim, 2005). In addition to helping remember important details later on, journal keeping becomes part of the analysis and interpretation process itself as researchers start to mull over new data and themes.

Diary studies of L2 learning by Bailey (1983), Bailey and Ochsner (1983), and Schmidt and Frota (1986) also revealed how in studies of one's own L2 learning, journals are not just a record of research, but also a kind of intervention: a platform for conceptualizing, noticing, articulating, or testing out new hypotheses or ideas.

4.13 Triangulation

An important principle in current qualitative research is that both insider (emic) and outsider (researcher/analyst) perspectives of phenomena should be incorporated to the extent possible in order to provide what is called a *triangulation* of data. This triangulation, or "crystallization", a more multifaceted metaphor (Richardson, 1994), increases the internal validity of the study. But triangulation can involve more than just the juxtaposition or integration of the perspectives of researchers and participants. Research methods themselves may also be triangulated (e.g., in mixed-method research), theory may be triangulated when the same phenomenon is examined through different theoretical lenses and from the standpoint of researchers in different fields, data collection techniques and results can be triangulated (e.g., observation, interviews, document analysis), and so on. Stake (2000) asserts that "seen from different worldviews and in different situations, the 'same' case *is* different" (p. 449).

Koschmann (1999) provides an example of the triangulation of diverse research perspectives in the analysis of discourse and interaction in a short medical tutorial (the case) that he invited different teams of researchers to analyze from their own epistemological and theoretical perspectives. Naturally, in this kind of triangulation, data sets (e.g., transcripts, video clips) shared for analysis already represent a certain theoretical perspective and preselection; thus, they cannot be construed as theory-neutral objects. But the exercise was an intriguing effort to see the "same" interactions from different perspectives.

Another innovative and experimental illustration of epistemological triangulation is a book by Wolf (1992), *A Thrice-Told Tale*. Wolf, an anthropologist, revisited some fieldnotes she had collected as an anthropologist in Taiwan Province of China some 30 years earlier about a "crazy" woman named Mrs. Tan, who "displayed symptoms of mental illness, spirit loss, possession by a god, and shamanism" for a period (p. 8). In the intervening years, Wolf noted that she herself, now a feminist anthropologist, the field of anthropology, and Taiwanese village life had all changed from what they had been back then. Wolf reflects:

I now have three texts describing in different ways what happened in the little village of Peihotien some thirty years ago. One is a piece of fiction written by me alone; another consists of unanalyzed fieldnotes recording interviews and observations collected by any of the several members of the field staff; and the third is entirely written in my voice.... Each text takes a different perspective, is written in a different style, and has different "outcomes", yet all three involve the same set of events. (p. 7)

Thus, there are many kinds of triangulation, some more experimental and postmodern than others, but the principal goal is to investigate the research problem from different perspectives in order to provide possibly more complex and ideally more valid insights into observed or tacit linguistic behavior and knowledge. Not all perspectives will necessarily converge, but such disjunctions themselves can be important findings.

4.14 Ethical Considerations

In many places in this book, I refer to ethical considerations in qualitative research and in case study research specifically. For example, I discussed ethical issues connected with Wolcott's (1994, 2002) study of Brad and its aftermath. Another case more closely connected with applied linguistics that was retrospectively scrutinized in terms of its legal, ethical, and scientific standards was that of Genie, studied by Curtiss (1977) and her colleagues. The case study received that degree of attention and publicity because not only had Genie's L1 not developed as hoped (see Chapter 2), but also there were other unforeseen consequences of the study:

- A series of disastrous foster placements for Genie, eventually leading to placement in a home for mentally challenged adults
- Her regression to the point of refusing to speak for months at a time
- Legal action taken against the original research team for allegedly excessive and invasive experimentation, testing, and exploitation, among other claims
- A television documentary detailing the promise, tragedy, and ethical dilemmas in the case
- Genie's enforced separation from Curtiss, who had been most devoted to her, professionally and personally, for so many years (Rymer, 1993)

Fortunately, most case study participants and researchers do not meet with such an unhappy fate.

Because ethical considerations are so closely connected with research design and data collection decisions, they are included in this chapter. I discuss the treatment of research ethics in our field in recent years, the role of institutional review boards (IRBs), whose job it is to review proposed research, and particular concerns in case study research and how to address them.

Within the biomedical, social science, humanities, and education fields, issues of ethical conduct by researchers or, in the absence of appropriate conduct or procedures, litigation, have surfaced in recent years. Reflecting the seriousness of the topic are entire books on research ethics (e.g., Kimmel, 1996) and sections and chapters of general education research methodology textbooks devoted to the subject (e.g., Christians, 2000; Cohen & Manion, 1994; Denzin & Lincoln, 2005b; Fraenkel & Wallen, 1996; Gall *et al.*, 1996; LeCompte, Millroy, & Preissle, 1992; Neuman, 1994; Punch, 1994). Surprisingly, however, one of the most cited case study methodologists (Yin, 2003a) does not have a section on ethics, nor is it listed in his subject index; Merriam (1998), another respected case study specialist, does address the issue.

Until the mid-1990s there was relatively little mention of research ethics in applied linguistics.[1] Mackey and Gass (2005) provide the most comprehensive guidance about research ethics among current applied linguistics (L2) research methodology textbooks, devoting an entire chapter to the topic, paying particular attention to L2 research, and appending numerous sample IRB review application documents.

Times have certainly changed with respect to the care and attention paid to research ethics in applied linguistics. Some journals now provide informed consent guidelines for contributors (e.g., at the back of each issue of the *TESOL Quarterly*), originally drafted out of concern for potential legal actions. The journal requires authors to indicate whether they have complied with

---

1   Research methods textbooks for L2 research by Hatch and Lazaraton (1991), Nunan (1992), and Brown and Rodgers (2002) do not include sections on research ethics or list ethics or ethical considerations in their subject indexes. Johnson (1992) made passing reference to ethical issues in experimental research or where teachers may feel coerced to participate in university-based research. Seliger and Shohamy (1989) devote a section (about a page and a half) to a discussion of ethical considerations in collecting research data (pp. 195–197). McKay (2006) also devotes several pages to "ethical research" in L2 classroom research. Ortega's (2005) special issue of the *Modern Language Journal* broaches broader issues of ethics in research on instructed SLA, though less in relation to methods and informed consent. Finally, Richards (2003) discusses ethics too, but mainly in connection with observation. See also Cameron, Frazer, Harvey, Rampton, and Richardson (1992) and Dufon (1993).

institutional human subjects review procedures or, for those not bound by such ethical review processes at their institutions (particularly outside of Canada and the United States), how they have complied with important principles of informed consent, including obtaining written consent to publish student work or obtaining parental consent for minors under age 18 to participate, and providing accessible, written L1 explanations for those whose English (L2) or intellectual abilities may make it difficult for them to understand explanations (see, e.g., *TESOL Quarterly*, *39*, 138–139). Many academic associations also publish ethical "best practice" guidelines for their members to voluntarily uphold.

Regardless of rules or guidelines that a researcher's institution, funders, or journal editors may have regarding research ethics, there must be an overriding commitment among researchers to protect the well-being of their research participants and respect their confidentiality, privacy, safety, and other legal and human rights. The "do no harm" (or "minimize risk") principle should be observed, and not just because a disgruntled participant might otherwise end up launching a lawsuit.

Most research-intensive Canadian and American universities have institutional review boards (IRBs) whose mandate is to promote ethical research and protect researchers (including students) who have followed guidelines appropriately, as well as to protect research participants themselves. These bodies also need to protect their institutions from expensive and ugly litigation and bad publicity, which may have serious ramifications for other researchers as well, leading, for example, to a sweeping moratorium on research in the city's or state's schools. The operationalization of such policies varies from campus to campus, however, although there is perhaps more consistency across Canadian universities, which have developed guidelines with major input from three national research (funding) agencies. For that reason, the requirements or procedures I associate with my own university in this section are likely shared by other Canadian universities.

In general, procedures of informed consent involve explaining, in writing, to potential participants what the study entails, who the researchers are, and how they or their supervisors or research officers can be contacted. The researchers must explain what the study is about, what the procedures or methods are, how much time is required, what risks or benefits are entailed in participating, how privacy or confidentiality (anonymity) will be ensured, what recourse participants have if they have any concerns (i.e., a third party they can contact, such as the director of the IRB), and what compensation or payment they will receive for participation, if any. There must be clear statements to the effect that participation is completely voluntary and that they may withdraw from the study at any point without negative repercussions. Also, it is common to state that participants may seek summaries of the results of the study afterward if they wish (see, e.g., UBC, 2006a). For IRBs, this information and additional documentation are usually needed: copies of questionnaires and observation or interview protocols, written permissions from agencies or authorities where research will be conducted, if needed, and a more detailed presentation of research purpose, methods/procedures, and sampling. If research participants who do not understand English or are not literate are recruited, additional measures must be taken to ensure that documents are translated into the participants' own languages or are comprehensible to them.

Normally (at my university), prospective participants are not supposed to be recruited initially by telephone, though exceptions can be made if this approach is well justified, as in telephone surveys. Furthermore, people who are asked to participate in most types of research are not required to respond immediately about their willingness to participate in other kinds of research, such as questionnaires. They must be given sufficient time (e.g., a day or more) to review the written documents and seek clarification or advice from others if needed, before signing and agreeing to participate.

The process of gaining approval from IRBs to conduct research, whether for student term papers, theses, or research by others, can take significant lead time, so it is important to plan ahead to prepare necessary documents carefully and submit them in a timely manner so that the research is not delayed. Preparing for ethical review actually has the advantage of forcing researchers to be as explicit and refined in their methods and instrumentation as possible, well in advance of commencing the study. Some universities now also require that faculty and students complete tutorials on ethical research practice before submitting requests for IRB approval. At my university, the review process from submission to notification of approval may take one to two months, although during vacation periods it may be slower. Fortunately, under pressure from those conducting research involving minimal risks outside of the life sciences, it is now possible to seek expedited reviews. A nonvideotaped interview-based study with consenting adults of the sort that is common in case studies (UBC, 2006a) would fall under this category. Such reviews may still take several weeks and require similar sorts of documentation and preparation, but they do not require full assembly and review of the entire IRB, or as many copies of applications. Research involving the following elements must still go through a review of the complete board (UBC, 2006a):

- Research on sensitive topics that could cause distress to research subjects/participants
- Action research
- Deception
- Focus groups
- Recruitment via telephone
- Database linkage where personal identifiers are used to probabilistically link one or more existing databases with new databases or surveys
- Plans to use oral consent or passive consent
- Inclusion of research subjects/participants who are less than 19 years of age
- Inclusion of research subjects/participants who are unable to be fully informed, such as those with mental disabilities or dementia
- Videotaping

Some forms of research that might seem quite straightforward and uncontroversial, such as autobiographical or biographical research, must now (at my university) go through ethical review as well—again, to protect people who might be identifiable by association with the focal cases.

Many teachers or other practitioners seek to conduct research in their own classrooms or other institutional contexts about the effectiveness of certain innovations they introduce. This is known as action research. They choose their own professional sites because of easy access and their intimate understanding of contextual factors. They may feel they have credibility and accountability within their own work contexts and rapport with students, parents, colleagues, or other participants. However, ethical review boards increasingly seem to frown upon action research carried out in one's own classes because it might be construed by potential research participants (e.g., students or employees) as coercive. These individuals may fear certain negative consequences—that their grades or status will suffer if they do not agree to participate or that they will miss out on better instruction—even with formal assurances to the contrary (e.g., UBC, 2006b). Steps must therefore be taken to assure concerned parties that students (parents) are indeed free to *not* participate without penalty. Elsewhere I have discussed ethical issues in classroom research in terms of both protections that should be in place for participants and the constraining effect that overly stringent procedures are having on certain kinds of research, which are becoming increasingly difficult to conduct (e.g., video-taped classroom research with minors, for purposes of discourse analysis) (e.g., Duff & Early, 1996; Duff, 2005).

Next I consider special issues related to ethics in case study research specifically. A small number of cases are involved in case study. This means that (1) the individuals' behaviors and lives will be analyzed quite extensively, and their privacy, welfare, and confidentiality concerns must be carefully taken into account, and (2) since participants are assured that they may withdraw themselves (and their data) from studies at any time without negative consequences, potential attrition in cases poses a great risk to the researcher who has invested heavily in such a study.

Regarding the first point, a high degree of trust must be cultivated between researcher and researched, and the former must take pains to withhold incriminating or clearly identifiable information (unless the incriminating behavior is also unlawful and reportable, such as child abuse). In some instances, this principle may require that certain nonkey details are omitted or altered. Simply using pseudonyms for people or places may not be sufficient to disguise their true identity (Duff & Early, 1996). Reporting findings honestly, accurately, and *responsibly* is the ethical duty of researchers.

Although most applied linguistics research is quite benign, critical research, in which particular cases may be singled out for criticism based on social justice concerns (oppressive or unfair practices), must tread very carefully so as not to be deemed libelous, slanderous, embarrassing, mean spirited or in violation of good-faith (trust) agreements between the researcher and participants (Duff, 2005).[1]

Regarding attrition in case studies, some strategies can help to keep participants engaged. Clear lines of communication are essential. Researchers must also be reasonable, flexible, and aware of any discomfort participants may be experiencing as a result of the study (e.g., by self-disclosures or

---

1   UBC (2006a) guidelines (19.8) follow: "If any subjects in an experimental setting, which is videotaped, decline to participate, researchers must take extra care to protect the rights of non-participants. On the one hand, it is unfair to require non-participants to sit outside camera range if this also excludes them from participating in the activity or marginalizes them in some other way. On the other hand, subjects' rights not to take part in the research must be respected. In any case, electronically distorting the facial features of non-participants does not honor the subject's wish not to participate. It is not a matter of non-identification but a matter of non-participation."

inability to perform as well as desired). Because a case study participant often dedicates a great deal of time to a project, involving multiple observations or interviews, especially in longitudinal research, it is wise to think of incentives or rewards for participation—not to coerce ongoing participation but to encourage or reward it. This practice is a form of reciprocity, the principle that both parties, researcher and researched, should gain from the enterprise. Although we may believe that participating in research has its own intrinsic benefits for participants (e.g., reflecting on their language use), more tangible compensation may also be warranted (see Section 4.7). Sharing the results may be compensation enough for some people, but there are other forms of reciprocity. I generally pay focal participants (such as Jim, Chapter 1) for their time or offer them gift certificates to local bookstores, music stores, or drugstores (depending on the study and population), often worth about $10 for each hour of a participant's time in the study. In studies involving considerable input and collaboration from teachers over time, I have been able to offer cash honoraria (e.g., $100 to $300). Other small gifts or services may also be rendered in the spirit of ongoing cooperation. My own university IRB now discourages offering generous gifts (e.g., more than $10/hour for interviews with student participants), citing this practice as coercive; they also require that compensation *not* be withheld until the end of the study, which is also considered coercive. In a study with several scheduled interviews during the year, for example, incentives must be given at the first interview meeting and not postponed, or even prorated based on interviews up to and including the final one. Thus, permissible incentives to keep participants involved in a study for its duration are somewhat limited, which is a concern in longitudinal case studies and a source of growing frustration to researchers.

A final area of research ethics is related to integrity in reporting and publishing research (see Chapter 6)—being fair minded and balanced in one's interpretations, being sensitive to possible unintended consequences of the research to the extent that these can be anticipated, and not flooding publications with exactly the same study content (and certainly not submitting the same works for review at the same time). It is of utmost importance to take measures to protect the cases we do research about or report on from harm or risk resulting from their involvement in the study, from the publication of results, or even from unforeseen interpretations and applications of research that may have negative and unintended consequences (Davidson, 1993). However, it is difficult to know how much responsibility researchers share with those who might use our results for their own "political agendas, to prove a point, or to justify unethical policies" (Shohamy, 2004, p. 730).[1]

4.15 Summary

This chapter has discussed how to conduct case studies by focusing on the initial conceptualizing and planning phases. In order to undertake any research, one's goals and research questions should be as clear as possible from the outset, although these may evolve over time as the case study progresses and new questions arise or as unexpected developments occur. The underlying constructs should be clear, although one of the contributions of the study may be to refine or revise these constructs. One of the most important early decisions the researcher must make is connected with the research design: whether the case study will be embedded within a larger study (e.g., one using mixed methods), whether a single case or multiple cases will be included and how cases will be selected or sampled, what the units of analysis will be, and what kinds and sources of data will be collected, and by what means. In the following chapter, we consider what to do once the data have been collected and examine approaches to data transcription, data analysis and representation, and criteria for evaluating case studies.

---

1   Shohamy gives an example of the Israeli Ministry of Education's misinterpretation of research she and her colleagues had done on Ethiopian immigrants and their academic achievement in Israeli schools. She laments: "Nothing in the research suggested any causal relationship between the number of Ethiopian immigrant students in schools and the schools' or students' levels of achievement; yet, the ministry interpreted the results as such" (p. 730). The fallout was that the number of Ethiopian students in schools was limited afterwards and students were transferred to other schools with better achievement profiles, a policy Shohamy criticized for being discriminatory and unethical.

CHAPTER 5

How to Conduct Case Studies (Part 2)
Analysis, Interpretation, and Evaluation

5.1 Introduction

This chapter builds on the previous one by describing how to analyze and interpret case study data and how to evaluate studies. I provide some of the basic principles of case study data analysis and illustrate them with some examples. It should be remembered, however, that many kinds of case study are carried out in applied linguistics—drawing upon methods in anthropology, sociology, psychology, linguistics, or related disciplines. The primary focus in some case studies is a structural analysis of patterns of linguistic development or use, as in my original analysis of Jim's L2 English production (see Chapter 1). In other studies, the goal is to understand or interpret the experiences and dilemmas of participants, such as teachers (e.g., Duff & Uchida, 1997) in light of various sociopolitical and other contextual factors. Thus, case study data analysis cannot assume a one-size-fits-all approach, although most have some elements of description, understanding/interpretation, and explanation. The units of analysis and degrees or types of triangulation can also vary greatly across types of case study. Therefore, they need to be consistent with the source (sub)disciplines and the goals of the research project itself.

5.2 Transcription

Although transcription might seem to be a very mechanical process of rendering oral data into a printed text that can be more easily analyzed at some later point, in qualitative research it is usually considered (1) an integral and important initial phase of data analysis, especially if the person transcribing (the researcher or research assistant) is also involved in the analysis and is able to make note of recurring patterns or other observations while transcribing; and (2) an activity that is very theory laden (Ochs, 1979). In this section, I describe different approaches to transcription and provide examples of transcription conventions or protocols. I also consider the role of transcription in the analytic or interpretive process.

Although many case studies involve data that must be transcribed, not all do. For example, studies of L2 writing development, Internet chat discourse, L2 diaries, or a country's language policies may not incorporate primarily oral data into the analysis. However, a great deal of applied linguistics research does involve the analysis of either oral raw data (e.g., speech samples or classroom interactions) or oral reflections on experiences (e.g., think-aloud protocols, introspective studies or stimulated recall, or interviews). Most of this interview and observation data is, in turn, transcribed, although not necessarily to the same degree of sophistication or detail across all studies.

Transcription is an art and science and also encapsulates theory. Like video-recording (where the camera is placed, what is captured, and how), transcribing is not theoretically neutral, and the various conventions that have been developed for transcription and the decisions researchers make while transcribing have their own epistemological precursors and interpretive consequences (Green, Franquiz, & Dixon, 1997; Markee, 2000; Ochs, 1979; Roberts, 1997). Transcription must therefore be seen as theory driven and theory saturated (Silverman, 2000). The conventions used in transcribing and the level of detail included also depend on what one is studying and the theoretical perspectives implicit in the transcriptions.

In my studies, I have used different kinds of transcription showing varying amounts of detail for different purposes. If the purpose of interviews is to get information about an interviewee's educational background, for example, and not to do an analysis of turn-taking behaviors or language proficiency based on the interview, it is probably unnecessary to measure the length of all pauses with a stopwatch to the nearest 10th or 20th of a second. Nor would it be useful to include mundane nonverbal behaviors, such as eye gaze, nose scratching, or heavy breathing. There are three reasons for not providing such detail in those cases:

1. It is very labor expensive and costly; it takes up to 20 hours to transcribe 1 hour of data that does not involve too many speakers or overlap if done in a very finely tuned way, compared to 4 to 8 hours for a less detailed transcription (depending on the type of discourse).
2. Those behaviors are likely to provide little theoretically interesting information related to the subject's education background.
3. When reporting the findings later, a very fine tuned transcription can interfere with readability, especially if all that is wanted is a brief description of the person's prior training, language instruction, degrees, and so on.

The same pragmatic principle can also be applied to how one provides glosses or translations for interviews or observations when multiple languages are present. If a linguistic analysis is planned, it may be crucial to provide a gloss for each language item (word, particle, or morpheme) and then a more holistic translation. If one is more interested in the gist of the utterance and less so in the linguistic detail, then an utterance-by-utterance or turn-by-turn translation will probably suffice. If, on the other hand, one is conducting a conversation analysis (CA) of a short recorded segment, a detailed transcription would normally be called for, using highly conventionalized procedures associated with CA (Markee, 2000).

In my study of Jim (see Chapter 1), exact pause length was not particularly important to me in some of my analyses. I therefore used a crude system of showing pauses with plus signs (+ represented a short pause and ++ a slightly longer pause), instead of timing micropauses (e.g., (0.2) for 2/10 of a second). In my initial transcription of the first 12 hours of data, it was simply not feasible to transcribe with more detail. But in Chapter 1, when I wanted to show how unforthcoming and seemingly disfluent Jim was on the second retelling of the same picture task (Excerpt 3), and the pause lengths were so painfully long, it seemed important and relevant to quantify the pauses.

A highly technical phonetic transcription is important in intended phonetic or phonological analyses (as well as certain other kinds of analysis) but may be less significant, and much less readable, when transcripts are to be used for other kinds of analysis. For example, I could have represented the first line of Excerpt 6 in Chapter 1 as follows: *yeh biikaz aa in + kaembowdiian in tha kantriisai z now baen* ["Yeah because uh in Cambodia in the countryside there are no banks"] as I did in an appendix in Duff (1993a). This system was used by researchers in Hawaii (e.g., Huebner, 1983; Sato, 1984, 1990). However, it would have made the analysis and presentation of data more cumbersome than necessary for me and other readers.

In contrast to the conventions I used with Jim in Chapter 1, presenting monologic, monolingual excerpts (taken from dialogic interaction), in Table 5.1 I illustrate the transcription system used in Duff (1995) and in some subsequent studies. That analysis dealt with one Hungarian teacher's English immersion history class at a Hungarian high school. Kati, the teacher, was calling on a student, Gabi, to come up and give a presentation (lecture).

The transcription conventions used in this excerpt, which are quite commonly used by others as well, are shown in Table 5.2.

Transcripts involving extensive use of other languages may be organized differently, as in Table 5.3 from Duff (1993c), showing a teacher's instructions to students in Hungarian to get ready for a *felelés*, or recitation on Roman history. An utterance-by-utterance global translation is provided on the right, but word-by-word or morpheme-by-morpheme literal

Table 5.1 Transcription of Classroom Discourse

Kati:	A::nd on: - decree on peace - Gabi (1.2) can give a lecture.
Gabi:	Right now?
Kati:	Right now.
	(9.8) ((Gabi comes up to front))
	And perhaps: - for that - you ((to class)) might as well open the Atlas. (1.6)
	[Okay?
S:	[(xxx)
Gabi:	It's on - 49. Page 49. ((in student atlas))
	(3.9)
Kati:	49?
S:	*Miről fogsz beszélni,* Gabi? ((What are you going to talk about Gabi?))
Gabi:	I('ll) write it on the board.

(Duff, 1995, pp. 519–520)

Table 5.2 Sample Transcription Conventions

- Participants: T = teacher; S = student; SS = two students; SSS = many students. Initials used for students identifiable by name (e.g., M, SZ, J) rather than the generic "S".
- Left bracket, [: The beginning of overlapping speech, shown for both speakers; second speaker's bracket occurs at the beginning of the line of the next turn, rather than in alignment with previous speaker's bracket (for word processing reasons only; many people align the exact point of overlap, but the formatting can easily become misaligned).
- Equal sign: For "latched" utterances; indicates speech across turns without any pause or break; shown for both speakers.
- (#): Marks the length of a pause; (.2) is 2/10 of a second; (2.0) is 2 seconds.
- (Words): The words in parentheses were not clearly heard; (x) = unclear word; (xx) = two unclear words; (xxx) = three or more unclear words.
- Underlined (or italicized) words: Spoken with emphasis.
- CAPITAL LETTERS: Loud speech.
- Double parentheses, ((: Researcher's comments, like "laughs", "coughs", "T writes on board", etc.; relevant details pertaining to interaction, or gloss for Hungarian when there is code-switching.
- Colon: Sound or syllable is unusually lengthened, e.g., rea::lly lo:ng.
- Period: Terminal falling intonation.
- Comma: Rising, continuing intonation.
- Question mark: High rising intonation, not necessarily at the end of a sentence.
- Unattached dash (-): A short, untimed pause (e.g., less than 0.2 seconds). In some transcripts, the same as plus sign (+).
- One-sided attached dash-: A cutoff, often accompanied by a glottal stop (e.g., a self-correction); a dash attached on both sides reflects spelling conventions or a glottal stop.
- Arrow: Flags something in the interaction to which the author is drawing attention.
- Numbering of lines: May also be used to facilitate reference to particular segments of discourse.

---

translations or glosses are not included because a syntactic analysis was not intended.

Sometimes journal or book editors will also ask for different kinds of transcription than the one provided. For example, in a book chapter I wrote about Hungarian classroom discourse, I was asked to take out the Hungarian (L1) and present only the translated talk in English for reasons of space (Duff, 1996). In other articles, I have been asked to take out certain kinds of redundancy in interview excerpts, such as false starts, repetitions, and so on, to enhance readability and to also shorten the excerpts, particularly since the

Table 5.3 Example of a Transcript in Another Language (Hungarian)

T: Na. Kérem szépen. Mindenféle gyönyör ség lesz ma. Nem biztos, hogy err l a rómaiak is így vélekedte:k. (8.0) Na kérem szépen. Könyveket becsukni (2.0), ((Ss close books)) füzetet is (4.0) Kicsit gyorsabban ...	Now then. There are going to be various kinds of fun things today. I'm not sure if the Romans thought the same. (8.0) Now then. Close your textbooks (2.0), ((Ss close books)) exercise books too (4.0) A bit more quickly...

Source: Duff (1993c, p. 183)

purpose of including the excerpts was to provide the content and include the voice of the interviewee. Formal properties of the talk were not of primary interest (e.g., Duff, 2001).

Transcription is a laborious and time-consuming task. It is therefore important to fully consider one's options and also the expectations of the field or domain in which one is working before collecting data. Also, the traditions that have developed for the preparation of transcripts for different kinds of discourse analysis have generally been carefully considered. If claiming to do a conversation analysis of case study interviews or observed interactions, then be sure to comply with the conventions established for that approach (Markee, 2000). If a more general discourse analysis is planned, then see what other options there are, how others have proceeded, and what conventions, analytic tools, and techniques they have used. Also, consider how the reader will react to the readability or clarity of excerpts.

It is therefore helpful and often necessary to use established transcription procedures when working within a particular tradition and research community. However, you can also develop new conventions if existing ones are inadequate for your purposes, but you must provide a key or appendix with the codes or conventions and then apply them consistently. Another word of advice is to have someone else (possibly the speakers themselves) listen to key excerpts you have transcribed to verify your interpretation of their utterances and the reliability of your transcript. For other examples and discussion of transcription, see Markee (2000), Richards (2003), Silverman (2001), and van Lier (1988).

On a very practical note, various kinds of tools exist for transcribing cassette tapes, such as conventional transcriber playback machines with foot pedals to easily replay an utterance and with voice speed controls and headphones to free up hands for typing. Some of my students have also successfully used voice recognition software, trained to their own voices, to revoice what they hear on recordings for easier (oral) inputting of data; this approach is especially suitable for content-based interviews with long stretches of interviewee talk. More applied linguists now also use digital recorders or digitized analog audio- or video-recordings to facilitate transcription, data management, and coding. Having digitized audio-video data facilitates the alignment of sound/video files and digitized transcripts when one event has been recorded; furthermore, it allows the alignment of data from multiple concurrently occurring events that have been recorded, when several groups are doing group work at the same time, for example. Having digitized files also permits the inclusion of audio and video tracks together with transcripts in digital presentations using PowerPoint or comparable programs. Some of these research tools can be downloaded free from the Web, such as SoundWriter from the University of California, Santa Barbara (http://www.linguistics.ucsb. edu/projects/transcription/tools.html).

5.3 Data Analysis

Many methodology textbooks and articles explore qualitative analysis in greater depth than I can here, and also differentiate among analytic techniques in various types of case studies (see, e.g., Bogdan & Biklen, 2003; Bromley, 1986; Bryman, 2004; Gall *et al.*, 2003; Merriam, 1998; Miles & Huberman, 1994; Patton, 1990; Silverman, 2000, 2001, 2004; Strauss & Corbin, 1998; Tesch, 1990; Wolcott, 1994; Yin, 2003a). In addition, Ellis and Barkhuizen (2005) present a recent overview of approaches to analyzing L2 learners' language, with many examples, using frequency analysis, functional analysis, interaction analysis, conversation analysis, sociocultural analysis, and critical analysis. Readers should become familiar with as many relevant applied linguistics case studies in their area as possible, examining the data analysis, chains of evidence, conclusions, and presentation techniques used especially.

In general though, qualitative case studies are increasingly associated with *iterative, cyclical,* or *inductive* data analysis, terms that are interrelated. From the earliest data collection and transcription stages, as noted above, data analysis is already taking place. Researchers may produce short (e.g., one-paragraph or one-page) summaries of an observation, interview, or document

149

highlighting the most salient points and themes, noticing things that may prove important in subsequent data collection. This kind of summary document is called a contact summary sheet; document summary sheets can be used in the same way. A salient point might be a statement, based on an interview with a principal, like "Teachers vary in their willingness to integrate special education students…". A theme is a short code word or phrase like *resistance* (Miles & Huberman, 1994, p. 54). Other examples of codes that might be used in some kinds of analysis in our field, especially related to L2 learning, are *motivation*, *anxiety*, *access*, and *agency*. The code may therefore be a theoretical construct, like motivation. Questions the researcher might ask when coding are "Of what general category is this item of data an instance?" or, basically, "What is happening here?" (Bryman, 2004, p. 408). Over time and with further analysis, codes or categories may change; they may be added, deleted, merged, or fine-tuned, and may also be linked to themes in existing research literature. Brice (2005) gives a firsthand, illustrated account of the process of coding qualitative L2 writing data and suggestions about how others might avoid some of the same troubles she encountered. Traditionally, coding involved colored pens and cutting and pasting chunks of data to flag noteworthy elements on documents and transcripts. While manual coding is still common, especially for novice researchers, technology offers many helpful tools to assist with this task (see following section).

Although qualitative data analysis is typically inductive and data driven, the codes may also be anticipated before analyzing the data (a priori codes), given the topic of the study, the research questions, and the issues likely to be encountered. Codes are very helpful in computer-assisted data management and analysis because similarly coded items can be sorted, retrieved, and reviewed easily. Miles and Huberman (1994) provide an extended discussion of different kinds of coding used throughout the process of data analysis and the importance of having an overall conceptual structure in generating codes. They also provide many concrete examples. They suggest that researchers seek patterns or associations among their coded elements once that stage has been completed. These *pattern codes* are less descriptive and more inferential and explanatory—related to apparent "rules" observed (e.g., "Don't talk about problems"), more general themes (e.g., "The immigrant participants feel powerless"), or explanations ("Attending extra language classes leads to success"). These pattern codes facilitate data reduction, the development of conceptual/

cognitive maps or schemas, and the basis for later cross-case analysis in multiple-case studies.

With a structured and coded linguistic or interactional analysis, the codes are likely related to the syntactic or discursive categories of items (e.g., *existential* vs. *possessive*, *topic marker*, *topic-comment*, etc. (Chapter 1)); or aspectual categories for verbs, such as *activity, accomplishment,* or *achievement,* used in studies of developing tense-aspect systems (e.g., Salaberry & Shirai, 2002). In classroom research, coding may also occur on various levels, for example, identifying the types of speech events or activities in different phases of a lesson or labeling different speech acts or moves, such as questions (directives or initiations), responses, and evaluation moves.

In my analysis of a speech event in Hungary known as the *felelés* (from the verb *felelni,* to answer or give an account), which is a kind of in-class recitation of the previous day's lesson, I analyzed the various phases of the lesson first, leading up to and following the *felelés,* and then analyzed the different phases of the *felelés* itself: the pre-*felelés* (six typical components), the *felelés* proper (three components), and the post-*felelés* phase (seven components) (Duff, 1993c; see Table 5.4). In coding, I used the shorthand codes PREFEL-1, FEL-3, POSTFEL-2, and so on, to look for patterns and variation in the speech event as enacted and negotiated within and across contexts.[1]

Interview and classroom transcripts then revealed the perspectives of teachers and students with respect to this traditional activity and the emerging new activities replacing it across three schools (Duff, 1995).

With narrative inquiry and analysis, in which coherent accounts of one's experiences may be sought, coding may not be used as much as in the highly structured approach just described (Bryman, 2004). However, regardless of the analytic procedures (inductive or interpretational analysis, grounded theory, narrative analysis, or structural analysis of the type used in linguistic and discourse analysis), the researcher must find ways of making sense of the various themes, accounts, or structures, or the relationships among them. The researcher must then be able to interpret them,

---

1   IRE (see Table 5.4) refers to initiation-response-evaluation question-answer sequences between the teacher and students.

Table 5.4 Coding Hungarian *Felelés* (Recitation) Components

Pre-*felelés*	*Felelés*	Post-*felelés*
1. Directive for students (Ss) to close books	1. Recitation • Uninterrupted spate of talk by S • IRE related to recitation (T-S-T)	1. Teacher (T) (or S) signals end of *felelés*
2. Warm-up question-answer period (IRE)		2. T thanks S
3. Statement of topic		3. T comments on S's performance
4. Selection of student (nomination)	2. Map quiz-IRE related to map (T/class-S-T)	4. T invites other Ss' comments; Ss' uptake
5. Specification of audience design	3. Other quizzing (names and dates) -IRE (T/class-S-T)	5. A number grade or adjective is assigned or deferred
6. Specification of *felelés* criteria		6. T records grade in grade book and closes it
		7. New lesson topic is introduced; Ss open books

Source: Duff (1993c, p. 169)

drawing inferences as appropriate, and report on them in a coherent and compelling manner (see Figure 4.1). Furthermore, in multiple-case studies researchers must determine the generality of the identified themes across cases. The connections between the findings and "theory" should also be explored. Miles and Huberman (1994) are strong proponents of visual displays of themes and relationships emerging from the data from the earliest stages of analysis, using mapping techniques, tables or charts (e.g., matrices), flowcharts, event-flow networks, tree diagrams, and other organizers.

Wolcott (1994) suggests that researchers should think in a finish-to-start manner, already anticipating, before even conducting the study, what form the final report will take and what the main emphasis will be. In a multiple-case study produced for a dissertation, students should consider in advance the likely overall structure of the dissertation, whether they will devote an entire chapter or section to each case or, rather, will choose emerging themes as the main organizers. Usually a detailed description of the cases, or *thick description*, is produced (Geertz, 1973), but more focused analyses may also be conducted.

When the fieldwork is over and any transcription is completed, the major analytic work begins. The researcher goes through the reams of amassed data (e.g., documents, fieldnotes, and transcripts) on multiple occasions as the analysis and interpretations evolve and as theory and data are linked. The result of this process is the identification of salient patterns, themes, clusters, or critical incidents that can then be discussed and interpreted in the report. Some case studies may seek meaningful metaphors or descriptors as a way of capturing themes creatively or to characterize contrasts across cases (e.g., "the silent observer", "the gregarious gatekeeper"). Analytic induction also requires that any inconsistent evidence or rival explanations or counter-examples also be dealt with.

Some kinds of data and analyses may involve coding using highly inferential categories involving a fair amount of judgment, subjectivity, or rich interpretation on the part of coders. In that case, coder checks, a kind of reliability to establish the consistency of coding, may be useful. This can by done by extracting potentially problematic portions of the data to be checked or randomly selected portions from the entire data set and, after training a colleague or research assistant using the coding scheme or categories you have adopted, seeing whether you reach agreement on coding decisions. This approach to establishing reliability or credibility is not as common in interpretive qualitative research as in positivist work, however.

As noted earlier, a variety of graphic organizers can also present in a distilled, compacted form the main features of cases (see Lynch, 1996, for examples from a language program evaluation). Although quantification is not centrally associated with qualitative research, it may be helpful to use descriptive statistics, graphics, and other forms of quantification to reduce data, show trends, and establish the strength of measurable differences between observations (if those are sought or found). A narrative or expository account of relationships, interactions, or other findings should also be provided.

Finally, the researcher needs to draw conclusions about the data and verify those conclusions based on the patterns that emerged. These conclusions need to be plausible and coherent and well supported by evidence. The representativeness of findings (and existence of exceptions or rival explanations, if any) should also be stated. Member checks (see below), feedback from participants, may also corroborate conclusions.

5.3.1 Cross-Case Analysis

In single-case studies (also called within-case analyses), researchers proceed to analyze data as outlined in the previous section. However, in multiple-case studies, they need to first analyze the individual cases and then conduct a comparative cross-case or collective analysis (e.g., Duff, 1993c; Duff & Uchida,

1997). For example, Duff and Uchida (1997) provided a general comparison of the four EFL teachers in Japan in their study after describing each one separately:

> None of the teachers in this study perceived their role as EFL teachers as necessarily involving the explicit teaching of cultural content, although the course description did mention that objective. However, in their observed practices and materials, implicit cultural transmission was evident. Danny emphasized sociopolitical issues and popular (U.S.) cultural media. Carol sought to foster autonomous learning by using communicative EFL teaching methods from American and British TEFL programs and publications, although she preferred Japanese themes during discussions. Miki's classes were largely structured around the interactive activities suggested in the textbook, including a game each lesson, and she attempted to bridge the cultural gap between Japanese high school EFL teaching and [their institution]. Finally, Kimiko engaged students in discussions of current, meaningful topics and had them express their personal opinions through public speaking activities. (p. 467)

We then examined them as a set in terms of two overriding themes affecting their approaches to teaching language and culture: a biographical/professional basis and a contextual basis.

Antonek *et al.*'s (2000) mixed-method program evaluation involved a cross-case analysis of six learners of Japanese, three of whom were intermediate and three novice. After describing the larger sample and then each of the six children, including information about their language proficiency, attitudes, and their results on the various measures of proficiency, the researchers examined the learners by subgroup (intermediate and novice). What follows is an excerpt from the cross-case analysis for the novice students and their seemingly paradoxical, inconsistent results. The focus here is their attitudes toward the Japanese language/culture, based on questionnaires and interviews:

> For the novice learners, the ratio of desirable to total responses is consistent across the novice learners (10/15 for Mallory and Isabel and 9/15 for Laurie). However, their attitude profiles are not as in "sync" as those of their intermediate counterparts. As examples, recall that while Mallory found Japanese boring, she would like to have the opportunity to study Japanese in the next school year. Isabel

reported not liking Japanese but wanting to learn a lot of foreign languages. Isabel enjoys speaking Japanese in class yet does not want to meet other Japanese speaking individuals. Isabel, like Mallory, responds negatively on two of the three categories comprising the parental support construct, leading us to conclude, therefore, that their parents are not as supportive as the other parents.

From examining these six students' attitudinal data, we have learned that certain positive responses are not linked categorically to high levels of proficiency—for example, wanting to learn other languages, wanting to speak in class, wanting to meet Japanese people. One could conceivably answer "no" to all these questions, as was the case with Lilly, and still be a very successful student. (pp. 346–347)

Cross-case analysis can also refer to the analysis of case studies conducted by different researchers (e.g., at different project sites) for commonalities, differences, and major themes. One such example was Burton's (1998) cross-case analysis of six funded Australian language education research projects involving teacher collaboration and action research. The cases were the research projects themselves. The projects had been conducted over a 10-year period in five sites, and Burton had been involved in all of them. She used a number of criteria to analyze the success of each project (e.g., revelation, robustness, reflection, reliability) and then ranked each one accordingly for each criterion on a scale of 1 (lowest) to 4 (highest).

I have ranked the NCP [National Curriculum Project] (1.1) first, reflecting my preference for research methodologies that include teachers as researchers and facilitate learning and development during the process of a project. The Desert Schools Project (3) scored one 4 amid mainly 1s and 2s because the national research management processes and political climate neither encouraged collaboration nor allowed for wide dissemination. The Languages Australia research nodes (Project 2) and the Thai EFL courses (Project 4) had relatively low scores because of low system sustainability outside the funded contexts or duration of the projects. The ALL [Australian Language Levels] project (1.2) fell in the middle position, because the research products failed to meet the expectations of many teachers for whom they were intended. In-service teacher education (Project 5) scored relatively highly because of its sustainability and facility for dissemination. (pp. 437–438)

A summary of the cross-case analysis outcomes is found in Table 5.5. (Her rating and ranking figures appeared separately.)

Tables and figures contrasting the different cases (or studies) can be very helpful for the purpose of comparing cases such as these (see other examples in Miles & Huberman, 1994). Different typologies of projects (e.g., most successful to least successful) with associated features could also be generated and graphically displayed.

Table 5.5 Example of a Cross-Case Analysis of Six Research Projects

Project	Outcome	Dissemination and Uptake
1.1. National Curriculum Project	Teaching products requiring supporting process	Wide during project; some dissemination of process after project; project model used for other contexts
1.2. Australian Language Levels project	Explicit teaching products requiring minimal supporting process	Limited adaptation possible during project; products capable of easy, wide dissemination after project
2. Languages Australia research nodes	Teaching support process with minimal products	Few products; little tangible dissemination beyond context members
3. Desert Schools Project	Research report	Publication with limited contexts of circulation
4. Thai EFL courses	Students enrolled in postgraduate study program	Decontextualised experience; teachers may not relate it to their own work context
5. In-service teacher education	Continuing teacher in-service education process; teaching products through assignments	Dissemination and communication across research, teacher education, and teaching contexts

Source: Burton, J., *TESOL Quarterly*, 32, p. 437, 1998. Published by Teachers of English to Speakers of Other Languages, Inc. This work is protected by copyright and it is being used with permission of Access Copyright. Any alteration of its content or further copying in any form whatsoever is strictly prohibited.

5.3.2 Some Examples of Data Analysis Procedures

In this section I provide detailed examples of data collection and analysis procedures reported by Leki (1995, 2001) and Morita (2004). First, in her study of nonnative English speakers' roles in group work connected with mainstream university course work, Leki (2001) sought answers to the following general research question: "What are the experiences of a group of NNES students in evaluated group work across the curriculum in higher education?" (p. 43). She provided a contextualization of the study by describing the American university at which the research took place, the demographics, and the backgrounds of her six focal participants. Next she described her data collection as follows:

> Data for this research, collected over the course of 5 years, consisted of complete transcriptions of in-depth weekly or biweekly interviews with the six NNES [non-native English speaking] students; fieldnotes of observations of their classes (from a minimum of one observation for some classes to weekly observations in others); transcriptions of interviews with their professors; documents given to them in classes, including syllabuses and course handouts; and their written work, including early drafts, for these classes. The varied data sources were intended to ensure data triangulation, though this report focuses primarily on findings from interview and observational data. (pp. 44–45)

With respect to her interviews, Leki notes that participants were asked open-ended questions about their lived experiences, according to a guide sheet, which she included in an appendix. Topics included their course work and educational life. Examples of questions from her interview guide follow:

- What are you working on now or what will you be working on in the next two weeks in each of your courses?
- Why do you think your teacher gave you this particular kind of assignment to do? (What is the professor's purpose in assigning it? What does the professor want you to learn from it or get out of it?)
- How is your group project going?
- How have you divided up the work? What part did you do/work on? When, where, how did you meet to work on the project? (p. 67)

Leki then described her data analysis strategies before providing an in-depth analysis of two of the cases, Ling and Yang, in their geography and nursing classes, respectively:

Data analysis followed typical procedures for qualitative research (Goetz & LeCompte, 1984). Data were read reiteratively, with all instances of mention of group work collated out. Basic categories were generated through content analysis of the interview, observational, and documentary data that involved "comparing, contrasting, aggregating, and ordering" (Goetz & LeCompte, 1984, p. 171) the data with a view to discovering logical groupings and links among categories that would shed light on the students' overall experiences in these group projects. Because I was after insights into how these collaborative experiences worked, even single instances attracted attention. Student interview transcripts were thus analyzed for both recurring and particularly salient themes. Salient themes were those that occasioned the most (positively or negatively) fraught or agitated comments from the students. (pp. 45–46)

Leki had followed the same general procedures in an earlier multiple-case study (Leki, 1995), which focused on the challenges faced by three graduate and two undergraduate international (visa) students from Europe and Asia in their first semester at an American university. Of interest were the English writing requirements in their disciplinary courses across the curriculum and their coping strategies, as newcomers to the local academic culture. The data presented include well-rounded profiles of five focal students (the cases), followed by a description and discussion of 10 general themes (strategies) that surfaced across the five students' experiences, as well as differences among them. Nine short quotations or excerpts from the students' interviews, journals, or assignments were included from the corpus of transcribed data. Neither study included excerpts of classroom discourse.

Morita's (2004) inductive analysis of classroom and interview data of six Japanese university students in Canada proceeded very similarly:

Categories and themes emerged mainly from the collected data, and preliminary hypotheses about the settings and participants were grounded in direct experience at the research site (Marshall & Rossman, 1995; Strauss & Corbin, 1998). Weekly reports, interview transcripts, and fieldnotes were reviewed multiple times throughout the project and salient themes and tentative categories were generated. The categories developed during the data collection phase were mostly "folk categories" (Delamont, 1992, p. 150), reflecting directly on the participants' own language, concepts, and classification scheme (e.g., class atmosphere, lack of confidence, nervousness, not wanting to make mistakes, obligation to speak). After the data collection was completed and certain recurring themes were identified, more theoretical categories and constructs were generated both from the data and relevant literature, and patterns and relations between the categories were explored. Such categories included competent participation, classroom membership, legitimacy, identity negotiation, power negotiation, personal agency, and so on. Once the data were coded according to salient themes and categories, tentative hypotheses were developed about each individual student. These hypotheses were then tested against the data about the particular student obtained from different data sources and were confirmed, revised, or rejected (i.e., *within-case analysis*: Merriam, 1998). Comparing a given student's experiences in different courses was particularly informative. Emergent hypotheses were also tested across the individual students (i.e., *cross-case analysis*). (pp. 581–582)

To reiterate, the approach to data analysis will crucially depend on the type and scope of study to be conducted and the conceptual framework guiding it. For example, if the case is an excerpt of classroom talk to be analyzed in great detail using conversation analysis techniques, an entirely different set of procedures and conventions will apply (Lazaraton, 2003; Markee, 2000).

5.3.3 Computer-Assisted Qualitative Data Analysis Software (CAQDAS)

Although many case study researchers in applied linguistics still code, retrieve, and analyze data using conventional means (e.g., colored pens, codes, file cards, or regular word processing software), new technologies and software programs are more widely available now for data analysis by qualitative researchers (see Berg, 2004, 2007; Coffey & Atkinson, 1996; Denzin & Lincoln, 2003; Fielding & Lee, 1998; Merriam, 1998; Ritchie & Lewis, 2003; Silverman, 2004; Weitzman, 2003; Weitzman & Miles, 1995). These programs or tools are commonly referred to as Computer-Assisted Qualitative Data Analysis Software (CAQDAS). Perhaps best known are N6 (the latest version of NUD*IST—Non-numerical Unstructured Data—Indexing, Searching and Theorizing), Atlas.ti, NVivo, MAX-QDA, Qualrus, HyperRESEARCH, ETHNOGRAPH, and XSight. For a discussion of the advantages and disadvantages of using CAQDAS in L2 research, see Séror (2005).

Some of these programs (e.g., Atlas.ti) have an in-built architecture using semantic or conceptual networks that depict connections between categories of information (codes, nodes) and therefore have theory-building capacity and not just text management and code-and-retrieval functioning (Miles & Huberman, 1994; Weitzman, 2000). However, these systems are not theory neutral—they have implicit assumptions about the nature of data (e.g., hierarchical conceptual relationships) that might lead researchers to view data differently than if they examined it without the constraints of an established program.

Learning to use these tools can require a significant initial investment of time and money to ensure that the tools are used to their full potential. However, when used well, the programs not only manage and consolidate large sets of data, but organize them, store notes and memos, cluster and represent related items in a logical and easily retrievable manner, and enable analysts to find relevant data efficiently and consistently at all levels of analysis (Weitzman, 2000).

For Ritchie and Lewis (2003), the hallmarks of qualitative data analysis facilitated by CAQDAS are that the analysis is both grounded in the data and synthetic, permits within- and between-case searches, and provides systematic, comprehensive coverage of the data set, and researchers can be flexible in their analysis yet transparent with respect to their chains of evidence or reasoning.

Many of my own (former) graduate students (e.g., Morita, 2000; Séror, 2005) have successfully used one or another of these programs, but also encountered challenges initially. Over time and with more experience, they have found them to be quite helpful. Toohey (2001) also used CAQDAS in her multiple-case study of children's disputes in classroom language learning contexts. A general recommendation for case study researchers expecting to handle large amounts of data might be to consider using Atlas.ti or NVivo, which are becoming more user-friendly than before.

5.4 Member Checks

According to Gall *et al.* (2005), member checking is "a procedure used by qualitative researchers to check their reconstructions of the emic perspective by having field participants review statements in the researchers' report for accuracy and completeness" (p. 551). Participants read transcripts or written reports before they are published, and then researchers incorporate their feedback or corrections. Or they are consulted in a recurring way during the analysis. Member checks, also known as member/respondent validation (Bryman, 2004), can enrich an analysis, help ensure the authenticity or credibility of interpretations, or shed new light on the analyses. It therefore is another form of triangulation or verification of perspectives and interpretations.

As Hornberger (2006) notes, member checking should be about more than just establishing the credibility of interpretations; it also relates to issues of (authorial) authority, collaboration (between those researching and those researched), and representation: Who gets to speak for or represent whom, and how? What are participants' rights? Where are their voices?

Doing member checks, however, assumes that the research participants have cognitive and linguistic maturity, technical sophistication to understand some kinds of analysis, and sufficient language proficiency, time, and reflexivity to examine documents containing transcripts, analyses, interpretations, or draft reports. If their L2 proficiency is not developed enough to reflect on such matters, a research assistant who speaks the same L1 should be brought in. In my study of Jim (Chapter 1), I unfortunately did not have access to a bilingual Khmer-speaking research assistant who might have helped me with interviews in Jim's L1 to get more details about his life and understandings than he could express easily in English.

Though laudatory in some respects as a straightforward way of improving an analysis, member checks can be risky—if, for example, the participant does not like or disagrees with the analysis, chooses to withdraw from the project based on what is shown (as is their right from a research ethics standpoint), or wants to edit or censor his or her original contributions substantially to leave a more favorable impression (e.g., by correcting non-target-like language, or by deleting unflattering aspects of the data or analysis). Kouritzen (1999), for example, recalls her frustration upon receiving feedback on the first case study narrative she had carefully prepared based on her subject Ariana's life history:

> I picked it up ... only to find out that she had crossed out half of the story.... All of the things that I had found particularly interesting in her story had been crossed out, and she had marked "Irrelevant, please delete" in the margins.... In the end she agreed that if I deleted some of the identifying features of her life and "toned down" her comments, that I could leave it intact. (pp. 32–33)

Early case study research in applied linguistics (e.g., SLA) did not usually seek out the emic perspectives of research participants, though their knowledge was solicited. The subjects were generally young children learning a first or second language or naturalistic, migrant learners of a second language with limited levels of formal prior education. Moreover, the studies did not embrace an interpretive epistemology or orientation to research and were often more positivist or post-positivist, interested in isolating causes, effects, stages, and relevant variables. That is, the goal was not to understand the learners'

161

own (emic) views of their linguistic behaviors or related attributes, but rather, for the applied linguist, using the tools of the trade, to describe, analyze, and explain the developmental patterns displayed. Introspective accounts or think-aloud or verbal reports, though they reveal participants' thoughts, are more a form of data collection or intervention than data validation or confirmation in our field. Similarly, chatting with research participants after an interview or observation is different—because it does not call on them to respond to a written analysis.

Member checks in research done from a critical theoretical perspective that positions research participants in ways they do not want to be positioned (e.g., as vulnerable or oppressed, on the one hand, or as authoritative, insensitive, or hegemonic, on the other) might also face opposition from participants. Gall *et al.* (2005) and others nevertheless consider member checking one of the criteria for sound contemporary case study research and a way of increasing the internal validity and accountability of a study.

5.5 Criteria for Evaluating Case Studies

Recently, because of the recognition that not all research—and certainly not all qualitative research—should be evaluated using the same criteria, there has been clarification about appropriate criteria for assessing both quantitative and qualitative research in applied linguistics (Edge & Richards, 1998). Examples of recent guidelines for some common types of qualitative research—conversation analysis, case study, and (critical) ethnography specifically—can be found in Chapelle and Duff (2003). Lazaraton (2003), in a separate article, also contrasted criteria for ethnography and conversation analysis; both are types of qualitative research, but ethnography requires a much more holistic, contextualized, triangulated, sustained involvement in the research site than does conversation analysis, which is designed to provide a turn-by-turn microanalysis of talk-in-interaction, with less regard for the larger social context, multiple perspectives (e.g., based on interviews), and so on (Lazaraton, 2003; Markee, 2000).

Importantly, the published guidelines underscore the need to situate research within a theoretical context, to select an issue of wider relevance and significance to the field, plus the need to collect and analyze data appropriate to the research questions asked and following the accepted conventions associated with a research tradition such as ethnography. Bachman (2004) argues that the more general principle underlying such research guidelines and criteria is the nature of the logical links made among *performance* (e.g., observed behaviors) → *observation results* (e.g., scores, verbal reports) → *interpretation* → *decision or generalization* (a principle mentioned earlier in terms of "chains of reasoning" from Krathwohl, 1993).

Sufficient evidence (e.g., data) must be provided for the interpretations and conclusions that are drawn from a study, and counter-examples, if any, should be explained. Furthermore, an explicit reflective account by researchers about their own role or history in a project and unanticipated influences over the findings is expected in many types of qualitative research nowadays, especially ethnography. The intent is not for researchers to apologize for "contaminating" research sites by their presence, but to recognize that researchers are themselves participants or instruments and are also learners in projects, and they should not pretend to be dispassionate, arm's-length, impersonal, and invisible research agents. They must acknowledge their role and presence and then try to understand how it might have inadvertently affected the kinds of data collected and interpretations made. For example, Valdés (1998) discloses:

> Lilian and Elisa are now young women of 18 and 19 with whom I have kept in close touch over a period of almost seven years. I have grown very fond of them and of their families. Some of this fondness will show through in this article. I do not claim detached objectivity. Rather, I claim to have had the opportunity to go beyond what most children show to adults in their schools and, for that reason, to be able to bring to you some special insights about how other young people like them may make the transition into our world. (p. 5)

Duff and Uchida (1997) included a final section before the conclusion in which we reflected on the collaborative research experience with the teachers and also reflected on their and our own changing subjectivities resulting from the research process itself. An excerpt follows:

> If examining sociocultural identity is like trying to track down a dynamic, often elusive, moving target, the research becomes even more challenging when the investigators' own sociocultural conceptions and identities are in flux. For example, Uchida had become more conscious of societal expectations regarding life as a Japanese woman (and teacher) in Japan and in America. Her views were both informed and transformed by the research participants, just as they too were changed by their collaborations on this project:

by Carol's critical, feminist views, by Kimiko's relativist attitude, by Miki's skillful role-switching depending on whether she was with Japanese-speaking or primarily English-speaking people, and by Danny's cultural (mis)understandings (as perceived by some of his colleagues) about Japanese women's happiness. (pp. 478–479)

These kinds of self-disclosures do not suit everyone's stylistic tastes or all kinds of case study research. However, they are becoming more mainstream.

According to Yin (2003a), case studies should be *significant, complete*, and *engaging*, display *sufficient evidence*, and consider *alternative perspectives*. It is perhaps because case studies are often very engaging and accessible to a general readership that they have been so well received among students in a variety of fields, and that the case method has become a fundamental component of much higher educational practice. However, above all, case studies must contribute to knowledge in the field. They should be timely and substantive, and help challenge, refine, or illustrate existing perspectives and theory.

5.5.1 Validity and Reliability: Conflicting Positivist/Interpretive Criteria in Case Study

There are at least two conflicting sets of criteria for case study research for which validity is the contested principle: one set of criteria is based on positivist approaches to case study (e.g., Miles & Huberman, 1994; Yin, 1994, 2003a), and the other set is based on interpretive approaches (e.g., Altheide & Johnson, 1994; Merriam, 1998). Here the two are briefly contrasted.

5.5.1.1 Positivist Criteria for Case Study

Yin (1994, 2003a) includes various kinds of *validity* and *reliability* as criteria for case studies. These concepts are closely associated with positivist quantitative research, which maintains that there is an external reality or truth that can be known objectively (Gall, Gall & Borg, 2003). Earlier in this chapter and in Chapter 4, we discussed the importance of constructs and a conceptual framework in contextualizing and interpreting research. Yin (2003a) notes that *construct validity* can be problematic in case studies because constructs (theoretical concepts) may be underspecified or ill-defined. In applied linguistics, topic prominence, language transfer, aptitude, investment, agency, interaction, and other such constructs that might be the focus of a study should be defined, explained, and illustrated.

Internal validity generally relates to the credibility of results and interpretations (e.g., regarding relationships among variables) based on the conceptual foundations and evidence that is provided. Gall, Gall & Borg, (2003) claim that internal validity is not a valid criterion in case study, which "does not seek to identify causal patterns in phenomena" (p. 460), though Miles and Huberman (1994) (positivist qualitative research methodologists like Yin) actually do look for causal relationships and chains in explanatory studies.

5.5.1.2 Interpretive Criteria for Case Study

According to Gall, Gall & Borg, (2003), the critique of positivist criteria in case study from interpretive researchers is captured by the following question:

> How does a researcher arrive at valid, reliable knowledge if each individual being studied constructs his or her own reality (the constructivist assumption), if the researcher becomes a central focus of the inquiry process (the "reflexive" turn in the social sciences), and if no inquiry process or type of knowledge has any authority over any other (the post-modern assumption)? (p. 461)

Thus, *interpretive validity*, or "judgments about the credibility of an interpretive researcher's knowledge claims" (p. 462), should be the target criterion according to Gall, Gall & Borg, (2002) and Altheide and Johnson (1994). A set of 11 features in this category (from Gall, Gall & Borg, 2003) with some brief comments are found in Table 5.6. They are listed according to three clusters of criteria: those reflecting sensitivity to readers' needs, use of sound research methods, and thoroughness of data collection and analysis (see Gall, Gall & Borg, 2005, pp. 319–323).

5.5.1.3 External Validity or Generalizability

External validity, or generalizability, is also a contentious criterion for good qualitative case studies, though not necessarily along positivist/interpretive lines (Duff, 2006; Chalhoub-Deville *et al.*, 2006). In Chapter 2, some of the arguments for or against the generalizability of case studies were summarized. Most case study researchers do not hold generalizability to populations as an achievable or desired goal; on the contrary, they usually assume an inherent lack of generalizability. However, many do argue that analytic generalizability (i.e., generalizing to theory or models as opposed to populations) is both possible and desirable, and in some cases, with careful sampling, generalization of findings to the wider sample population may also be warranted. One of the key ways in which case study researchers might avoid the criticism of unique or idiosyncratic findings whose impact on knowledge more broadly may be difficult to assess or assert is to choose *typical* or *representative* sites or participants to study and not just those that are most convenient or easily accessible and whose representativeness is unclear. This is not a goal shared by all qualitative researchers, though, who may choose to study people and sites already known to them or to which they have access; most accessible, of course, are the researchers themselves through introspective (e.g., diary/ narrative) studies, memoirs, and auto-ethnographies (Schumann, 1997). Researchers must also bear in mind that the typicality of a case within one context (e.g., a Cambodian learner in Canada) may not equate with typicality in another (e.g., a Cambodian learner in Cambodia).

Another method for enhancing the potential generalizability as well as credibility of qualitative research is to conduct multisite or multiple-case studies, not all of which may have the same attributes (as in my study of three different immersion programs in Hungary; Duff, 1993c). Schofield (1990) asserts that "a finding emerging from the study of several very heterogeneous sites would be more robust and thus more likely to be useful in understanding various other sites than one emerging from the study of several very similar sites" (p. 212). We could also replace "sites" with "people".

Researchers might also look for an aggregation or (meta)synthesis of case studies, comparable to a meta-analysis of quantitative studies, to corroborate findings across studies (Noblit & Hare, 1988; Norris & Ortega, 2006). Researchers may also include participants' own judgments about generalizability or representativeness to assist them with interpretations about typicality (Hammersley, 1992). Finally, longitudinal studies with data collected from multiple sources or task types also have the potential to increase the nature of inferences that can be drawn about learning because the developmental pathways (consistent, incremental, erratic, or very dynamic) can be shown, as well as interactions in the acquisition of several interrelated structures over time (Huebner, 1983).

Table 5.6 Criteria for Evaluating Case Studies (see Gall *et al.*, 2005, pp. 319–323)

Sensitivity to readers' needs	1. Strong chain of evidence; audit trail (provision of links between research questions, data, analysis, and conclusions; audit trail involves documentation of entire process and provision of examples in text or appendix) 2. Truthfulness of representation; "verisimilitude", "a style of writing that draws the reader so closely into the subjects' worlds that these can be palpably felt" (Adler & Adler, 1994, p. 381) 3. Usefulness (e.g., of reports to readers or of research to participants themselves)
Use of sound research methods	1. Triangulation (also called "crystallization"; Richardson, 1994): corroboration from different sources of data during the study; data may be convergent or divergent 2. Coding checks (consistency or reliability of coding) 3. Disconfirming case analysis: an "outlier analysis" (of extreme cases or negative evidence that can strengthen the validity of claims and interpretations) 4. Member checking (another way of achieving corroboration and getting emic perspectives on a researcher's report or interpretations, after the fact)
Thoroughness of data collection and analysis	1. Contextual completeness (comprehensiveness of description of setting, participants, activities, etc.); multivocality (different points of view included from participants and their "tacit knowledge" and "ecology of understanding"; Altheide & Johnson, 1994, p. 492) 2. Long-term observation (provides more consistent, stable evidence from observations) 3. Representativeness check (verification of the typicality of sites, participants, observations, etc.) 4. Researcher's self-reflection (or reflexivity, researcher positioning; subjectivities that may affect interpretations)

5.5.1.4 Reliability

Despite some disagreement about the concept and applicability of reliability to qualitative research, *consistency* in sampling, interviewing, and data analysis procedures is generally considered to be a virtue in rigorous research, whether quantitative or qualitative, positivist or interpretive. However, philosophical differences exist regarding the criterion of reliability as the replicability of findings. Gall *et al.* (2003), taking a relatively positivist perspective, define reliability in case study as follows: "the extent to which other researchers would arrive at similar results if they studied the same case using exactly the same procedures as the first researcher" (p. 635). But an interpretive perspective disputes "the assumption that there is a single reality and that studying it repeatedly will yield the same results" (Merriam, 1998, p. 205). In interpretive qualitative research, "researchers seek to describe and explain the world as those in the world experience it. Since there are many interpretations of what is happening, there is no benchmark by which to take repeated measures and establish reliability in the traditional sense" (Merriam, 1998, p. 205). Triangulation in qualitative research shows that even with multiple observers or analysts, interpretations or conclusions reached about the observations may be nonconvergent. Thus, the notion that reliable procedures will lead to predictable or uniform outcomes is flawed, a point that Merriam (1998) makes forcefully below:

> Because what is being studied in education is assumed to be in flux, multifaceted, and highly contextual, because information gathered is a function of who gives it and how skilled the researcher is at getting it, and because the emergent design of a qualitative case study precludes a priori controls, achieving reliability in the traditional sense is not only fanciful but impossible. (p. 206)

She suggests, following Lincoln and Guba (1985), that dependability and consistency are more appropriate criteria, to ensure that the results "make sense" to others. One way of ensuring that goal is by having an "audit trail" about decision making throughout.

5.5.2 Accuracy, Truthfulness, and "Thinking Outside the Box"

It should go without saying that researchers must be as accurate and truthful in conducting and reporting research as possible. Professional ethics and expectations of personal integrity require it, although as I reported earlier, some factual details about a case may need to be altered slightly to protect the identity of participants. Accuracy in qualitative research does not mean that researchers have obtained the correct solution to a research problem or found the truth or reality, but rather that they have handled data and conveyed perspectives, observations, and biases with care and attention paid to meaningful details and have been accountable to the data. Withholding information about counter-examples and giving the impression that all data fit neatly into certain patterns is not really honest reporting, although some simplification of complex cases may be necessary to convey main trends and patterns in short articles or presentations. These considerations are all related to the trustworthiness and credibility of the researcher and the results.

Bromley (1986) argues that, in the context of case study research, the lack of relevant information can be a problem—but not because information is willfully withheld:

> A particularly subtle source of error in case-study materials is the *absence* of information and ideas. The possibilities that no-one thought of, and the facts that were not known, must have invalidated numerous case-studies, simply because people's attention tends to be concentrated on the information actually presented. It is important in case-studies and in problem-solving generally to go "beyond the information given" to "what might be" the case. Naturally, such speculations need to be backed up by reasoned argument and by a search for relevant evidence. (p. 238)

There is always the possibility, then, that other crucial pieces of information—or alternate explanations—have been overlooked. This factor is not so much one of truth or accuracy as creative speculation or "thinking outside of the box".

5.6 Summary

In order to conduct a case study, it is important to determine not only one's research questions and design, but also one's epistemological stance and the traditions one is building upon: more positivist or more interpretive. Data analysis, interpretation, and claims follow accordingly. Finally, evaluative criteria also vary to some extent according to ontological assumptions related to the objective versus subjective nature of reality, although some general principles related to validity apply.

Writing the Case Study Report

6.1 Introduction

Writing up research is a matter of representing the research process and findings, through printed text and images or other modalities, and disseminating findings or new knowledge within a particular community. Without publishing the results, even if the results have been presented orally, the study will have only a limited impact on the field and on subsequent research and practice. Consequently, the efforts and insights of the researcher and participants will benefit very few others. Thus, writing up and disseminating one's case study, as with other forms of research, is very important.

This final chapter contains an overview of how to prepare a case study report, in consideration of a number of relevant factors: the intended audience, purpose and focus, contents, organization, stylistic matters, voice and reflexivity, visual displays, ethics, appendices, and other practical considerations. In what follows, I make the assumption that the intended report is a stand-alone case study or multiple-case study, and is not embedded within a mixed-method design, in which the report would be organized somewhat differently and less emphasis would be placed on the cases themselves. Readers should also consult other helpful resources on how to write up case studies (e.g., Merriam, 1998; Stake, 1995; Yin, 2003a) and other qualitative research (e.g., Holliday, 2002; Silverman, 2000; Wolcott, 1990), or applied linguistic research more generally (Mackey & Gass, 2005); see also the publication manual of the American Psychological Association (APA, 2001), which is widely used in applied linguistics (although the guidelines reflect a positivist psychological bent and reporting style). Finally, reading other recently published case studies in reputable journals, books, or dissertations is another excellent way of becoming familiar with currently acceptable writing practices and topics.

6.2 Audience, Publication Venue, and Focus: Preparing the Report

Writing up case studies is in many respects similar to the preparation of other kinds of research reports regardless of the inquiry tradition or methodology. This chapter discusses aspects that are both common to all research and specific to case studies. The first considerations in preparing a case study report are common ones: (1) identifying the intended audience or readership, (2) selecting an appropriate venue for publication, and (3) determining the main focus and content of a prospective publication. The organization, content, and presentation of reports follow from these. Therefore, before even beginning to prepare a manuscript based on the study, it is crucial to consider all of these factors, which will determine the report's length, format, genre, and so on.

6.2.1 Audience

With respect to the intended audience, the following questions should be addressed:

- Are the intended readers the project funders to whom a final report must be submitted, and if so, what is the expected length, format, and genre?
- Is the report a synthesis of findings primarily for the research participants in the study?
- Is the audience a dissertation committee, the editorial board of a journal, a book editor, the general public, practitioners, or policy makers?
- If it is a manuscript in preparation for a journal, which journal is most suitable for the type of study conducted and the intended focus of this manuscript, and what are the genres and page or word restrictions for that journal?

The intended readership and the specific policies of various publishers (e.g., journals) determine, to a large degree, the acceptable length of the manuscript, the amount and type of theoretical contextualization required or possible, the scope and depth of coverage permitted, and the genres or rhetorical styles that are acceptable. Regardless of audience, however, or the length of the report that is prepared, the case should ideally be contextualized and described as fully as possible, evidence for claims should be provided, and the main purpose and findings of the study must be clear.

6.2.2 Publication Venue and Type

Because the best journals in a field normally have a rigorous review and revision process for manuscripts, and many now are widely accessible internationally through various Internet-based online databases, journals are a preferred publication venue. Book chapters, though they may also have gone through an internal or external review by the editors or publication house, are mainly an option for those who have had a manuscript solicited by the volume editor in connection with a given theme.

To illustrate issues connected with publication venue and type, let us consider the case studies by Schmidt (1983) and Schmidt and Frota (1986). The audience for the articles, both of which were book chapters, was graduate students and established L2 researchers. The focus was a Japanese man's English L2 development over an extended period (Schmidt, 1983) and Schmidt's own L2 development in Brazilian Portuguese over a five-month period and his metalinguistic reflections on the process (Schmidt & Frota, 1986). Normally, unless authors wanted to write a complete book about each case, which is mainly done with dissertations or multiple-case studies, they would choose an appropriate journal to submit a manuscript to (e.g., journals that publish exploratory SLA research in this instance).

Schmidt published his pieces in volumes edited by colleagues in applied linguistics. What was very unusual (and fortuitous) about the resulting publications, and may have been a factor in the tremendous impact they have had on the field—besides the important theoretical insights that the case studies generated—was the depth of analysis possible because of the length of the book chapters: 37 and 89 pages, respectively. In contrast, the average length of other chapters in the same books was 13 and 19 pages, respectively (about a third or a quarter of the length of his chapters).[1] Had the same articles been submitted to a journal, or to more typical edited volumes, considerably shorter versions would normally have been required and some of the invaluable contextualization, data excerpts, and analysis would have been reduced as

---

1   The case studies in Hatch (1978), including Schumann's (1978) case study of Alberto, were approximately 10 to 20 printed pages each.

a result.[1]

Most journals in applied linguistics (e.g., *Applied Linguistics, Language Learning, Modern Language Journal, Studies in Second Language Acquisition*) call for manuscripts between 20 and 30 double-spaced pre-publication pages (4,000 to 8,000 words, though some publish up to 10,000 words) (TESOL, 2007).[2] Page allowances are an important consideration in determining how much of the context and analysis can satisfactorily be captured and illustrated in an article, especially since qualitative research articles typically require more space or words than quantitative ones do. Therefore, case study authors must carefully plan how and where they will submit/publish their work. Duff and Li's (2004) case study of a Mandarin teacher and her instructional dilemmas appeared in *System*, a journal with a 4,000-word limit for articles (a limit we had failed to notice when submitting the article for review). As a result, most of the carefully chosen excerpts in the original manuscript, plus an entire section on L1-L2 code-switching, had to be deleted prior to publication. In retrospect, we should probably have submitted the manuscript to a journal with more generous page allowances but had not realized how strictly article length would be enforced at the time of submission.

6.2.3 Focus

The focus and scope of an article are connected to the intended audience, the author's main purpose, and the venue and type of publication. Furthermore, decisions about the focus of any one publication should take into account other planned publications based on the same study. Typically, dissertations can be turned into more than one publication, highlighting different aspects of the study in the same journal or in other places. Duplication of publications is of course not normally permitted. For a short article, the cases could be described and then one or two main themes could be highlighted with at most a few short examples. In a longer article, greater contextualization and description of the case are possible, and more excerpts from data and more themes could potentially be included.

If the intended audience is not other scholars, as in Schmidt's (1983) case, but rather is the research participants themselves, members of the public, or

---

1   Of course, there are always exceptions: Spack's (1987) case study was nearly 60 journal pages long.
2   Readers should consult a very helpful online publication, "How to Get Published in ESOL and Applied Linguistics Serials", for descriptions of journals in our field and features of manuscript submissions and reviews (TESOL, 2007).

practitioners, the author would likely write in a more accessible, less technical, less theoretical, and less analytic style, with special care given to protecting the identities of participants, especially with sensitive data, since participants will be more easily identified within the original community. The article might also be much shorter and submitted to teachers' journals, newsletters, or for private circulation among the focal participants, with some concrete practical pedagogical or policy implications provided.

6.3 Organization and Content of the Report

The typical organization of the social science research report published in journals is abstract, introduction, literature review or background/context, research design and methods (including a full description of the case or cases), results or findings, discussion, and conclusions. Sometimes the results and discussion are combined (Mackey & Gass, 2005), especially in interpretive qualitative research. There can be some leeway in the actual headings used, though, and some journals or books encourage (or tolerate) creativity more than others.

Here I provide examples of the organization and headings in three of my own published case studies.

6.3.1 Example 1

The first example, shown in Table 6.1, comes from my original publication about Jim (see Chapter 1) in *Studies in Second Language Acquisition* (Duff, 1993a). This organization reflects a typical structural/positivist approach. The contextualization in this article was primarily theoretical and linguistic, as opposed to personal or sociocultural. The analysis was of Jim's development across three stages that emerged from the data, out of four possible stages for the structure in question. In retrospect, the many points between Discussion and Conclusion, in Table 6.1, should probably have appeared as subsections under Discussion. That is, I did not pay enough attention to the different levels of headings used.

Table 6.1 Article Organization: Example 1 (Duff, 2003a)

- Abstract
- [Introduction with excerpt/vignette but without a section title]
- Typological Sketch: The Semantics of P [Possessives] and E [Existentials]
- SLA: Theoretical Approach
- Previous SLA Studies of P/E Acquisition or Use
- Present Study: Longitudinal Case Study of P/E in Cambodian-ESL
  - Methods
  - Grammatical Sketch of Cambodian
  - Analysis
- Results
  - Stage I
  - Stage II
  - Stage III
- Discussion
- A Case of "Transfer Plus"
- Further Cross-Linguistic Evidence Concerning P/E Overlap
  - Creole Languages
  - Dialect Variation
- Language Contact and Variation
- Transfer Plus: The Nature of the English Input
- Some Predictions Concerning SLA
- Conclusion
- Notes
- References
- Appendices
  - A: Partial list of coded features
  - B: Excerpts that illustrate developmental trends, by time

---

6.3.2 Example 2

The second example, shown in Table 6.2, is of the organization in an interpretive qualitative multiple-case study of English as a foreign language (EFL) teachers in Japan that appeared in *TESOL Quarterly* (Duff & Uchida, 1997). The focus was the four teachers' sociocultural identities and professional socialization. In this article, the literature was organized around these two central themes, research on learners' identities, and language socialization or acculturation. In the presentation of the study, we included the usual components, but under Findings, we discussed each case in turn. We then returned to the overarching theme of identity (the article appeared in a special issue on identity) in two successive sections and next examined themes that emerged in the inductive analysis of all four cases. The Discussion then summarized and commented on these themes, particularly the notion that teachers are "culture workers". The section on Collaboration and Change was our reflective commentary about our collaboration, especially about Uchida's involvement in the study, and the four teachers' reflections on their own involvement and new insights based on their involvement.

Table 6.2 Article Organization: Example 2 (Duff & Uchida, 1997)

- Abstract
- [Introduction, untitled]
- Background: Researching Sociocultural Identity and Socialization in TESOL
  - ○ Research on Learners' Identities
  - ○ Research on Language Socialization
- English Education in Japan
- The Study
  - ○ Research Questions
  - ○ Methodology
  - ○ The Site
  - ○ The Participants
  - ○ Analysis
  - ○ Findings
    - Danny
    - Carol
    - Miki
    - Kimiko
    - Teachers' Profiles: Summary
- Conceptualizing and Contextualizing Teachers' Sociocultural Identity in TEFL
  - ○ Biographical/Professional Basis
  - ○ Contextual Basis
- Emergent Themes
  - ○ The Complexity of Sociocultural Identity Formation, Cultural Transmission, and Change
  - ○ The Pursuit of Interpersonal and Intercultural Connection
  - ○ The Desire for Educational and Personal Control
- Discussion
- Collaborative Research and Change
- Conclusion
- References

6.3.3 Example 3

Finally, Duff and Li's (2004) short report (case study) of a university-level Mandarin teacher's instructional practices in a semester-long course had the following organization: Abstract, Introduction, the Study (Context, Research Methods, Instructor and Course), Results, Summary and Conclusion.

Therefore, the organization and content of a study are determined by a number of interrelated factors. Some variation in these occurs, even in journal publications by the same author, based on purpose, the mandate of the journal, length constraints, the type of analysis conducted, and the number of cases involved.

Table 6.3 Article Organization: Example 3 (Duff & Li, 2004)

- Abstract
- Introduction
- The Study
    - Context
    - Research Methods
    - The Instructor and Course
- Results: Emerging Themes and Issues
    - Fostering a Focus on Form, Linguistic Interaction, and a Positive Affective Climate
        - Pair Work vs. Teacher-Fronted Instruction and Practice
        - Focus on Form through Grammar Presentation, Repetition, Explanation, and Practice
        - Corrective Feedback
- Summary and Conclusion

6.3.4 Organization and Content of Graduate Theses and Dissertations

Dissertations usually organize chapters in a very traditional, formulaic order that is determined by convention within a university, discipline, or academic department, by committees and the author, and by the kind and number of case studies reported upon. The basic components are (1) Introduction, (2) Literature Review, (3) Methodology, (4) Results, (5) Discussion, and (6) Conclusion. Alternatively, in lieu of one Results chapter containing the presentation of findings by case or theme, a chapter might be devoted to each case or major theme (ideally just a small number of them, e.g., up to four, as in Li (1998) or three focal pairs, as in Morita (2002)).

In his recent dissertation, a multiple-case study of Japanese university students' performance of tasks/activities at a Canadian university, Kobayashi (2004) had chapters with the titles and thematic focus shown in Table 6.4.

Table 6.4 Organization of PhD Dissertation (Kobayashi, 2004)

1. Introduction
2. Sociocultural Perspectives on Task-Based L2 Research: Review of the Literature
3. Research Methodology
4. Community Context of Tasks
5. Student Agency and Collaboration in L2 Task Preparation
6. Students' Performance on Oral Presentations
7. Students' Learning across Tasks and Contexts
8. Conclusions and Implications

The first three chapters followed the usual model, and the fourth was a broad contextualization of the study. The next three chapters discussed three different themes using data from different focal research participants (cases) who best illustrated the theme. Then the final chapter summarized and discussed the major findings in the dissertation, according to salient themes and presented a number of implications for both pedagogy and future research.

Publishers usually do not like to publish what seem to be unrevised dissertations written in fulfillment of a university's or doctoral committee's requirements. Thus, case studies based on dissertations that are to be submitted as book manuscripts often need to be reorganized or edited in certain ways. However, they may still feature a primary case or theme per chapter and will certainly contextualize the study within relevant literature, but possibly with different chapter titles. For example, "Literature Review" might be changed to the central theme of the review, such as "Researching Identity and Language Learning" (see Norton, 2000, based on her revised dissertation literature review chapter). Before making such changes, however, it is wise to consult with the publishing house, obtain a copy of sample prospectus (proposal) guidelines, and understand what steps are needed in order to get a prospectus approved. Normally, an overview and rationale for the book, a table of contents, and three sample chapters must be submitted for review before a contract is issued.

Case studies provide in-depth descriptions and analyses of cases, but the discussion of findings (or results) should also attempt to link back particularities of the individual cases and the study itself to the larger literature on the topic in applied linguistics. For dissertations or other large projects (e.g., books) that have taken years to complete, this point will necessitate becoming familiar with important recent studies relevant to one's own research, as well as the literature already reviewed earlier in the dissertation writing or in the process of conceptualization and designing the study, in order to make a more significant, timely, and topical contribution to knowledge in the field.

6.3.5 Other Organizational and Content Issues

Some creative writers depart from the traditional formula for presenting research by using different rhetorical and organizational strategies, such as presenting the cases at the outset and then providing contextualizing information, research questions, and so on; or they may forego explicitly stating research questions entirely. Others may choose metaphors or salient themes as major organizing tools. If the case study is prepared for publication in an academic journal, it is important to familiarize yourself with the style of writing and format most commonly associated with that journal to increase the likelihood that the article will be acceptable to reviewers, from a stylistic or rhetorical standpoint, and will be compatible with other articles, although different types of research may be written up in somewhat different ways. If a book manuscript is prepared, it is important to see other books that have been published by the publisher in the same content area or series and to examine those books carefully for compatibility.

Above all, the unique contribution of the research, the gap in existing knowledge that is being filled, or the insights that have been generated must be emphasized. Also, research questions posed earlier in the article need to be systematically answered. To be explicit about this and to remind readers of what the main goals of the study were, authors may organize their research findings by restating and then addressing each research question in turn.

Case studies often involve many different sources of data, with interview transcripts from students, teachers, and other stakeholders or participants, transcripts from audio- or video-recorded observations, test scores, and so on. For some writers, it can be a daunting task to capture the essence of the case, its most interesting and theoretically important characteristics, and also to incorporate sufficient amounts and types of discursive data to support claims. In both single- and multiple-case studies, one of the earliest decisions affecting the written report is which (and how many) cases to select for extended discussion, especially when cases have been sampled from a larger pool. Second, if multiple cases (say, two to six) are involved, writers must decide how much space and detail should be accorded to each case without making the report too long, repetitious, or complicated. Stake (1995) devotes a short chapter to the topic of writing the case study report, in which he stresses the importance of learning to "ruthlessly winnow and sift" (p. 121) through massive amounts of data that may have been collected for reporting purposes. His own stylistic strategy is to organize case study reports as shown in Table 6.5, book-ended by vignettes to engage the reader. (See Stake, 2005, p. 123, for an elaboration of these points.)

Table 6.5 Sample Organization of Case Report

- Entry vignette
- Issue identification, purpose, and method of study
- Extensive narrative description to further define case and contexts
- Development of issues
- Descriptive detail, documents, quotations, triangulating data
- Assertions
- Closing vignette

Source: Adapted from Stake, R., *The Art of Case Study Research*, Sage, Thousand Oaks, CA, 1995, p.123. Adapted with the permission of Sage Publications.

Vignettes are included at the beginning of a report to engage readers. These vignettes may be short quotations from interviews or short descriptions of case participants that are then elaborated on in the report. Examples of opening vignettes used in Duff and Uchida (1997) are shown in italics in the left column in Table 6.6 for Danny and Carol, two American teachers in Japan. The vignettes in this case are interview excerpts that capture elements of the teachers' profiles to be developed and compared in a cross-case analysis. These vignettes were then followed (in turn) by descriptions of each teacher (shown in the right column), with respect to their backgrounds and orientation to teaching language and culture. Instead of a quotation, the vignettes might alternatively have contained the description of a critical incident, such as an episode reflecting conflict between teachers' ideologies of language/culture teaching and those of students, administrators, or other teachers.

Table 6.6 Sample Introduction to a Case or Case Study

Case (Teacher)	Opening Vignette (Interview Excerpt)	Case Description Immediately Following Vignette
Danny	*I guess I kind of almost learned [to teach] to be like David Letterman does his talk show stuff.... Like he teases his guests a lot.... So I'm Letterman, the student I'm teasing is the guest, the audience is the rest of the class. It's one of those things, everyone gets into it. (Interview: 11/10/93)*	Born, raised, and educated on the West Coast of the United States with little previous travel experience, Danny had a strong attachment to American popular media and was a committed vegetarian, nonsmoker, feminist, and environmentalist.... (p. 461)
Carol	*I think [teaching culture is] a BS issue. When people are teaching culture or things like body language, who cares? ... It comes down to a very personal interpretation. That's what I don't like about it.... It's basically teaching what's inside you. And I don't want that much power. (Interview: 11/4/93)*	Carol was also American, the same age as Danny, and, as it turns out, from the same hometown as well. A short brunette, who was occasionally mistaken for a Japanese woman, Carol embraced strong feminist convictions and a positive self-image as a resourceful, well-educated, committed TESL professional.... (p. 462)

Notice that in writing this book, although it is not a case study report, I decided to front-end a long descriptive narrative of my case study of one language learner (Chapter 1) for the same reason, and then to intersperse excerpts from that and other studies throughout the remainder of the text. A different approach to reporting case studies does not use opening vignettes or extended descriptive narratives at the beginning but integrates them within the text and commentary (Merriam, 1998).

6.4 Stylistic Matters

Writers need to be persuasive and provide compelling but sound arguments and evidence.[1] Adler and Adler (1994) suggest that researchers' writing or reporting style itself contributes a great deal to the impact of qualitative research on readers and their perceptions of its credibility and authenticity, and

---

1   Stake (1995) provides a fairly standard checklist for case study reports, with 20 questions, such as "Is the report easy to read? ... Has the writer made sound assertions ...? ... Is the role and point of view of the researcher nicely apparent? ... Were data sources well chosen and in sufficient number?" (p. 131).

that researchers should strive to achieve what they call "verisimilitude" in their writing—"a style of writing that draws the reader so closely into the subjects' worlds that these can be palpably felt" (p. 381). In addition to well-written prose, most case studies require the artful interweaving of texts from different sources: carefully chosen, representative, ideally vivid excerpts that illustrate points (e.g., aspects of performance or perspective) or that characterize different participants well. There is no best way of making decisions about how many and which excerpts or examples to include. It is an intuitive as well as practical matter of not bogging readers down with excessive data. Having other people read drafts of your work with selected excerpts and examples and provide feedback on which ones are most effective and on how much evidence is sufficient can be very helpful.

Richardson (1990, 2000) discusses different rhetorical options for people writing up qualitative research, especially for junior researchers, from the traditional to the highly creative and unconventional. Richardson and St. Pierre (2005), in an updated *Handbook* chapter based on Richardson's (2000) earlier version, again stress that writing itself (like transcription) is a method of inquiry and that it not only *reflects* "social reality but *produces* meaning and *creates* social reality" (p. 961, italics added). Richardson suggests five criteria for evaluating manuscripts for publication that incorporate her interest in the quality of both content and presentation:

- substantive contribution to our understanding of social life
- aesthetic merit (i.e., the piece is engaging)
- reflexivity—about ethical issues, epistemology, methodology, and accountability
- impact on readers (Richardson, 2000; Richardson & St. Pierre, 2005)
- expression of a reality ("a fleshed out, embodied sense of lived experience", a "credible account"; Richardson, 2000, p. 937)

Having others respond to your work (friends, colleagues, or reviewers), her fourth point, can provide concrete feedback on readability, the apparent logic of the research, and the merits or shortcomings of the discourse itself. Another of her suggestions is to begin writing sooner rather than later in order to record decisions about sampling and methods during the research process itself, while the information is fresh. Similarly, it is often highly desirable, though sometimes logistically difficult, to write fieldnotes and begin transcribing data immediately, while still conducting fieldwork. Not only does this ensure that information is not lost as it recedes from memory, but also the writing and transcribing themselves may help provide clarity and insights to the researcher.

> Although we usually think about writing as a mode of "telling" about the social world, writing is not just a mopping-up activity at the end of a research project. Writing is also a way of "knowing"—a method of discovery and analysis. By writing in different ways, we discover new aspects of our topic and our relationship to it. Form and content are inseparable. (Richardson, 2000, p. 923)

Richardson decries the "boring" nature of much published qualitative research, which cannot be easily skimmed or scanned in the same way that quantitative results can in tables and figures, for example, but which, she says, suffers from "acute and chronic passivity: passive-voiced author, passive 'subjects'" (p. 924). She recommends using vivid and novel metaphors, and blending approaches to conducting and writing up research from the humanities and social sciences (see Richardson & St. Pierre, 2005).

6.5 Voice and Reflexivity

Writing well involves developing a voice and style as author, something that most of us spend a lifetime trying to achieve. The issue of voice, stance, and representation in the reporting of research has come to the fore in recent years, especially in qualitative research. Capturing one's authorial voice or stance, and also the voice of case study participants, is important. Increasingly, the involvement of the researcher in the study, the perspectives and biases (or subjectivities) of the researcher, and also the reflections of the researcher on the research experience and findings are acknowledged explicitly in many, but certainly not all, types of qualitative research, including case studies. For example, case study researchers will reveal how they became acquainted with the case participant and how they established and maintained rapport, or their personal history with the case site, at a minimum.

Van Maanen (1988) describes three types of accounts, conventions, or narrative modes (in ethnography) that are also used in case study: *realist*, *confessional*, and *impressionist*. Realist "tales" are commonly associated with both positivist, quantitative research and much existing qualitative research: they are dispassionate, concrete, detailed, objective, arm's-length accounts of observations; "the fieldworker, having finished the job of collecting data, simply vanishes behind a steady descriptive narrative" (p. 46). Van Maanen also wryly calls this "interpretive omnipotence" (p. 51) based on "an assumed Doctrine of Immaculate Perception" (p. 73), which tends to preclude alternative interpretations or perspectives. The main authorial voice is institutional or professional, but the "native's point of view" or emic perspective may be carefully conveyed through the extensive use of representative quotations. Realist discourse is the dominant tradition in the social sciences, but it has been evolving over the past decade or two. Although this description may seem critical of such an approach, especially as it was practiced in previous generations, newer versions of realism do have legitimacy in educational and social research, and Van Maanen advises students to start with "sensitive" versions of a realist approach.

Confessional tales, according to Van Maanen (1988), refers to accounts that are more reflexive, personal insights into contingencies that led to emergent research decisions, unplanned scenarios, and unexpected findings and consequences of research. While at the extreme, these can be melodramatic and sensationalistic autobiographic accounts, their goal is to supplement realist accounts by capturing the story behind the story. They also convey the researcher's dilemmas or rapport with those researched and with writing up the research—a different kind of contextualization, but not one that calls into question the veracity of the researcher's interpretations or claims or their legitimacy. This "confessional" style of discourse is normally produced by established scholars.

Merriam *et al.* (2002) present the full-length sociological case study of an American school with a large proportion of Arab Americans and the role of the school in assimilating immigrant students (Enomoto & Bair, 1999), followed by a three-page retrospective account by the original authors (Enomoto & Bair, 2002) that Merriam seems to have solicited. In the latter, they describe the negotiation of access to the school, the challenges both researchers faced, as non-Arab Americans, and learning to conduct qualitative research in that setting. Duff and Early (1996) argue that more reflexivity about the research process should be contained *within* reports, space permitting, and not just in short solicited follow-up pieces such as the one by Enomoto and Bair (2002).

Finally, *impressionist* accounts or tales often contain dramatic representations of events and the use of metaphors, personal experience, and powerful narrative. Like impressionist paintings, these accounts are meant to be vibrant and evocative. They are more experiential than analytical, following literary as opposed to social-scientific reporting strategies, and they may be embedded within realist accounts. Van Maanen concedes that most researchers do not have the literary talent to write effectively in this manner about critical incidents, and it can therefore be risky.

These three approaches are not mutually exclusive. Perhaps the most telling research includes measured amounts of all three, typically dominated by the first approach, although writers are experimenting across genres nowadays. In applied linguistics research, realist accounts are certainly most common, but contemporary case studies often contain some of the following features: reflexive comments about the case and about issues of representation, a critical stance (e.g., of prevailing power structures), autobiographical comments from researchers about their involvement, collaborative accounts by researchers and those researched, and vivid examples or telling cases. These could be viewed as "rich points" (Hornberger, 2006).

Holliday (2004) suggests that case study researchers should be more "progressive" and flexible, so they can change direction and explain new directions in their research, as local contingencies allow or dictate, and that the contingencies themselves become part of the larger story. He gives the example of a doctoral student whose planned research in China was blocked by the SARS (Severe Acute Respiratory Syndrome) epidemic in that country a few years ago, but who reportedly found a new, very meaningful way of approaching his topic first from outside of China and then later within China.

Gall *et al.* (2003), in a somewhat less extreme and less postmodern characterization of approaches to writing than Van Maanen's, describe two approaches to case study reporting: *reflective* reporting and *analytic* reporting. Though the two can co-occur, one impulse usually dominates. Reflective reporting, in their view, involves the use of literary devices to "bring the case alive" (p. 467) for readers, and they illustrate this approach with Wolcott's (1994) "sneaky kid" life history research of "Brad", reviewed elsewhere in this book. More creative, dramatic accounts, from a literary standpoint, might include fictionalizations and poetry, though these "creative analytic writing practices" (Richardson, 2000, p. 941) are still quite rare in published applied linguistic studies.

6.6 Visual Displays of Information

A rather naïve view of the difference between quantitative and qualitative research is that the former is characterized by numbers and measurement, and the latter by words. While there is some truth to that distinction, the challenge for research in any paradigm is to do justice to the data that are collected and to present findings in a meaningful, efficient, and effective manner. With large amounts of linguistic or narrative data to cull and present, many qualitative researchers can be assisted in analysis, data reduction, and the presentation of results by using a variety of graphic organizers, such as figures, tables, conceptual maps, and boxes, as exemplified by Miles and Huberman (1994). They might appear as flowcharts, conceptual frameworks or networks, bar charts, or intricate matrices that illustrate coding practices and results. Comments and themes may or may not be quantified, but the representativeness of observations, the existence of counter-examples, or gradations in findings may be shown visually, as well as through prose, by signifying frequencies through the use of symbols (e.g., + for each positive comment and – for each negative one; see examples from language program evaluation in Lynch (1996)). Such decisions are based on the author's (or sponsor's and supervisor's) stylistic and epistemological preferences.

If one is conducting a structuralist/positivist study of language learning, including a graphic that captures change over time based on frequencies, proportions or tallies of some kind might be highly appropriate. In multiple-case studies comparing and contrasting the experiences of four individuals based on L1, country of origin, L2 proficiency level, gender, and learning outcomes, a table might be sufficient. To summarize interview comments from a large and disparate group of research participants, a matrix (clustered summary table) containing themes, representative responses, and an indication of the number of people sharing the same view would be in order. Typically, in applied linguistics case studies, graphic organizers, if used at all, are straightforward tables and figures, but new software makes other forms of images simpler to create or import.

6.7 Research Ethics

Chapter 4 discussed research ethics in some depth. It is also customary in current research reports to explain how the principles of ethical research were upheld. When a great deal of contextualizing information is provided about individual people or sites, the risk of identification increases. Researchers should not provide enough information about research subjects or sites that they can be identified. In some research, special permissions have been granted to reveal participants' identities because it is their desire to be so named (publicly recognized), or it is not possible or desirable to mask the identity, as in the case study of a well-known public official (a so-called "elite case") or of a showcase program. Generally, however, such disclosures are to be avoided.

Writers must also, for example, be sure that they have substituted pseudonyms for subjects consistently in reports and transcripts (since some researchers continue to use the real names during analysis in order to keep track of data with the intention of substituting pseudonyms prior to publication). In some instances it becomes necessary to alter aspects of the case (e.g., location, gender, language, age) in order to protect the case.

6.8 Appendices

Appendices often contain information from data-gathering tools such as questionnaires, interview protocols, consent form templates, coding schemes or samples of coding, and extended tables, transcripts, or descriptions that are too large to incorporate in the body of the text but are nevertheless deemed useful to better contextualize and interpret the findings.

6.9 Evaluating the Written Report

Earlier in this chapter we considered features that contribute to a report's readability, transparency, and persuasiveness. Johnson (1992) presents a list of questions for analyzing case studies. In Table 6.7, I provide a related list of general criteria for evaluating a written report, to which many additional criteria could be added.

Table 6.7 Some Criteria for Evaluating the Written Report

- The study reads well and is interesting and timely, and references are current.
- The theoretical orientation and role of the researcher are evident.
- The author has situated the study in relation to existing research on the topic.
- The study's research questions are clear.
- The research context is carefully described.
- The research participants (or sites) and their specific characteristics and selection criteria are carefully described.
- Data collection procedures, timelines, and findings are explained.
- Conclusions are clearly presented and logically related to the descriptive data and to the original research questions.
- The study contributes knowledge to the field of applied linguistics.

6.10 Summary

In this chapter, I have presented some of the choices available to writers of case study reports. These choices are related to publication venues, different rhetorical styles for different audiences, the organization of theses/dissertations versus books or articles, the notion of developing an authorial voice in one's writing, and criteria for evaluating written reports of case studies. I also pointed out that some of the traditional genres for writing social science research are themselves evolving. The rhetorical modes con- sidered acceptable are determined largely by consensus within the commu- nity (e.g., the editorial boards of scholarly journals) for which the writing is done. Even within the same disciplines or communities, there may be quite distinct discursive representations of research; one journal (e.g., in the area of L2 writing) may welcome more personal, creative narratives of the research process, reflecting the unique voice of the researcher, whereas others may prefer a more realist presentation.

6.11 Conclusion

This book has shown that case studies have a long, distinguished history within applied linguistics and have collectively had a considerable impact on the subfields of L2 acquisition and L2 education. However, until recently, qualitative research methods were not very well represented or explained in research methods textbooks and courses in our field. Case study methods have, at best, been allocated a single chapter in broad surveys of research methodology in L2 studies. The current expansion of qualitative approaches in applied linguistics and in publications on methodology reflects similar trends across the health sciences, social sciences, humanities, and general education. An increased awareness of the importance of ecological validity, and the social, cultural, situational, embodied, and performative nature of experience (e.g., language, learning, and knowledge accumulation) implicit in much case study research has also come to the fore in 21st-century academia.

Whereas qualitative research in the past leaned toward (post)positivism and structuralism, relying on researchers' structured elicitations, analyses, and interpretations of a relatively narrow band of observed linguistic (or other) behavior sometimes designed to test specific hypotheses, current strands of research lean toward more unapologetically subjective, dialectical accounts, incorporating different, sometimes contradictory perspectives of the same phenomenon, and grappling more intentionally with issues of position, voice, and representation (Edge & Richards, 1998). The personal accounts and narratives of language teachers, learners, and others, often across a broader span of time, space, experience, and languages, have now become a major focus in some qualitative research. Evidence of this is in first-person narratives, diary studies, autobiographies, and life histories of learning, teaching, or losing aspects of one's language and identity (e.g., Bailey & Nunan, 1996; Kouritzen, 1999; Schumann, 1997). Studies now examine individuals using language in and across social contexts that were investigated to a lesser degree in the past (e.g., in professional or academic settings; Spack, 1997), in the home/family, community, workplace, and other social institutions. Members of minority groups or populations previously underrepresented in research are being represented to a greater degree as new scholars from inside and outside those communities conduct exploratory, descriptive, or explanatory case study research.

Although interpretive accounts are often quite compelling, these newer approaches to research in applied linguistics are not necessarily supplant- ing older ones, but rather are complementing them, providing alternatives and challenges to the discourses of traditional research, and to erstwhile accepted notions of authenticity and legitimacy (Edge & Richards, 1998). Categorical labels and unacknowledged bias have been the subject of analysis and critique in connection with race, class, culture, language, gender, sexuality, nativeness versus nonnativeness, inner- versus outer-circle Eng- lishes in World Englishes, indigenous versus "Western" ways of knowing (or "knowledges") and researching, and so on.

Future generations of case study researchers in applied linguistics will continue to add significant new thematic areas to those surveyed in this book (especially in Chapter 3), as well as enrich (or complicate) our understanding of existing themes. The new technologies and software programs at our disposal for research purposes and for publishing multimodal and heteroglossic texts will also transform case study research as we know it. Applied linguistic knowledge about discourse, language-as-system, of multilingual and multimodal language learning, use, and loss; about language teaching and assessment; about language and the brain; about the changing ways in which languages are used in contemporary globalized societies by ever-changing populations and institutions; and about research practices, epistemologies, and representation themselves will be transformed. New cases will offer insights about phenomena and contexts (both disciplinary and geographical) that have never before been considered. We therefore have much to look forward to in case study research in applied linguistics.

研究案例

外语教师课堂决策研究
——优秀外语教师个案研究 *†

北京外国语大学　张　莲

提要：本文以定性的多例个案研究试图回答两个问题：1）教师课堂决策参照系的内容及其结构是什么？2）教师如何形成和发展这样的参照系？研究涉及的数据包括课前深度访谈、课堂实录及课后追溯访谈、学生态度与认识调查问卷。研究结果表明，教师课堂决策的参照系是教师关于外语教学的理论知识、个人信念以及一般性假设交织在一起的个人理论；参照系形成的过程就是教师建构和发展个人理论的过程，即教师学习教书、谋求职业成长和发展的过程。

关键词：课堂决策、个人理论、个案研究

[中图分类号] H319　[文献标识码] A　[文章编号] 1000-0429（2005）04_0265-6

1. 前言

　　教师是课堂的决策者和执行者，教育的改革和发展最终都要通过教师的课堂实践来实现。因此，教师或教师教育研究已经成为当前各国教育界共同关注的热点。

　　教师认知研究把教学（包括外语教学）看做一个决策过程（Shavelson & Stern 1981; Calderhead 1984; Woods 1996; Hativa & Goodyear 2002），教师是这个过程的理性决策者（rational decision-maker）。在具体的课堂中，教师的决策体现为课堂事件发生的方向和形式。这些是表面的、可见的，而为何决策则是深层的、不可见的。正是这些深层的东西充当了教师采取不同课堂行动的"参照系"（frame of reference）（Dewey 1938/1963: 6），决定了具体课堂决策的发生与否。所谓"参照系"，是指个体或群体用以感知、理解、判断和行动的观念、价值、基本假设或评估标准体系，它有选择地制约这一系列活动的过程和结果（Bullock & Trombley 1999）。

---

* 本文转载自《外语教学与研究》，2005 年第 4 期。

† 本研究是中国外语教育研究中心承担的教育部人文社科重点基地重大项目"外语教师教育与发展研究"（01JAZJD740010）的子课题成果。本文写作过程中得到导师吴一安教授的悉心指导，谨此致谢。

教师课堂决策研究在国外已有较长的历史，积累了丰富的经验和成果，但国内的相关研究还比较少，特别是针对优秀外语教师课堂决策的实证研究更为罕见。参照系的内容和结构是什么，以及教师如何建立并发展这样的参照系，是本文试图回答的两个核心问题。

2．研究方法

本研究采用了多例个案研究方法（multiple-case approach）。深度访谈、课堂实录以及学生态度与认识的问卷调查是本研究设计的三个层面。

2.1　设计的理据

设计主要基于以下两点考虑。

三十多年的教师行为研究已经证明，外在行为研究的简单化描写和量化评估不足以揭示教师教学行为背后复杂的深层原因。教师认知研究已经发现教师外在的、显性的课堂行为源自他们内心潜在的、隐性的认识和观念。Miles & Huberman（1994: 10）认为，定性研究有三个优势：一是对现实生活的有力把握，二是对潜在的、隐性的问题的理解和解释，三是能够揭示问题的复杂性。教师教育研究的核心是"理解并关注课堂事件"（Tsui 2003: 32），而课堂就是教师的"现实生活"，其最大特点是它的复杂性和混沌性。复杂和混沌的背后是教师潜在的决策动机，所以定性研究范式成为首选方法论。

其次，正如 Rosenshine（1971，转见 Shulman 2000: 249）所言，所有忽略学生学习是否发生的教师研究都是"自我陶醉式的、不道德的研究"。对课堂的关注和研究必然要考虑学生对教师课堂行为的态度和认识，所以对学生态度和认识的调查成了研究设计的另一重要组成部分。

2.2　研究对象

六位优秀高校英语教师参与了本研究。表 1 是这些教师的基本情况。

表 1. 六位教师的基本情况

姓名	性别	年龄	教龄（年）	学历	职称
张红	女	35	9	硕士	副教授
李明	男	39	18	硕士	副教授
方英	女	37	12	硕士	副教授
陈磊	男	37	13	博士	副教授
孟莉	女	47	25	硕士	副教授
刘梅	女	38	11	硕士	讲师

注：1）表中姓名均为假名；2）每位教师在近五年均多次获得国家级、省市级或校级教学奖。

2.3 研究工具

本研究所使用的工具主要有三个：一是课前访谈纲要，二是课后追溯访谈提要，三是学生调查问卷，均为研究者自行设计。纲要和问卷中的问题编制分三步：首先，研究者从相关文献中收集、整理出研究问题所涉及的主题和维度，然后将这些主题和维度编制成试点访谈纲要，最后对试点研究结果进行提炼、梳理，完成所有问题的编制。

课前访谈纲要由两个核心问题衍生出的五个框架问题组成，其中每个框架问题又细化为四至五个延伸问题。问题之间相互印证。

课后访谈提要由六个较为固定的问题和许多即时的"为什么?"、"如何?"、"怎样?"等问句组成。追溯访谈的目的在于了解教师对自己课堂决策的定义和解释，访谈的内容既要回应课前访谈中出现的问题，又要兼顾流动画面中的动态课堂事件，所以课后访谈的问题有很强的情景性和即时性。

学生调查问卷由六个问题组成，涉及学生对教师和课堂的一般性和即时的评价、态度和认识。共有六所学校六个班 196 名学生参加了问卷调查，收回有效问卷 195 份。

2.4 研究步骤

首先对研究对象进行课前访谈，然后进行课堂录像并在课后作学生问卷调查。一周后（或更长）[1]，请研究对象观看录像并同时进行追溯式访谈。所有的访谈均录音并转录为文字，并经研究对象确认。获得的研究资料为 12 小时的课堂录像、740 分钟的访谈录音和 195 份调查问卷。

3. 结果和讨论

3.1 数据分析方法

本研究综合借鉴了语篇分析中"主题一致"（thematic coherence）的分析方法（Linde 1980；Agar & Hobbs 1983）。所谓"主题一致分析"是指在语料中搜索不断重复的主题并考察主题间的关系是否呈现一致性。通过比较不同情景和时间里所发生的事件（instances）并找到其间的一致性或模式，可以推断出一个人隐性或显性的知识（knowledge）、信念（belief）和假设（assumption），从而获得对某一特定文化的认识。在本研究中，这种方法的重要性和有效性表现在研究者可以把课堂事件、决策和决策背后的潜在内容联系起来，而这些潜在的东西正是本研究要回答的第一个问题。

分析分两个层面：第一个层面是个案内分析（within-case analysis）（Miles & Huberman 1994），即分析一个研究对象在三个不同语境（课前、课堂和课后）中表现出的一致性；第二个层面是个案间分析 (cross-case analysis)（同上），即六个研究对象在同一个语境中所呈现的一致性。两个层面的分析都采用三个程序：数据剥离（reduction）、数据陈列 (display) 和文本分析（text analysis）(Miles & Huberman 1994)。因篇幅所限，详细的数据剥离、陈列和文本分析均从略（详见张莲 2004），下面只对主要结果加以讨论。

3.2 结果和讨论

本文对第一个核心问题的回答涉及研究者对三个语境 / 文本（课前、课堂和课后）的分析和推断，所涉及的内容分别是：

（1）研究对象对自己教学方法（包括课堂）的描述、解释和辩白，对优秀外语教师素质的理解，对成功外语学习者的定义以及他们对一个假设情景题的回答（"如果您现在被学校指定去帮助一个刚进入教学岗位的年轻老师，您认为自己最想告诉他 / 她的是什么？"）。

（2）研究者对课堂事件的观察、描述和理解。

（3）研究对象在课后访谈中对课堂事件的定义和诠释。

结果与讨论如下：

1）六位教师在被要求描述自己的教学方法并评价其主要特征时，均能给出明确的回答，详见表 2。显然，突显的主题一致性是"学生"和"学习"。换句话说，教师的教学方法和特征是以学生和学习是否发生为价值导向。这一点在课后随即进行的学生问卷中也得到了印证（表 3）。

表 2. 教师对自己教学方法及特征的描述

教师	教学方法总描述	主要特征
张红	讲解课文时比较传统，但练习听说时会变得比较靠近"交际法"；核心原则是学生要能比较有效地掌握语言知识和提高语言能力。	折中法
李明	以学生为中心；在具体的训练活动中培养学生运用语言能力。	以学生为中心
方英	教师是组织者，学生有更多的练习机会；激发学生，最大限度地保证学生的学习；学生必须说，而不只是听老师说。	综合的方法
陈磊	指导原则是学生是否在积极思考；语言知识和技能都重要，但不是中心，意义的建立和交流才是目标；要考虑学生的学习效果。	比较综合的方法
孟莉	越来越以学生为中心；主要原则是教师是组织者，起宏观指导作用；学生有很大的自主性。	以学生为中心

（待续）

（续表）

教师	教学方法总描述	主要特征
刘梅	给学生很大的自主性，激发他们学习的兴趣和积极性；主要特点是师生间的互动。	交际法特征比较明显，但也是多种方法的运用。

表 3. 学生对课堂教学的评价

教师	班级人数	问卷数	很喜欢	比例(%)	喜欢	比例(%)	不知道	比例(%)	不太喜欢	比例(%)	不喜欢	比例(%)
张红	37	37	24	64.9	13	35.1						
李明	56	55*	37	67.3	14	25.5	1	1.8			1	1.8
方英	24	24	18	75	5	20.8	1	4.2				
陈磊	32	32	16	50	15	46.9	1	3.1				
孟莉	21	21	13	61.9	8	38.1						
刘梅	26	26	16	61.5	9	34.6			1	3.9		

　　表中显示所有相关班级的学生对六位教师的教学满意度非常高。什么是好的教学？好的教学能激发、促进学生有效学习的发生（Dewey 1904/1964; Gage & Berliner 1998; Ramsden 2003）；好教师便是能进行有效教学的教师。

　　2) 六位教师均能清晰地解释自己的课堂教学。所呈现的主题一致性是他们的定义和诠释频繁地诉诸于和外语教学相关的理论和原理，如语言的本质、二语习得的规律和原则、学习理论、应用语言学及其他教育心理学相关内容。如张红在描述和解释自己的教学方法时明确谈到自己对外语学习中"有意识的学习"（conscious learning）和"交际法"的平衡问题的理解。李明和刘梅在解释他们分析课文的方法时都提到了信息加工理论中"图式"概念对他们的影响；陈磊则很清楚地把语言学习的主要目的定义为意义的交流和建构，他的课堂设计了大量学生与学生之间及师生之间观点的交流活动，充分体现了他对语言学习的定义。显然，这一发现和许多相关研究关于教师具有两套理论即"信仰的理论"（espoused theory）和"实践的理论"（theory-in-use）的假设（Schön 1983; Hativa, Barak & Simhi 2001）是不一致的。换句话说，在这些教师身上并不存在所谓信仰理论和实践理论的分裂。

---

* 该班有效问卷数为 55，但对于"学生对课堂教学的评价"这一题项，可能有两位被试漏答。

3）六位教师关于优秀外语教师应具备的素质的陈述也呈现了高度的主题一致性，见表 4 左栏。

表 4. 教师和学生对优秀外语教师素质的描述比较

教师的描述	学生的描述
1) 扎实的语言基本功（准确、优美的语音语调，流利、地道的口语表达）。 2) 广博的文化知识（文化、历史、社会、人文地理等）。 3) 丰富的教育教学方法（如课堂教学方法灵活多样、气氛活跃，能激发学生的学习积极性）。 4) 善于建立良好的师生关系（如有幽默感，热爱、尊重学生，善于与学生沟通，主动了解学生的需求）。 5) 有敬业精神（高度的责任感、使命感）。 6) 善于学习、反思、总结并能有目的地开展实践。	1) 英语水平高，特别是口语好，语音语调标准地道。 2) 善于激发、调动学生的学习积极性（如知道怎么教，方法灵活多样，善于创造活泼积极的课堂气氛）。 3) 善于和学生相处（如爱学生，理解、体谅、宽容学生，有耐心等）。 4) 各方面知识渊博。 5) 有敬业精神，有责任感。 6) 能够清楚地解答问题。 7) 有幽默感。

通过对这些主题词及相关文本话语的进一步分析，我们可以看出：（1）六位教师对优秀外语教师应具备的素质的描述和认识基本一致。这一点和其他一些研究结果不太一致（Wideen *et al.* 1996）。虽然本研究为个案性质，研究目的不是为了推导出一般性结论，但研究对象在这个问题上所表现出来的一致性和相似性不应忽视。（2）这些关于优秀外语教师素质的描述和六位教师对自己教学方法的描述、课堂行为以及他们对自己课堂行为的解释和辩白呈现了不同语境下的主题一致性。（3）教师和学生对什么是优秀教师的看法呈现出惊人的一致性，些许不同也只是表述方面的差异。这一发现的重要性在于明确指出这些优秀教师提升自己的教学能力、改进课堂教学的努力方向与学生的期待是一致的。

4）六位教师对成功外语学习者的描述和定义也基本一致。在他们看来，成功的外语学习者应该是"愿意学习"，"刻苦学习"，"能独立思考"。没有一位老师表示希望自己的学生只是一个"专注的听讲者"。他们希望自己的学生"思考"、"积极、主动"、"参与"、"回应"、"感兴趣"等等，总之，"行动"起来，亦即学习是否在发生是他们定义成功外语学习者的重要标准。

综合以上几点分析和讨论，可以看出研究对象在回答相关问题时实际涉及的内容是他们所拥有的关于外语教学各相关要素的知识、理解、信念、认识和假设。这些要素涉及什么是语言、语言的本质是什么、二语习得的规律和原则、什么是有效学习以及他们对职业道德的理解。所有这些理论知识、个人理解 / 信念或一般性假设 / 认识交织在一起，形成一种以教师"个人理论"（personal theory）为表现形式的知识结构。三个范畴之间并没有明确、清晰的界线，它们彼此重叠、交织，构成教师用于课堂决策的参照系。至此，我们回答了第一个问题。

研究的第二个核心问题是：教师们如何建构与发展这样的决策参照系？有哪些关键因素在起作用？通过对数据的剥离、陈列和文本分析，可发现如下几点：

1）"教学经历 / 体验"是教师形成与发展教学方法过程中的一个必要因素。诸如"我多年的教学经验告诉我……"，"根据我的经验……"这样的表述在研究对象的陈述中复现率很高。经验包括教师自己作为外语学习者的学习经历（Britzman 1991）、课堂教学实践（Galiego 2001）、同事间的互相观摩和交流，以及在教学生涯中发生的一些关键事件等等。但 Dewey（1938/1963: 39）曾指出经验是"一种动力"，但"不是所有的经验都有教育意义"（educative），有的经验可能是"误导性的"，它们会"阻碍或扭曲未来经验的积累和增长"（同上：25）。所以经验可以是资源，但也可能是陷阱（Galiego 2001: 313）。

2）"理论知识"是另一个复现率很高的主题词。研究对象认为理论知识是他们建构与发展教学思想的过程中至关重要的因素，均反复强调应用语言学知识对外语教师的重要性[2]，但同时也都特别指出，他们不会把理论知识照搬进自己的课堂。他们会"选择"、"尝试"、"检验"、"适应"和 / 或"调整"，其中适合自己的教学实际并取得好的效果的就"沉淀"下来，吸收、纳入自己的教学思想，或个人理论，反之则放弃或"淘汰"。他们还认为教学时间越长，获取更丰厚的理论知识的愿望就越迫切，教学反思才会更有效。应该说，这一点从另一个角度回应了经验在教师成长过程中的作用：教学时间的长短和经验的多少是重要的，但它们并不能使一位教师自动成为优秀教师。

3）"反思"是另一个被反复提及的重要主题词。研究对象认为反思是他们职业成长与发展过程中非常重要的因素。它是过去和现在、理论和实践之间的一座桥梁。但同时，他们也特别指出反思不是凭空"遐想"，而是对自己已有经验和理论知识的再思考。反思使过往的经验成为有教育意义的经验（Dewey 1938/1963），从而使反思成为有效反思（effective reflection，见 Loughran 2002）。

4）教师形成和发展自己的教学方法基本上是一个渐进的过程，但这并不意味着这个过程一直是匀速发展的历时过程。数据分析显示，在教师的教学生涯中发生的一些"关键事件"可能给教师带来顿悟的机会，从而在他们的教学思想和行为上引发巨大的变化。这一发现表明，对有经验的教师进行再教育是必要的。

5）"敬业精神"是另一个在个案间分析中呈现高度一致性的主题词。教学从本质上是一种认知活动，但它一定是涵盖了"道德维度"的认知活动（Goodlad, Soder & Sirotnik 1990）。这一点在以往许多关于教师教育观念框架的研究中（Schön 1983；Shulman 1987）一直是被忽略的。分析结果表明这个道德维度在教师建构和发展个人理论的过程中的作用是决定性的，因为"一个教师是否愿意改进自己的教学"，"是否愿意花时间思考、反思"，甚至"是否乐意找到不同的方法做同一个课堂活动"都和他的职业态度有关。

综上所述，我们可以用一个流程图表来表示这样一个过程（图1）：

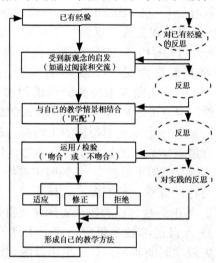

图 1. 建构与发展个人理论的过程

从图 1 中，我们可以看到四个主要特点。

（1）这个过程的本质是建构的。这一点和建构主义所提倡的认识论、学习观是吻合的。建构主义学习观认为个体学习者通过已有的知识、信念和新的观点、事件与活动之间的互动来创建新的知识和理解（Roberts 1998）。学习者根据自己对世界的已有认识"过滤"新的信息并建构自己对新信息的理解，然后把这种理解与他们之前的相关知识表征进行"匹配"。匹配包括对已有知识表征的确认，即吻合，或否认，即不吻合。如吻合，建立或接纳新的意义或认识；如不吻合，则修改已有知识表征以接纳新信息，或者将新信息过滤、清除掉（Roberts 1998）。

（2）这个过程是互动的，即教师在"学习教书"时，教书过程本身就提供了大量的学习机会和经验。

（3）教师的职业道德、责任感是这个过程的启动机制。虽然流程图没有包括道德维度，但并不意味着它不重要。恰恰相反，正如前文分析指出，也是本文要着重指出的是，道德维度在整个个人理论建构和发展的过程中不是一个程序的问题，而是一个可能性的问题，即这个过程是否会发生。

（4）虽然研究对象在建构和发展自己的个人理论的过程中表现出很高的主题一致性和相似性，但也存在一定程度上的差别。不同教师的个人成长背景、受教育环境、工作情景以及个人努力的程度方面都存在差异，所以某一特定因素在不同的教师身上可能会产生不同程度的影响，表现了教师建构和发展个人理论的过程的"个性化"、"情景化"特征。至此，我们回答了第二个核心问题。

4．小结

本文用定性的多个案研究方法对六位高校优秀外语教师进行了课堂决策的研究。研究发现教师作出课堂决策的参照系是他们历经多年的教学实践过程逐渐建立和发展起来的个人理论，包括他们关于外语教学的理论知识、个人信念和一般性假设，以知识结构的形式指引他们的教学行为。就研究对象而言，建构和发展个人理论的过程也就是教师学习教书、谋求职业成长和发展的过程。在这个过程中有诸多因素起作用，其中，经验、理论知识、不间断的实践与反思以及敬业精神是最重要的几个因素。这些因素彼此互动，成就了这些优秀教师。

注　释

1. 一般认为课前访谈和课后追溯访谈的时间间隔较短为好，但有时也可能因为一些技术原因，如课堂录像不能及时供研究对象观看或其他原因而导致间隔时间过长。

2. 传统上，应用语言学被看做外语教师知识基础的一个重要组成部分，但由此产生的一个悖论是：教师很难取得完全专业地位（Freeman 2001）。

参考文献

Agar, M. & J. Hobbs. 1983. Interpreting discourse: coherence and the analysis of ethnographic interviews [J]. *Discourse Processes* 5: 1-32.

Britzman, D. P. 1991. *Practice Makes Practice: A Critical Study of Learning to Teach* [M]. New York: State University of New York Press.

Bullock, A. & S. Trombley. 1999. *The Norton Dictionary of Modern Thought* [Z]. New York: W. W. Norton & Company.

Calderhead, J. 1984. *Teachers' Classroom Decision-Making* [M]. London: Holt, Rinehart and Winston Ltd.

Connelly, F. & D. Clandinin. 1988. *Teachers as Curriculum Planners: Narratives of Experience* [M]. New York: Teachers College Press.

Dewey, J. 1904/1964. The relation of theory to practice in education [A]. In R. Archambault (ed.). *John Dewey on Education* [C]. Chicago: Chicago University Press.

Dewey, J. 1938/1963. *Experience and Education* [M]. New York: Collier Books.

Freeman, D. 2001. Second language teacher education [A]. In R. Carter & D. Nunan (eds.). *The Cambridge Guide to Teaching English to Speakers of Other Languages* [C]. Cambridge: Cambridge University Press.

Gage, N. L. & D. C. Berliner. 1998. *Educational Psychology* [M]. Boston: Houghton Mifflin Company.

Galiego, M. A. 2001. Is experience the best teacher? [J] *Journal of Teacher Education* 52/4: 312-325.

Goodlad, J. I., R. Soder & K. A. Sirotnik. 1990. *The Moral Dimension of Teaching* [C]. San Francisco: Jossey-Bass.

Hativa, N., R. Barak & E. Simhi. 2001. Exemplar university teachers: knowledge and beliefs regarding effective teaching dimensions and strategies [J]. *Journal of Higher Edcuation* 72: 699-729.

Hativa, N. & P. Goodyear. 2002. *Teacher Thinking, Beliefs and Knowledge in Higher Education* [C]. Dordrecht: Kluwer Academic Publishers.

Linde, C. 1980. Investigating language learning/teaching belief systems. Unpublished manuscript [A]. Cited in D. Woods. 1996. *Teacher Cognition in Language Teaching* [M]. Cambridge: Cambridge University Press.

Loughran, J. J. 2002. Effective reflective practice: in search of meaning in learning about teaching [J]. *Journal of Teacher Education* 53/1: 33-43.

Miles, M. B. & A. M. Huberman. 1994. *Qualitative Data Analysis: An Expanded Sourcebook* [M]. Thousand Oaks: Sage Publications.

Polanyi, M. 1967. *The Tacit Dimension* [M]. London: Routledge & Kegan Paul.

Ramsden, P. 2003. *Learning to Teach in Higher Education* [M] (2nd ed.). London: Routledge.

Richards, J. C. & D. Nunan. 1990. *Second Language Teacher Education* [C]. Cambridge: Cambridge University Press.

Roberts, J. 1998. *Language Teacher Education* [M]. London: Arnold.

Rosenshine, B. 1971. *Teaching Behaviors and Student Achievement* [M]. London: National Foundation for Educational Research.

Schön, D. 1983. *The Reflective Practitioner: How Professionals Think in Action* [M]. New York: Basic Books.

Shavelson, R. J. & P. Stern. 1981. Research on teachers' pedagogical thoughts, judgments, decisions, and behavior [J]. *Review of Educational Research* 51/4: 455-498.

Shulman, L. S. 1987. Knowledge and teaching: foundations of the new reform [J]. *Harvard Educational Review* 57: 1-22.

Shulman, L. S. 2000. Truth and consequences?: inquiry and policy in research on teacher education [J]. *Journal of Teacher Education* 53/3: 248-253.

Tsui, A. B. M. 2003. *Understanding Expertise in Teaching: Case Studies of Second Language Teachers* [M]. Cambridge: Cambridge University Press.

Wideen, M. F. , J. A. Mayer-Smith & B. J. Moon. 1996. Knowledge, teacher development and change [A]. In F. Ivor & A. Hargreaves (eds.). *Teachers' Professional Lives* [C]. London: Falmer.

Williams, M. & R. L. Burden. 1996. *Psychology for Language Teachers* [M]. Cambridge: Cambridge University Press.

Woods, D. 1996. *Teacher Cognition in Language Teaching* [M]. Cambridge: Cambridge University Press.

陈向明, 2003, 实践性知识：教师专业发展的基础 [J],《北京大学教育评论》第 1 期。

张　莲, 2004, 外语教师个人理论研究：教师教育之概念重构（博士论文, 北京外国语大学）。

References

Abraham, R. G., & Vann, R. J. (1987). Strategies of two language learners: A case study. In A. Wenden & J. Rubin (Eds.), *Learner strategies in language learning* (pp. 85–102). Englewood Cliffs, NJ: Prentice Hall/International.

Achiba, M. (2003). *Learning to request in a second language: A study of child interlanguage pragmatics*. Clevedon, UK: Multilingual Matters.

Adler, P. A., & Adler, P. (1994). Observational techniques. In N. K. Denzin & Y. S. Lincoln (Eds.), *Handbook of qualitative research* (pp. 377–392). Thousand Oaks, CA: Sage.

Allport, G. W. (1961). *Pattern and growth in personality*. New York: Holt, Rinehart.

Altheide, D. L., & Johnson, J. M. (1994). Criteria for assessing interpretive validity in qualitative research. In N. K. Denzin & Y. S. Lincoln (Eds.), *Handbook of qualitative research* (pp. 485–499). Thousand Oaks, CA: Sage.

Andersen, R., & Shirai, Y. (1994). Discourse motivations for some cognitive acquisition principles. *Studies in Second Language Acquisition, 16*, 133–156.

Antonek, J., Donato, R., & Tucker, G. R. (2000). Differential linguistic development of Japanese language learners in elementary school. *Canadian Modern Language Review, 57*, 325–351.

APA [American Psychological Association]. (2001). *Publication manual of the American Psychological Association* (5th ed.). Washington, DC: APA.

Bachman, L. (2004). Research guidelines in TESOL: Alternative perspectives linking observations to interpretations and uses in TESOL research. *TESOL Quarterly, 38*, 723–728.

Bailey, K. M. (1983). Competitiveness and anxiety in adult second language learning: Looking *at* and *through* the diary studies. In H. W. Seliger & M. H. Long (Eds.), *Classroom oriented research in second language acquisition* (pp. 67–103). Rowley, MA: Newbury House.

Bailey, K. M., & Nunan, D. (Eds.). (1996). *Voices from the language classroom: Qualitative research in second language education*. New York: Cambridge University Press.

Bailey, K. M., & Ochsner, R. (1983). A methodological review of the diary studies: Windmill tilting or social science? In K. M. Bailey, M. H. Long, & S. Peck (Eds.), *Second language acquisition studies* (pp. 88–98). Rowley, MA: Newbury House.

Belcher, D., & Connor, U. (Eds.). (2001). *Reflections on multiliterate lives*. Clevedon, UK: Multilingual Matters.

Bell, J. S. (2002). Narrative inquiry: More than just telling stories. *TESOL Quarterly, 36*, 207–213.

Belz, J., & Kinginger, C. (2002). The cross-linguistic development of address form use in telecollaborative language learning: Two case studies. *Canadian Modern Language Review, 59*, 189–214.

Berg, B. L. (2004). *Qualitative research methods for the social sciences* (5th ed.). Boston: Pearson.

Berg, B. L. (2007). *Qualitative research methods for the social sciences* (6th ed.). Boston: Pearson.

Blum-Kulka, S. (1997). *Dinner talk*. Mahwah, NJ: Lawrence Erlbaum.

Bogdan R. C., & Biklen, S. K. (2003). *Qualitative research for education: An introduction to theories and methods* (4th ed.). Boston: Allyn & Bacon.

Borg, S. (1998). Teachers' pedagogical systems and grammar teaching: A qualitative study. *TESOL Quarterly, 32*, 9–38.

Breen, M. (1985). The social context for language learning: A neglected situation? *Studies in Second Language Acquisition, 7*, 135–158.

Brice, C. (2005). Coding data in qualitative research on L2 writing: Issues and implications. In P. K. Matsuda & T. Silva (Eds.), *Second language writing research* (pp. 159–175). Mahwah, NJ: Lawrence Erlbaum.

Briggs, C. (1986). *Learning how to ask*. Cambridge: Cambridge University Press.

Bromley, D. B. (1986). *The case-study method in psychology and related disci-plines*. New York: John Wiley & Sons.

Brown, J. D. (1988). *Understanding research in second language learning*. Cambridge: Cambridge University Press.

Brown, J. D., & Rodgers, T. S. (2002). *Doing second language research*. Oxford: Oxford University Press.

Brown, R. (1973). *A first language*. Cambridge, MA: Harvard University Press.

Bryman, A. (2004). *Social research methods* (2nd ed). Oxford: Oxford University Press.

Budwig, N. (1995). *A developmental-functionalist approach to child language*. Mahwah, NJ: Lawrence Erlbaum.

Burton, J. (1998). A cross-case analysis of teacher involvement in TESOL research. *TESOL Quarterly, 32*, 419–446.

Butterworth, G., & Hatch, E. (1978). A Spanish-speaking adolescent's acquisition of English syntax. In E. Hatch (Ed.), *Second language acquisition* (pp. 231–255). Rowley, MA: Newbury House.

Cameron, D., Frazer, E., Harvey, P., Rampton, B., & Richardson, K. (1992). *Researching language: Issues of power and method.* London: Routledge.

Cancino, H., Rosansky, E., & Schumann, J. (1978). The acquisition of English negatives and interrogatives by native Spanish speakers. In E. Hatch (Ed.), *Second language acquisition* (pp. 207–230). Rowley, MA: Newbury House.

Caracelli, V. W., & Greene, J. C. (1993). Data analysis strategies for mixed-method evaluation designs. *Educational Evaluation and Policy Analysis, 15,* 195–207.

Casanave, C. P. (1992). Cultural diversity and socialization: A case study of a Hispanic woman in a doctoral program in sociology. In D. E. Murray (Ed.), *Diversity as resource: Redefining cultural literacy* (pp. 148–182). Alexandria, VA: TESOL.

Casanave, C. P. (1998). Transitions: The balancing act of bilingual academics. *Journal of Second Language Writing, 7,* 175–203.

Casanave, C. P. (2002). *Writing games: Multicultural case studies of academic literacy practices in higher education.* Mahwah, NJ: Lawrence Erlbaum.

Casanave, C. P. (2003). Looking ahead to more sociopolitically-oriented case study research in L2 writing scholarship (But should it be called "post-process"?). *Journal of Second Language Writing, 12,* 85–102.

Casanave, C. P., & Schecter, S. (Eds.). (1997). *On becoming a language educator: Per- sonal essays of professional development.* Mahwah, NJ: Lawrence Erlbaum.

Cazden, C., Cancino, H., Rosansky, E., & Schumann, J. (1975). *Second language acquisition in children, adolescents and adults* (final report). Washington, DC: National Institute of Education, Office of Research and Grants. (Grant NE-6-00-3-014)

Chalhoub-Deville, M., Chapelle, C., & Duff, P. (Eds.). (2006). *Inference and generalizability in applied linguistics: Multiple perspectives.* Amsterdam: John Benjamins.

Chapelle, C., & Duff, P. (Eds.). (2003). Some guidelines for conducting quantitative and qualitative research in TESOL. *TESOL Quarterly, 37,* 157–178.

Christians, C. (2000). Ethics and politics in qualitative research. In N. Denzin & Y. S. Lincoln (Eds.), *Handbook of qualitative research* (2nd ed., pp. 133–162). Thousand Oaks, CA: Sage.

Coffey, A., & Atkinson, P. (1996). *Making sense of qualitative data: Complementary research strategies.* London: Sage Publications.

Cohen, L., & Manion, L. (1994). *Research methods in education* (4th ed.). London: Routledge.

Coughlan, P., & Duff, P. (1994). Same task, different activities: Analysis of a SLA [second language acquisition] task from an activity theory perspective. In J. Lantolf & G. Appel (Eds.), *Vygotskian perspectives on second language research* (pp. 173–193). Norwood, NJ: Ablex.

Creswell, J. (1994). *Research design: Qualitative and quantitative approaches.* Thousand Oaks, CA: Sage.

Creswell, J. (1998). *Qualitative inquiry and research design: Choosing among five traditions.* Thousand Oaks, CA: Sage.

Curtiss, S. (1977). *Genie: A psycholinguistic study of a modern-day "wild child".* New York: Academic Press.

Curtiss, S. (1994). Language as a cognitive system: Its independence and selective vulnerability. In C. Otero (Ed.), *Noam Chomsky: Critical assessments* (pp. 211–255). London: Routledge.

Dagenais, D., & Day, E. (1999). Home language practices of trilingual children in French immersion. *Canadian Modern Language Review, 56,* 99–123.

Davidson, F. (1993). Some comments on the social impact of research in TESOL. *TESOL Quarterly, 27,* 160–162.

Davis, K. (1995). Qualitative theory and methods in applied linguistics research. *TESOL Quarterly, 29,* 427–453.

Day, E. (2002). *Identity and the young English language learner.* Clevedon, UK: Multilingual Matters.

de Courcy, M. (2002). *Learners' experiences of immersion education: Case studies of French and Chinese.* Clevedon, UK: Multilingual Matters.

de la Pietra, M., & Romo, H. (2003). Collaborative literacy in a Mexican immigrant household: The role of sibling mediators in the socialization of preschool learners. In R. Bayley & S. Schecter (Eds.), *Language socialization in bilingual and multilingual societies* (pp. 44–61). Clevedon, UK: Multilingual Matters.

Denzin, N. K. (1994). The art and politics of interpretation. In N. Denzin & Y. S. Lincoln (Eds.), *The handbook of qualitative research* (pp. 500–515). Thousand Oaks, CA: Sage.

Denzin, N. K., & Lincoln, Y. S. (1994a). Introduction: Entering the field of qualitative research. In N. K. Denzin & Y. S. Lincoln (Eds.), *The handbook of qualitative research* (pp. 1–17). Thousand Oaks, CA: Sage.

Denzin, N. K., & Lincoln, Y. S. (Eds.). (1994b). *The handbook of qualitative research.* Thousand Oaks, CA: Sage.

Denzin, N. K., & Lincoln, Y. S. (Eds.). (2000). *The handbook of qualitative research* (2nd ed.). Thousand Oaks, CA: Sage.

Denzin, N. K., & Lincoln, Y. S. (Eds.). (2003). *Collecting and interpreting qualitative materials*. Thousand Oaks, CA: Sage.

Denzin, N. K., & Lincoln, Y. S. (2005a). Introduction: The discipline and practice of qualitative research. In N. K. Denzin & Y. S. Lincoln (Eds.), *The handbook of qualitative research* (3rd ed., pp. 1–32). Thousand Oaks, CA: Sage.

Denzin, N. K., & Lincoln, Y. S. (Eds.). (2005b). *The handbook of qualitative research* (3rd ed.). Thousand Oaks, CA: Sage.

Diamond, M. C., Scheibel, A. B., Murphy, G. M., Jr., and Harvey, T. (1985). On the brain of a scientist: Albert Einstein. *Experimental Neurology, 88*, 198–204.

Dobson, C. B., Hardy, M., Heyes, S., Humphreys, A., & Humphreys, P. (1981). *Understanding psychology*. London: Weidenfeld and Nicolson.

Donmoyer, R. (1990). Generalizability and the single-case study. In E. Eisner & A. Peshkin (Eds.), *Qualitative inquiry in education: The continuing debate* (pp. 175–200). New York: Teachers College Press.

Duff, P. (1985). *Syntacticization of topic in Japanese and Mandarin students' English: A test of Rutherford's model*. Unpublished master's thesis, University of Hawaii, Manoa.

Duff, P. (1988, March). *The progression toward subject prominence in the interlanguage of Chinese middle school students*. Paper presented at the Eighth Second Language Research Forum, University of Hawaii, Manoa.

Duff, P. (1990). Developments in the case study approach to second language acquisition research. In T. Hayes & K. Yoshioka (Eds.), *Proceedings of the First Conference on Second Language Acquisition and Teaching* (pp. 34–87). Tokyo: International University of Japan.

Duff, P. (1993a). Syntax, semantics, and SLA: The convergence of possessive and existential constructions. *Studies in Second Language Acquisition, 15*, 1–34.

Duff, P. (1993b). Tasks and interlanguage performance: An SLA [second language acquisition] research perspective. In G. Crookes & S. Gass (Eds.), *Tasks in language learning: Integrating theory and practice* (pp. 57–95). Clevedon, UK: Multilingual Matters.

Duff, P. (1993c). *Changing times, changing minds: Language socialization in Hungarian-English schools*. Unpublished PhD dissertation, University of California, Los Angeles.

Duff, P. (1995). An ethnography of communication in immersion classrooms in Hungary. *TESOL Quarterly, 29*, 505–537.

Duff, P. (1996). Different languages, different practices: Socialization of discourse competence in dual-language school classrooms in Hungary. In K. Bailey & D. Nunan (Eds.), *Voices from the language classroom: Qualitative research in second language acquisition* (pp. 407–433). New York: Cambridge University Press.

Duff, P. (2001). Language, literacy, content, and (pop) culture: Challenges for ESL students in mainstream courses. *Canadian Modern Language Review, 59,* 103–132.

Duff, P. (2002a). Research methods in applied linguistics. In R. Kaplan (Ed.), *Handbook of applied linguistics* (pp. 13–23). Oxford: Oxford University Press.

Duff, P. (2002b). The discursive co-construction of knowledge, identity, and difference: An ethnography of communication in the high school mainstream. *Applied Linguistics, 23,* 289–322.

Duff, P. (2005, July). *The life and afterlife of second-language classroom research: Epistemological, ethical, methodological, and sociopolitical issues.* Paper presented at the World Congress of Applied Linguistics, Madison, WI.

Duff, P. (2006). Beyond generalizability: Context, credibility and complexity in applied linguistics research. In M. Chalhoub-Deville, C. Chapelle, & P. Duff (Eds.), *Inference and generalizability in applied linguistics: Multiple perspectives* (pp. 65–95). Amsterdam: John Benjamins.

Duff, P., & Early, M. (1996). Problematics of classroom research across sociopolitical contexts. In S. Gass & J. Schachter (Eds.), *Second language classroom research: Issues and opportunities* (pp. 1–30). Hillsdale, NJ: Lawrence Erlbaum.

Duff, P., & Hornberger, N. H. (Eds.). (in press). *Language socialization. Encyclopedia of language and education: Vol. 8.* Boston: Springer.

Duff, P., & Li, D. (2004). Issues in Mandarin language instruction: Theory, research, and practice. *System, 32,* 443–456.

Duff, P., & Uchida, Y. (1997). The negotiation of teachers' sociocultural identities and practices in postsecondary EFL classrooms. *TESOL Quarterly, 31,* 451–486.

Duff, P., Wong, P., & Early, M. (2000). Learning language for work and life: The linguistic socialization of immigrant Canadians seeking careers in healthcare. *Canadian Modern Language Review, 57,* 9–57. (Reprinted in Duff, P., Wong, P., & Early. M. (2002). Learning language for work and life: The linguistic socialization of immigrant Canadians seeking careers in healthcare. *Modern Language Journal, 86,* 397–422.)

Dufon, M. (1993) Ethics in TESOL research. *TESOL Quarterly, 27,* 157–160.

Duranti, A., & Goodwin, C. (Eds.). (1992). *Rethinking context: Language as an interactive phenomenon.* Cambridge: Cambridge University Press.

Edge, J., & Richards, K. (1998). May I see your warrant, please? Justifying outcomes in qualitative research. *Applied Linguistics, 19,* 334–356.

Ehrman, M. E. (1972). *Contemporary Cambodian: Grammatical sketch.* Washington, DC: Foreign Service Institute.

Ehrman, M. E. (1996). *Understanding second language learning difficulties.* Thousand Oaks, CA: Sage.

Eisner, E., & Peshkin, A. (Eds.). (1990). *Qualitative inquiry in education: The continuing debate.* New York: Teachers College Press.

Ellis, N., & Larsen-Freeman, D. (2006). Language emergence: Implications for applied linguistics. *Applied Linguistics, 27,* 558–589.

Ellis, R. (1992). Learning to communicate in the classroom: A study of two language learners' requests. *Studies in Second Language Acquisition, 14,* 1–23.

Ellis, R. (1994). *The study of second language acquisition.* Oxford: Oxford University Press.

Ellis, R., & Barkhuizen, G. (2005). *Analysing learner language.* Oxford: Oxford University Press.

Enomoto, E., & Bair, M. (1999). The role of the school in the assimilation of immigrant children: A case study of Arab Americans. *International Journal of Curriculum and Instruction, 1,* 45–66. (Reprinted in Merriam, S. *et al.* (Eds.). (2002). *Qualitative research in practice* (pp. 181–197). San Francisco: Jossey-Bass.)

Enomoto, E., & Bair, M. (2002). Reflections on our own inner lives. In S. Merriam *et al.* (Eds.), *Qualitative research in practice* (pp. 198–200). San Francisco: Jossey-Bass.

Faltis, C. (1997). Case study methods in researching language and education. In N. H. Hornberger & D. Corson (Eds.), *Encyclopedia of language and education: Research methods in language and education* (Vol. 8). London: Kluwer.

Fielding, N., & Lee, R. M. (1998). *Computer analysis and qualitative research.* Thousand Oaks, CA: Sage.

Fontana, A., & Frey, J. H. (1994). Interviewing: The art of science. In N. K. Denzin & Y. S. Lincoln (Eds.), *Handbook of qualitative research* (pp. 361–176). Thousand Oaks, CA: Sage.

Fraenkel, J. R., & Wallen, N. E. (1996). *How to design and evaluate research in education* (3rd ed.). New York: McGraw-Hill.

Gall, J. P., Gall, M. D., & Borg, W. T. (2005). *Applying educational research* (5th ed.). Boston: Pearson Education.

Gall, M. D., Borg, W. R., & Gall, J. P. (1996). *Educational research* (6th ed.). White Plains, NY: Longman.

Gall, M. D., Gall, J. P., & Borg, W. T. (2003). *Educational research* (7th ed.). White Plains, NY: Pearson Education.

Galloway, L. (1981). *Contributions of the right cerebral hemisphere to language and communication.* PhD dissertation, University of California, Los Angeles.

Gass, S., Madden, C., Preston, D., & Selinker, L. (Eds.). (1989). *Variation in second language acquisition: Psycholinguistic issues.* Clevedon, UK: Multilingual Matters.

Gass, S. M., & Selinker, L. (2001). *Second language acquisition* (2nd ed.). Hillsdale, NJ: Lawrence Erlbaum.

Geertz, C. (1973). Thick description: Toward an interpretive theory of culture. In C. Geertz (Ed.), *The interpretation of cultures* (pp. 3–30). New York: Basic Books.

George, A. L., & Bennett, A. (2005). *Case studies and theory development in the social sciences*. Cambridge, MA: MIT Press.

Givón, T. (1979). *On understanding grammar.* New York: Academic Press.

Glaser, B. G., & Strauss, A. L. (1967). *The discovery of grounded theory: Strategies for qualitative research*. Hawthorne, NY: Aldine de Gruyter.

Goldstein, T. (1997). *Two languages at work: Bilingual life on the production floor.* Berlin: Mouton de Gruyter.

Granger, C. A. (2004). *Silence in second language learning: A psychoanalytic reading.* Clevedon, UK: Multilingual Matters.

Green, J., Franquiz, M., & Dixon, C. (1997). The myth of the objective transcript. *TESOL Quarterly, 31*, 172–176.

Grimshaw, G., Adelstein, A., Bryden, P., & MacKinnon, G. (1998). First language acquisition in adolescence: Evidence for a critical period for verbal language development. *Brain and Language, 63*, 237–255.

Guardado, M. (2002). Loss and maintenance of first language skills: Case studies of Hispanic families in Vancouver. *Canadian Modern Language Review, 58*, 341–363.

Hakuta, K. (1976). A case study of a Japanese child learning English. *Language Learning, 26*, 321–351.

Halliday, M. (1975). *Learning how to mean.* London: Edward Arnolds.

Hamel, J., Dufour, S., & Fortin, D. (1993). *Case study methods. Qualitative research methods* (Vol. 32). Newbury Park, CA: Sage.

Hammersley, M. (1992). *What's wrong with ethnography?* London: Routledge.

Han, Z.-H. (1998). *Fossilization: An investigation into advanced L2 learning of a typologically distant language.* Unpublished PhD dissertation, University of London, UK.

Han, Z.-H. (2004). *Fossilization in adult second language acquisition.* Clevedon, UK: Multilingual Matters.

Harklau, L. (1994a). ESL versus mainstream classes: Contrasting L2 learning environments. *TESOL Quarterly, 28*, 241–272.

Harklau, L. (1994b). Tracking and linguistic minority students: Consequences of ability grouping for second language learners. *Linguistics and Education, 6*, 217–244.

Harklau, L. (1999). Representing culture in the ESL writing classroom. In E. Hinkel

(Ed.), *Culture in second language teaching and learning* (pp. 109–130). New York: Cambridge University Press.

Harklau, L. (2000). From the 'good kids' to the 'worst': Representations of English language learners across educational settings. *TESOL Quarterly, 34*, 35–67.

Hatch, E. (Ed.). (1978a). *Second language acquisition*. Rowley, MA: Newbury House.

Hatch, E. (1978b). Introduction. In E. Hatch (Ed.), *Second language acquisition* (pp. 1 –18). Rowley, MA: Newbury House.

Hatch, E. (1978c). Discourse analysis and second language acquisition. In E. Hatch (Ed.), *Second language acquisition* (pp. 401–435). Rowley, MA: Newbury House.

Hatch, E. (1983). *Psycholinguistics: A second language perspective*. Rowley, MA: Newbury House.

Hatch, E., & Farhady, H. (1982). *Research design and statistics for applied linguistics*. Rowley, MA: Newbury House.

Hatch, E., & Lazaraton, A. (1991). *The research manual: Design and statistics for applied linguistics*. Boston: Heinle and Heinle.

Hatch, J. A. (2002). *Doing qualitative research in education settings*. Albany: State University of New York Press.

Hesse-Biber, S. N., & Leavy, P. (2006). *The practice of qualitative research*. Thousand Oaks, CA: Sage.

Hilles, S. (1991). Access to Universal Grammar in second language acquisition. *Point counterpoint: Universal Grammar in the second language* (pp. 305–338). Amsterdam: John Benjamins.

Hoffman, E. (1989). *Lost in translation: A life in a new language*. New York: Penguin Books.

Holliday, A. (1994). *Appropriate methodology and social context*. Cambridge: Cambridge University Press.

Holliday, A. (2002). *Doing and writing qualitative research*. Thousand Oaks, CA: Sage.

Holliday, A. (2004). Issues of validity in progressive paradigms of qualitative research. *TESOL Quarterly, 38*, 731–734.

Holstein, J. A., & Gubrium, J. F. (1997). Active interviewing. In D. Silverman (Ed.), *Qualitative research: Theory, method, and practice* (pp. 113–129). Thousand Oaks, CA: Sage.

Hornberger, N. (2006). Negotiating methodological rich points in applied linguistics research: An ethnographer's view. In M. Chalhoub-Deville, C. Chapelle, & P. Duff (Eds.), *Inference and generalizability in applied linguistics: Multiple perspectives* (pp. 221–240). Amsterdam: John Benjamins.

Hornberger, N., & Ricento, T. (Eds.). (1996). Language planning and policy [special issue]. *TESOL Quarterly, 30,* 3.

Huang, J., & Hatch, E. (1978). A Chinese child's acquisition of English. In E. Hatch (Ed.), *Second language acquisition* (pp. 118–147). Rowley, MA: Newbury House.

Hudelson, S. (1989). A tale of two children: Individual differences in ESL children's writing. In D. M. Johnson & D. H. Roen (Eds.), *Richness in writing: Empowering ESL students* (pp. 84–99). White Plains, NY: Longman.

Huebner, T. (1979). Order-of-acquisition vs. dynamic paradigm: A comparison of method in interlanguage research. *TESOL Quarterly, 13,* 21–28.

Huebner, T. (1983). *A longitudinal analysis of the acquisition of English.* Ann Arbor, MI: Karoma.

Hunter, J. (1997). Multiple perceptions: Social identity in a multilingual elementary classroom. *TESOL Quarterly, 31,* 603–611.

Ioup, G. (1989). Immigrant children who have failed to acquire native English. In S. Gass, C. Madden, D. Preston, & L. Selinker (Eds.), *Variation in second language acquisition: Psycholinguistic issues* (pp. 160–175). Clevedon, UK: Multilingual Matters.

Ioup, G. (1995). Age in second language development. In E. Hinkel (Ed.), *Handbook of research in second language teaching and learning* (pp. 419–436). Mahwah, NJ: Lawrence Erlbaum.

Ioup, G., Boustagui, E., El Tigi, M., & Moselle, M. (1994). Re-examining the critical period hypothesis: A case study of successful adult second language acquisition in a naturalistic environment. *Studies in Second Language Acquisition, 16,* 73–98.

Itoh, H., & Hatch, E. (1978). Second language acquisition: A case study. In E. Hatch (Ed.), *Second language acquisition* (pp. 76–88). Rowley, MA: Newbury House.

Ivani , R. (1998). *Writing and identity: The discoursal construction of identity in academic writing.* Philadelphia: John Benjamins.

Jacobs, B. (1988). Neurobiological differentiation of primary and secondary language acquisition. *Studies in Second Language Acquisition, 10,* 303–337.

Jarvis, S. (2003). Probing the effects of the L2 on the L1: A case study. In V. Cook (Ed.), *Effects of the second language on the first* (pp. 81–102). Clevedon, UK: Multilingual Matters.

Johnson, D. M. (1992). *Approaches to research in second language learning.* New York: Longman.

Kanno, Y. (2003). *Negotiating bilingual and bicultural identities: Japanese returnees betwixt two worlds.* Mahwah, NJ: Lawrence Erlbaum.

Kaplan, A. (1993). *French lessons: A memoir.* Chicago: University of Chicago Press.

Kenyeres, A. (1938). Comment une petite Hongroise de sept ans apprend le français. *Archives de Psychologie, 26,* 321–366.

Kimmel, A. J. (1996). *Ethical issues in behavioral research.* Oxford: Blackwell.

Klein, W., & Perdue, C. (1992). *Utterance structure: Developing grammars again.* Philadelphia: John Benjamins.

Kobayashi, M. (2003). The role of peer support in ESL students' accomplishment of oral academic tasks. *Canadian Modern Language Review, 59,* 337–368.

Kobayashi, M. (2004). *A sociocultural study of second language tasks: Activity, agency, and language socialization.* Unpublished PhD dissertation, University of British Columbia, Vancouver.

Koschmann, T. (Ed.). (1999). Meaning making [special issue]. *Discourse Processes, 27,* 2.

Kouritzen, S. (1999). *Face[t]s of first language loss.* Mahwah, NJ: Lawrence Erlbaum.

Kramsch, C. (Ed.). (2002). *Language acquisition and language socialization: Ecological perspectives.* New York: Continuum.

Krathwohl, D. (1993). *Methods of educational and social science research.* White Plains, NY: Longman.

Krueger, R. A. (1994). *Focus groups: A practical guide for applied research.* Thousand Oaks, CA: Sage.

Kvale, S. (1996). *InterViews: An introduction to qualitative research methods.* Thousand Oaks, CA: Sage.

Labov, W. (1966). *The social stratification of English in New York City.* Washington, DC: Center for Applied Linguistics.

Lam, W. S. E. (2000). L2 literacy and the design of the self: A case study of a teenager writing on the Internet. *TESOL Quarterly, 34,* 457–482.

Lam, W. S. E. (2004). Second language socialization in a bilingual chat room: Global and local considerations. *Language Learning & Technology, 8,* 44–65.

Lamberth, J., McCullers, J. C., & Mellgren, R. L. (1976). *Foundations of psychology.* New York: Harper & Row.

Lantolf, J. P. (Ed.). (2000). *Sociocultural theory and second language learning.* New York: Oxford University Press.

Lantolf, J. P., & Thorne, S. L. (2006). *Sociocultural theory and the genesis of second language development.* Oxford: Oxford University Press.

Lardiere, D. (1998a). Case and tense in the "fossilized" steady state. *Second Language Research, 14,* 1–26.

Lardiere, D. (1998b). Dissociating syntax from morphology in a divergent L2 end-state grammar. *Second Language Research, 14,* 359–375.

Lardiere, D. (2006). *Ultimate attainment in second language acquisition: A case study.* Mahwah, NJ: Lawrence Erlbaum.

Larsen-Freeman, D. (1997). Chaos/complexity science and second language acquisition. *Applied Linguistics, 18,* 141–165.

Larsen-Freeman, D., & Long, M. H. (1991) *An introduction to second language acquisition research.* New York: Longman.

Lather, P. (1991). *Getting smart: Feminist research and pedagogy with/in the postmodern.* New York: Routledge.

Lave, J., & Wenger, E. (1991). *Situated learning: Legitimate peripheral participation.* Cambridge: Cambridge University Press.

Lazaraton, A. (1995). Qualitative research in applied linguistics: A progress report. *TESOL Quarterly, 29,* 455–472.

Lazaraton, A. (2000). Current trends in research methodology and statistics in applied linguistics. *TESOL Quarterly, 34,* 175–181.

Lazaraton, A. (2003). Evaluating criteria for qualitative research in applied linguistics: Whose criteria and whose research? *Modern Language Journal, 87,* 1–12.

Leather, J., & van Dam, J. (Eds.). (2003). *Ecology of language acquisition.* Dordrecht: Kluwer Academic Publishers.

LeCompte, M. D., Millroy, W. L., & Preissle, J. (Eds.). (1992). *The handbook of qualitative research in education.* New York: Academic Press.

Leki, I. (1995). Coping strategies of ESL students in writing tasks across the curriculum. *TESOL Quarterly, 29,* 235–260.

Leki, I. (2001). "A narrow thinking system": Nonnative-English-speaking students in group projects across the curriculum. *TESOL Quarterly, 35,* 39–67.

Leopold, W. (1939, 1947, 1949a, 1949b). *Speech development of a bilingual child: A linguist's record.* Vol. 1, *Vocabulary growth in the first two years.* Vol. 2, *Sound learning in the first two years.* Vol. 3, *Grammar and general problems in the first two years.* Vol. 4, *Diary from age 2.* Evanston, IL: North-western University Press.

Leopold, W. (1954). A child's learning of English. *Georgetown University Round Table on Languages and Linguistics, 7,* 19-30. (Reprinted in Hatch, E. (Ed.). (1978). *Second language acquisition* (pp. 24–32). Rowley, MA: Newbury House.)

Lewin, M. (1979). *Understanding psychological research.* New York: John Wiley & Sons.

Lewis, O. (1961). *The children of Sanchez: Autobiography of a Mexican family.* New York: Random House.

Li, C., & Thompson, S. (1976). Subject and topic: A new typology of language. In C. Li (Ed.), *Subject and topic* (pp. 457–490). New York: Academic Press.

Li, D. (1998). *Expressing needs and wants in a second language: An ethnographic study of Chinese immigrant women's requesting behavior.* Unpublished doctoral dissertation, Teachers College, Columbia University, New York.

Li, D. (2000). The pragmatics of making requests in the L2 workplace: A case study of language socialization. *Canadian Modern Language Review*, *57*, 58–87.

Li, D., & Duff, P. (in press). Issues in Chinese heritage language education and research at the postsecondary level. In A. W. He & Y. Xiao (Eds.), *Chinese as a heritage language*. Honolulu: National Foreign Language Resource Center.

Lightbown, P., & White, L. (1987). The influence of linguistic theories on language acquisition research: Description and explanation. *Language Learning*, *37*, 483–510.

Lincoln, Y., & Guba, E. G. (1985). *Naturalistic inquiry*. Beverly Hills: Sage.

Lincoln, Y., & Guba, E. G. (2000). Paradigmatic controversies, contradictions, and emerging confluences. In N. K. Denzin & Y. S. Lincoln (Eds.), *Handbook of qualitative research* (2nd ed., pp. 163–188). Thousand Oaks, CA: Sage.

Long, M. (2003). Stabilization and fossilization in interlanguage development. In C. Doughty & M. Long (Eds.), *Handbook of second language acquisition* (pp. 487–536). Oxford: Blackwell.

Long, M., & Sato, C. (1984). Methodological issues in interlanguage studies: An interactionist perspective. In A. Davies, C. Criper, & A. P. R. Howatt (Eds.), *Interlanguage* (pp. 253–279). Edinburgh: Edinburgh University Press.

Losey, K. M. (1997). *Listen to the silences: Mexican American interaction in the composition classroom and community*. Norwood, NJ: Ablex.

Lynch, B. (1996). *Language program evaluation: Theory and practice*. Cambridge: Cambridge University Press.

Lyovich, N. (1997). *The multilingual self: An inquiry into language learning*. Mahwah, NJ: Lawrence Erlbaum.

Mackey, A., & Gass, S. (2005). *Second language research: Methodology and design*. Mahwah, NJ: Lawrence Erlbaum.

Madriz, E. (2000). Focus groups in feminist research. In N. K. Denzin & Y. S. Lincoln (Eds.), *Handbook of qualitative research* (2nd ed., pp. 835–850). Thousand Oaks, CA: Sage.

Malinowski, B. (1953). *Argonauts of the Western Pacific*. London: Routledge & Kegan Paul. (Original work published 1922)

Markee, N. P. (2000). *Conversation analysis*. Mahwah, NJ: Lawrence Erlbaum.

Markee, N. P. (2006). A conversation analytic perspective on the role of quantification and generalizability in second language acquisition. In M. Chalhoub-Deville, C. Chapelle, & P. Duff (Eds.), *Inference and generalizability in applied linguistics: Multiple perspectives* (pp. 135–162). Philadelphia: John Benjamins.

Marshall, C., & Rossman, G. (1995). *Designing qualitative research* (2nd ed.). Thousand Oaks, CA: Sage.

Marx, N. (2002). Never quite a "native speaker": Accent and identity in the L2 and the

L1. *Canadian Modern Language Review, 59,* 264–281.

McKay, S. (2006). *Researching second language classrooms.* Mahwah, NJ: Lawrence Erlbaum.

McKay, S., & Wong, S. C. (1996). Multiple discourses, multiple identities: Investment and agency in second-language learning among Chinese adolescent immigrant students. *Harvard Educational Review, 66,* 577–608.

Mellow, J. D. (1996). *A longitudinal study of the effects of instruction on the development of article use by adult Japanese ESL learners.* Unpublished doctoral dissertation, University of British Columbia, Vancouver.

Mellow, J. D., Reeder, K., & Forster, E. (1996). Using time-series research designs to investigate the effects of instruction on SLA. *Studies in Second Language Acquisition, 18,* 325–350.

Merriam, S. (1988). *Case study research in education: A qualitative approach.* San Francisco: Jossey-Bass.

Merriam, S. (1998). *Qualitative research and case study applications in education* (2nd ed.). San Francisco: Jossey-Bass.

Merriam, S., & Associates (Eds.). (2002). *Qualitative research in practice.* San Francisco: Jossey-Bass.

Miles, M., & Huberman, A. M. (1994). *Qualitative data analysis* (2nd ed.). Thousand Oaks, CA: Sage.

Miller, J. (1997). Case study research in second language teaching. *Queensland Journal of Educational Research, 13,* 33–53.

Miller, J. (2003). *Audible difference.* Clevedon, UK: Multilingual Matters.

Miller, J., & Glassner, B. (1997). The "inside" and the "outside": Finding realities in interviews. In M. Silverstein (Ed.), *Qualitative research: Theory, method and practice* (pp. 99–112). Thousand Oaks, CA: Sage.

Mishler, E. (1986). *Research interviewing: Context and narrative.* Cambridge, MA: Harvard University Press.

Mitchell, R., & Miles, F. (2004). *Second language learning theories* (2nd ed.). London: Edward Arnold.

Mori, K. (1997). *Polite lies: On being a woman caught between cultures.* New York: Henry Holt.

Morita, N. (2000). Discourse socialization through oral classroom activities in a TESL graduate program. *TESOL Quarterly, 34,* 279–310.

Morita, N. (2002). *Negotiating participation in second language academic communities: A study of identity, agency, and transformation.* Unpublished doctoral dissertation, University of British Columbia, Vancouver.

Morita, N. (2004). Negotiating participation and identity in second language academic communities. *TESOL Quarterly, 38,* 573–603.

Naiman, N., Frohlich, M., Stern, D., & Todesco, A. (1978). *The good language learner.* Toronto: Ontario Institute for Studies in Education.

Neuman, S. B., & McCormick, S. (Eds.). (1995). *Single-subject experimental research: Applications for literacy.* Newark, DE: International Reading Association.

Neuman, W. L. (1994). *Social research methods: Qualitative and quantitative approaches* (2nd ed.). Boston: Allyn & Bacon.

Noblit, G. W., & Hare, R. D. (1988). *Meta-ethnography: Synthesizing qualitative studies.* Thousand Oaks, CA: Sage.

Norris, J. M., & Ortega, L. (2006). The value and practice of research synthesis for language learning and teaching. In J. Norris & L. Ortega (Eds.), *Synthesizing research on language learning and teaching* (pp. 3–50). Philadelphia: John Benjamins.

Norton, B. (Ed.). (1997). Language and identity [special issue]. *TESOL Quarterly, 31,* 3.

Norton Peirce, B. (1995). Social identity, investment, and language learning. *TESOL Quarterly, 29,* 9–31.

Norton, B. (2000). *Identity and language learning: Gender, ethnicity and educational change.* London: Longman/Pearson Education.

Norton, B., & Toohey, K. (2001). Changing perspectives on good language learners. *TESOL Quarterly, 35,* 307–322.

Novoa, L., Fein, D., & Obler, L. K. (1988). Talent in foreign languages: A case study. In L. Obler & D. Fein (Eds.), *The exceptional brain: Neuropsychology of talent and special abilities* (pp. 294–302). New York: Guilford Press.

Nunan, D. (1992). *Research methods in language learning.* Cambridge: Cambridge University Press.

Obler, L. (1989). Exceptional second language learners. In S. Gass, C. Madden, D. Preston, & L. Selinker (Eds.), *Variation in second language acquisition,* Vol. II, *Psycholinguistic issues* (pp. 141–149). Clevedon, UK: Multilingual Matters.

Obler, L., & Fein, D. (Eds.). (1988). *The exceptional brain: Neuropsychology of talent and special abilities.* New York: Guilford Press.

Ochs, E. (1979). Transcription as theory. In E. Ochs & B. Schieffelin (Eds.), *Developmental pragmatics* (pp. 43–72). New York: Academic Press.

Ortega, L. (Ed.). (2005). Methodology, epistemology, and ethics in instructed SLA research [special issue]. *Modern Language Journal, 89,* 3.

Ortega, L., & Iberri-Shea, G. (2005). Longitudinal research in second language acquisition: Recent trends and future directions. *Annual Review of Applied Linguistics, 25,* 26–45.

Palys, T. (1997). *Research decisions: Quantitative and qualitative perspectives* (2nd ed.). Toronto: Harcourt, Brace, Jovanovich.

Paradis, M. (1977). Bilingualism and aphasia. In H. Whitaker & H. Whitaker (Eds.), *Studies in neurolinguistics* (Vol. 3, pp. 65–121). New York: Academic Press.

Patton, M. Q. (1990). *Qualitative evaluation methods* (2nd ed.). Thousand Oaks, CA: Sage.

Pavlenko, A. (2002). Narrative study: Whose story is it, anyway? *TESOL Quarterly, 36*, 213–218.

Pavlenko, A., & Lantolf, J. P. (2000). Second language learning as participation and the (re)construction of selves. In J. P. Lantolf (Ed.), *Sociocultural theory and second language learning* (pp. 155–177). New York: Oxford University Press.

Peck, S. (1978). Child-child discourse in second language acquisition. In E. Hatch (Ed.), *Second language acquisition* (pp. 383–400). Rowley, MA: Newbury House.

Pennycook, A. (2001). *Critical applied linguistics: A critical introduction.* Mahwah, NJ: Lawrence Erlbaum.

Peshkin, A. (1993). The goodness of qualitative research. *Educational Researcher, 22*, 24–30.

Peters, A. (1983). *The units of language acquisition.* Cambridge: Cambridge University Press.

Pienemann, M. (1998). *Language processing and second language development: Processability theory.* Philadelphia: John Benjamins.

Prior, P. (1998). *Writing/disciplinarity: A sociohistoric account of writing in the academy.* Mahwah, NJ: Lawrence Erlbaum.

Punch, K. (1998). *Introduction to social research: Quantitative and qualitative approaches.* Thousand Oaks, CA: Sage.

Punch, M. (1994). Politics and ethics in qualitative research. In N. K. Denzin & Y. S. Lincoln (Eds.), *Handbook of qualitative research* (pp. 83–97). Thousand Oaks, CA: Sage.

Ragin, C., Shulman, D., Weinberg, A., & Gran, B. (2003). Complexity, generality, and qualitative comparative analysis. *Field Methods, 15*, 323–340.

Rankin, J., & Becker, F. (2006). Does reading the research make a difference? A case study of teacher growth in FL German. *Modern Language Journal, 90*, 353–372.

Richards, K. (2003). *Qualitative inquiry in TESOL.* New York: Palgrave Macmillan.

Richardson, J. T. E. (Ed.). (1996). *Handbook of qualitative research methods for psychology and the social sciences.* Leicester, UK: British Psychological Society.

Richardson, L. (1990). *Writing strategies: Reaching diverse audiences.* Thousand Oaks, CA: Sage.

Richardson, L. (1994). Writing: A method of inquiry. In N. K. Denzin & Y. S. Lincoln

(Eds.), *Handbook of qualitative research* (pp. 516–529). Thousand Oaks, CA: Sage.

Richardson, L. (2000). Writing: A method of inquiry. In N. K. Denzin & Y. S. Lincoln (Eds.), *Handbook of qualitative research* (2nd ed., pp. 923–948). Thousand Oaks, CA: Sage.

Richardson, L., & St. Pierre, E. A. (2005). Writing: A method of inquiry. In N. K. Denzin & Y. S. Lincoln (Eds.), *Handbook of qualitative research* (3rd ed., pp. 959–978). Thousand Oaks, CA: Sage.

Ritchie, J., & Lewis, J. (Eds). (2003). *Qualitative research practice: A guide for social science students and researchers*. Thousand Oaks, CA: Sage.

Roberts, C. (1997). Transcribing talk: Issues of representation. *TESOL Quarterly, 31*, 167–171.

Ronjat, J. (1913). *Le développement du langage observé chez un enfant bilingue*. Paris: Champion.

Rutherford, W. (1983). Language typology and language transfer. In S. Gass & L. Selinker (Eds.), *Language transfer in second language learning* (pp. 358–370). Rowley, MA: Newbury House.

Rymer, R. (1993). *Genie: A scientific tragedy*. New York: HarperCollins.

Salaberry, R., & Shirai, Y. (Eds.). (2002). *The L2 acquisition of tense-aspect morphology*. Amsterdam: John Benjamins.

Saldaña, J. (2003). *Longitudinal qualitative research: Analyzing change through time*. Walnut Creek, CA: AltaMira Press.

Sasaki, M. (1990). Topic prominence in Japanese EFL students' existential constructions. *Language Learning, 40*, 337–368.

Sato, C. (1984). Phonological processes in second language acquisition: Another look at interlanguage syllable structure. *Language Learning, 34*, 43–57.

Sato, C. (1990). *The syntax of conversation in interlanguage development*. Tübingen, Germany: Gunter Narr.

Savage-Rumbaugh, S., Shanker, S. G., & Taylor, T. J. (1998). *Apes, language, and the human mind*. New York: Oxford University Press.

Schachter, J. (1974). An error in error analysis. *Language Learning, 24*, 205–214.

Schecter, S., & Bayley, R. (1997). Language socialization practices and cultural identity: Case studies of Mexican-descent families in California and Texas. *TESOL Quarterly, 31*, 513–542.

Schecter, S., & Bayley, R. (2002). *Language as cultural practice: Mexicanos en el Norte*. Mahwah, NJ: Lawrence Erlbaum.

Schieffelin, B., & Ochs, E. (Eds.). (1986). *Language socialization across cultures*. Cambridge: Cambridge University Press.

Schmidt, R. (1983). Interaction, acculturation and the acquisition of communicative competence. In N. Wolfson & E. Judd (Eds.), *Sociolinguistics and language acquisition* (pp. 137–174). Rowley, MA: Newbury House.

Schmidt, R., & Frota, S. (1986). Developing basic conversational ability in a second language: A case study of an adult learner of Portuguese. In R. Day (Ed.), *Talking to learn: Conversation in second language acquisition* (pp. 237–326). Rowley, MA: Newbury House.

Schneiderman, E. I., & Desmarais, C. (1988a). A neuropsychological substrate for talent in second language acquisition. In L. Obler & D. Fein (Eds.), *The exceptional brain: Neuropsychology of talent and special abilities* (pp. 103–126). New York: Guilford Press.

Schneiderman, E. I., & Desmarais, C. (1988b). The talented language learner: Some preliminary findings. *Second Language Research, 4,* 91–109.

Schofield, J. W. (1990). Increasing the generalizability of qualitative research. In E. Eisner & A. Peshkin (Eds.), *Qualitative inquiry in education: The continuing debate* (pp. 201–232). New York: Teachers College Press.

Schostak, J. (2006). *Interviewing and representation in qualitative research.* Berkshire, UK: Open University Press.

Schumann, J. (1978). *The pidginization process: A model for second language acquisition.* Rowley, MA: Newbury House.

Schumann, J. (1993). Some problems with falsification: An illustration from SLA research. *Applied Linguistics, 14,* 295–306.

Schumann, J. (1997). *The neurobiology of affect in language.* Malden, MA: Blackwell.

Scollon, R. T. (1976). *Conversations with a one year old: A case study of the developmental foundation of syntax.* Honolulu: University of Hawaii Press.

Seidman, I. (2006). *Interviewing as qualitative research: A guide for researchers in education and the social sciences* (3rd ed.). New York: Teachers College Press.

Seliger, H. W., & Shohamy, E. (1989). *Second language research methods.* New York: Oxford University Press.

Séror, J. (2005). Computers and qualitative data analysis: Paper, pens, and highlighters vs. screen, mouse, and keyboard. *TESOL Quarterly, 39,* 321–328.

Shapira, R. (1978). The non-learning of English: Case study of an adult. In E. Hatch (Ed.), *Second language acquisition* (pp. 246–255). Rowley, MA: Newbury House.

Shaughnessy, J. J., & Zechmeister, E. B. (1985). *Research methods in psychology.* New York: Alfred A. Knopf.

Shi, L. (2003). Writing in two cultures: Chinese professors return from the West. *Canadian Modern Language Review, 59,* 369–391.

Shohamy, E. (2004). Reflections on research guidelines, categories, and responsibility.

TESOL Quarterly, 38, 728–731.

Siegal, M. (1994). *Looking East: Learning Japanese as a second language in Japan and the interaction of race, gender and social context.* Unpublished PhD dissertation, University of California, Berkeley.

Siegal, M. (1996). The role of learner subjectivity in second language sociolinguistic competency: Western women learning Japanese. *Applied Linguistics, 17,* 356–382.

Silverman, D. (2000). *Doing qualitative research: A practical handbook.* Thousand Oaks, CA: Sage.

Silverman, D. (2001). *Interpreting qualitative data: Methods for analysing talk, text and interaction* (2nd ed.). Thousand Oaks, CA: Sage.

Silverman, D. (2004). *Qualitative research: Theory, method and practice* (2nd ed.). Thousand Oaks, CA: Sage.

Singleton, D. (1987). Mother and other tongue influence on learner French. *Studies in Second Language Acquisition, 9,* 327–346.

Skehan, P. (1989). *Individual differences in second-language learning.* London: Edward Arnold.

Slobin, D. (Ed.). (1985). *The cross-linguistic study of language acquisition,* Vol. 1, *The data.* Hillsdale, NJ: Lawrence Erlbaum.

Smith, N., & Tsimpli, I. (1991). Linguistic modularity? A case study of a *"savant"* linguist. *Lingua, 84,* 315–351.

Spack, R. (1997). The acquisition of academic literacy in a second language: A longitudinal case study. *Written Communication, 14,* 3–62.

Spada, N., & Lyster, N. (1997). Macroscopic and microscopic views of the L2 classroom. *TESOL Quarterly, 31,* 787–795.

Spradley, J. P. (1979). *The ethnographic interview.* New York: Holt Rinehart and Winston.

Stake, R. (1995). *The art of case study research.* Thousand Oaks, CA: Sage.

Stake, R. (2000). Case studies. In N. K. Denzin & Y. S. Lincoln (Eds.), *Handbook of qualitative research* (2nd ed., pp. 435–454). Thousand Oaks, CA: Sage.

Stake, R. (2005). Qualitative case studies. In N. K. Denzin & Y. S. Lincoln (Eds.), *Handbook of qualitative research* (3rd ed., pp. 443–466). Thousand Oaks, CA: Sage.

Strauss, A., & Corbin, J. (1998). *Basics of qualitative research: Techniques and procedures for developing grounded theory* (2nd ed.). Thousand Oaks, CA: Sage.

Tarone, E., Gass, S. M., & Cohen, A. (1994). *Research methodology in second-language acquisition.* Hillsdale, NJ: Lawrence Erlbaum.

Tarone, E., & Liu, G-Q. (1995). Situational context, variation and second-language acquisition theory. In G. Cook & B. Seidlhofer (Eds.), *Principles and practice in the study of language and learning: A festschrift for H. G. Widdowson* (pp. 107–124). Oxford: Oxford University Press.

Tashakkori, A., & Teddlie, C. (1998). *Mixed methodology: Combining qualitative and quantitative approaches.* Thousand Oaks, CA: Sage.

Tesch, R. (1990). *Qualitative research: Analysis types and software tools.* New York: Falmer.

TESOL. (2007). How to get published in ESOL and applied linguistics serials. Retrieved from http://www.tesol.org/s_tesol/seccss.asp?CID=334&DID=1026 &DOC=FILE.PDF. Retrieved May 29, 2007.

Toohey, K. (2000). *Learning English at school: Identity, social relations and classroom practice.* Clevedon, UK: Multilingual Matters.

Toohey, K. (2001). Disputes in child L2 learning. *TESOL Quarterly, 35,* 257–278.

UBC Behavioural Research Ethics Board. (2006a). Guidance Notes for Application for Behavioral Ethical Review. Retrieved April 28, 2006, from http://www.ors.ubc.ca/ethics/clinical/CREB_GN/BREB_Guidance_Notes.html

UBC Behavioural Research Ethics Board. (2006b) Guidance Note: Appendix 3. Action Research. Retrieved April 28, 2006, from http://www.ors.ubc.ca/ethics/forms/BREB%20Appendix%203%20(Action%20Research).doc

Valdés, G. (1998). The world outside and inside schools: Language and immigrant children. *Educational Researcher, 27,* 6, 4–18.

van Lier, L. (1988). *The classroom and the language learner.* New York: Longman.

van Lier, L. (1997). Observation from an ecological perspective. *TESOL Quar-terly, 22,* 783–787.

van Lier, L. (2004). *The ecology and semiotics of language learning: A sociocultural perspective.* Heidelberg: Kluwer Academic.

van Lier, L. (2005). Case study. In E. Hinkel (Ed.), *Handbook of research in second language teaching and learning* (pp. 195–208). Mahwah, NJ: Lawrence Erlbaum.

Van Maanen, J. (1988). *Tales of the field: On writing ethnography.* Chicago: University of Chicago Press.

Wagner-Gough, J. (1978). Comparative studies in second language learning. In E. Hatch (Ed.), *Second language acquisition* (pp. 155–171). Rowley, MA: Newbury House.

Watson, R. (1995). *The philosopher's demise: Learning French.* Columbia: University of Missouri Press.

Webster, J. (Ed.). (2003). *The language of early childhood* (Vol. 4 in the collected works of M. A. K. Halliday). New York: Continuum.

Weitzman, E. (2000). Software and qualitative research. In N. K. Denzin & Y. S. Lincoln (Eds.), *Handbook of qualitative research* (2nd ed., pp. 803–820). Thousand

Oaks, CA: Sage.

Weitzman, E. (2003). Software and qualitative research. In N. K. Denzin & Y. S. Lincoln (Eds.), *Collecting and interpreting qualitative materials* (2nd ed., pp. 310–339). Thousand Oaks, CA: Sage.

Weitzman, E., & Miles, M. B. (1995). *Computer programs for qualitative data analysis.* Thousand Oaks, CA: Sage.

Whitaker, H. (1976). A case of isolation of the language function. In H. Whitaker & H. Whitaker (Eds.), *Studies in neurolinguistics* (Vol. 2, pp. 1–58). New York: Academic Press.

Whyte, W. F. (1993). *Street corner society: The social structure of an Italian slum* (4th ed.). Chicago: University of Chicago Press. (Original work published 1943)

Willett, J. (1995). Becoming first graders in an L2: An ethnographic study of language socialization. *TESOL Quarterly, 29,* 473–504.

Willis, P. E. (1977). *Learning to labor.* Westmead, UK: Saxon House.

Wolcott, H. F. (1983). Adequate schools and inadequate education: The life history of a sneaky kid. *Anthropology and Education Quarterly, 14,* 3–32.

Wolcott, H. F. (1990). *Writing up qualitative research.* Newbury Park, CA: Sage.

Wolcott, H. F. (1994). *Transforming qualitative data: Description, analysis, and interpretation.* Thousand Oaks, CA: Sage.

Wolcott, H. F. (2002). *The sneaky kid and its aftermath: Ethics and intimacy in fieldwork.* Walnut Creek, CA: Altamira.

Wolf, M. (1992). *A thrice-told tale.* Stanford, CA: Stanford University Press.

Wong-Fillmore, L. (1979). Individual differences in second language acquisition. In C. Fillmore, D. Kempler, & W. Wang (Eds.), *Individual differences in language ability and language behavior* (pp. 203–228). New York: Academic Press.

Yim, Y. K. (2005). *Second language speakers' participation in computer-mediated discussions in graduate seminars.* Unpublished doctoral dissertation, University of British Columbia, Vancouver.

Yin, R. (1993). *Applications of case study research.* Newbury Park, CA: Sage.

Yin, R. (1994). *Case study research: Design and methods.* Thousand Oaks, CA: Sage.

Yin, R. (2003a). *Case study research: Design and methods* (3rd ed.). Thousand Oaks, CA: Sage.

Yin, R. (2003b). *Applications of case study research* (2nd ed.). Thousand Oaks, CA: Sage.

Young, R., & He, A. W. (Eds.). (1998). *Talking and testing: Discourse approaches to the assessment of oral proficiency.* Philadelphia: John Benjamins.

Yow, V. R. (1994). *Recording oral history.* Thousand Oaks, CA: Sage.

Author Index

167, 186

Gall, M. D., 14, 17, 19–20, 27, 30, 40, 48,
93, 100, 109, 135, 149, 160–162,
164–165, 167, 186

Galloway, L., 62

Gass, S., 29, 34, 36, 63, 67, 94, 118, 135,
171, 175

Geertz, C., 152

George, A. L., 21, 23, 40

Givón, T., 6, 64

Glaser, B. G., 50

Glassner, B., 122

Goldstein, T., 127

Goodwin, C., 115

Granger, C. A., 72

Green, J., 144

Greene, J. C., 40, 102

Grimshaw, G., 43

Guardado, M., 34

Guba, E. G., 26, 48, 168

Gubrium, J. F., 122

H

Hakuta, K., 42, 63

Halliday, M., 64

Hamel, J., 23–24, 80

Hammersley, M., 166

Han, Z.-H., 13, 75–76

Hardy, M., 23, 30, 45, 47

Hare, R. D., 50, 166

Harklau, L., 81, 113

Hatch, E., 24, 34, 36, 49–50, 55, 60–61,
62, 64–65, 110, 118, 135, 173

Hatch, J. A., 94, 104, 118

He, A. W., 124

Hesse-Biber, S. N., 25, 52

Hilles, S., 107

Hoffman, E., 72–73

Holliday, A., 25, 29, 115, 171, 186

Holstein, J. A., 122

Hornberger, N., 34, 80, 160, 186

Huang, J., 65

Huberman, A. M., 25, 41, 53, 93–94, 105,
115, 149–150, 152, 156, 160, 164,
187

Hudelson, S., 37

Huebner, T., 4–6, 35, 53, 146, 166

Hunter, J., 82

I

Iberri-Shea, G., 37, 43

Ioup, G., 43, 69–71, 97, 110

Itoh, H., 65

Ivanič, R., 85

J

Jacobs, B., 42

Jarvis, S., 120

Johnson, D. M., 30, 31–32, 36, 115, 188

Johnson, J. M., 116, 164–165

K

Kanno, Y., 87

Kaplan, A., 72–73

Kenyeres, A., 60

Kimmel, A. J., 135

Kinginger, C., 78

Klein, W., 50

Kobayashi, M., 115, 128, 132, 179

Subject Index